# *Soloveitchik* ON REPENTANCE

*Pinchas Peli*

# Soloveitchik ON REPENTANCE

PAULIST PRESS
New York/Ramsey

Library of Congress
Catalog Card Number: 83-82017

ISBN: 0-8091-2604-4

Published by Paulist Press
545 Island Road, Ramsey, N.J. 07446

Printed and bound in the
United States of America

*Contents*

*Walter S. Wurzburger*

# PREFACE

Within a remarkably short span of time, Rabbi Soloveitchik's *On Repentance* has been acclaimed as a major classic of religious literature. The enthusiastic reception of this treatise, which was brilliantly written and edited by Professor Pinchas Peli, attests to the extraordinary impact of Rabbi Soloveitchik's seminal contributions to contemporary Jewish thought.

What renders Rabbi Soloveitchik's approach so unique as well as so authentically Jewish is the utilization of Halakhah (Jewish Law) as the matrix for the formation of a religious philosophy. To be sure, traditional Jewish thinkers always emphasized that Judaism revolves around obedience to Halakhah. After all, there is a wide consensus that the Law constitutes the very core of Judaism. Some Jewish as well as non-Jewish thinkers went even further and, following in the footsteps of Spinoza and Moses Mendelssohn, asserted that Judaism was not a religion at all but only revealed Law.

Although the acceptance of the primacy of Halakhah as the supreme normative authority was axiomatic for traditional Jewish philosophies, this did not necessarily lead to the development of systems of thought which reflected the spirit of the Halakhah. As a general rule, philosophy merely co-existed with Halakhah. The paramount goal of Jewish philosophers was the creation of systems which managed to avoid outright conflict with the norms and the beliefs mandated by the Halakhah.

Most Jewish philosophical positions either mirrored the basic outlook of schools of philosophy in vogue (with whatever minor revisions were necessary to make them conform to the dictates of the Halakhah) or were based largely upon the non-legal sources of Biblical and Rabbinic Judaism.

But it is one thing to construct the philosophy which can be reconciled with Halakhah, and another to produce a philosophy which actually reflects the data, methods and pre-suppositions of the Halakhah itself.

As a renowned authority on Jewish Law—and as an eminent philosopher, "The Rav"—as Rabbi Soloveitchik is referred to by devotees all over the world—is superbly suited for the task of plumbing the depth of Halakhah in order to extract from it a Jewish axiology and metaphysics.

*On Repentance* represents a paradigm of a philosophy of Halakhah. Analysis in depth of the various components of Halakhic norms yields a rich harvest of psychological, ethical, metaphysical and religious insights. Especially striking is the complete avoidance of all apologetics and the unabashed willingness to face up to the complexities which are so frequently overlooked by philosophers in quest of a master formula designed to unify all experience.

As Raphael Morris Cohen puts it, "Philosophers are usually right in what they see, and wrong in what they fail to see." Rabbi Soloveitchik guards against the tendency toward over-simplification which frequently vitiates the work of philosophers, who, instead of being totally open to all experience, want to force their ideas into a Procrustean bed of pre-conceived categories.

Rabbi Soloveitchik's rigorous phenomenological approach reveals rather than conceals the enormous diversity as well as the disparities of our experience. He is not prepared to sacrifice depth to neatness, complexity to spurious unity. In *On Repentance* no attempt is made to explain (or, better, to explain away) the multiplicity of irreducible elements which Halakhic analysis discerns in the conception of repentance. He is not troubled by the inescapability of paradoxes and dialectical tensions. As he so convincingly argues in his *Lonely Man of Faith*, dialectical tensions need not necessarily be attributed to historic or socio-cultural factors; they frequently arise from the incongruities and contradictions which are rooted in the very nature of the human condition. Since dialectical tension is not a disturbance to be resolved or overcome but an ontological necessity, it is not surprising that Rabbi Soloveitchik advocates a two-tiered ethics as formulated in his *Majesty and Humility*.

Rabbi Soloveitchik's phenomenological method also accounts for what some might regard as a shortcoming of his approach. He nowhere seeks to demonstrate the validity of the Halakhah. But having been exposed to the influence of a Kant, Cohen, Kierkegaard and Barth, it is readily understandable that he eschews the pretensions of natural theology. All he seeks is to provide a phenomenology of a religious experience which accepts the need for unconditional submission to the divinely revealed will as stipulated by the Halakhah.

The Rav does not argue for his position. He is content with employing his brilliance and literary skills to describe and analyze the meaning of *his* experience of the teachings of Halakhah. Adopting the stance of a religious existentialist, his objective is not to build a system, but to do justice to the religious reality as perceived by one who is deservedly hailed as one of the most original, creative and profound minds of the age.

*RABBI WALTER S. WURZBURGER,* editor of *Tradition,* a journal of Orthodox Jewish Thought, is adjunct Professor of Philosophy at Yeshiva University, former President of the Rabbinical Council of America and immediate past president of the Synagogue Council of America.

# BIOGRAPHICAL NOTES

*SOLOVEITCHIK, JOSEPH DOV* (1903– ) U.S. Talmudic scholar and religious philosopher, and scion of a preeminent Lithuanian rabbinical family, known as *Bet Harav.* Soloveitchik was born in Pruzhan, Poland where his maternal grandfather, Elijah Feinstein, was the rabbi. Soloveitchik spent his early years in Hasloviz, Belorussia, where his father, Moses, served as rabbi. Until his early twenties, Soloveitchik devoted himself almost exclusively to the study of Talmud and *halakhah.* Under his father's tutelage, he mastered his grandfather's (Rav Hayyim Soloveitchik) method of Talmudic study, with its insistence on incisive analysis, exact classification, critical independence, and emphasis on Maimonides' *Mishneh Torah.* In his late teens Soloveitchik received the equivalent of a high school education from private tutors, and at the age of twenty-two entered the University of Berlin. He majored in philosophy and was attracted to the neo-Kantian school. In 1931 he received his doctorate for his dissertation on Hermann Cohen's epistemology and metaphysics. That same year he married Tonya Lewit (d. 1967), herself the recipient of a doctorate in education from Jena University, who ably assisted him in all his endeavors. In 1932 they emigrated to the United States. A few months after his arrival, Soloveitchik became rabbi of the Orthodox Jewish community of Boston, the city which remained his home. He founded the first Jewish day school in New England, the Maimonides School, and also conducted post-graduate Talmudic classes for young scholars who gathered around him. In 1941 Soloveitchik succeeded his father as professor of Talmud at the Rabbi Isaac Elchanan Theological Seminary of Yeshiva University. For many years he also lectured at the university's Bernard Revel Graduate School, where he served as professor of Jewish philosophy. In these positions Soloveitchik became the spiritual mentor of the majority of the American-trained Orthodox rabbis, and for decades inspired students to follow his teachings.

Soloveitchik is looked up to in North America as the unchallenged leader of enlightened Orthodoxy and is popularly known simply as "the Rav." His main influence is through his lectures and public discourses. As a Talmudic and Halakhic expositor, Soloveitchik has an unusual facility for explaining difficult technical problems. He is also an orator of note in his native Yiddish, as well as in English and Hebrew. The annual halakhic and aggadic discourses which he delivers at Yeshiva University on the anniversary of his father's death attract thousands of listeners and are regarded as the major academic event for United States Orthodox Jewry.

excerpts from the Encyclopedia Judaica

*PELI, PINCHAS HACOHEN* (1930– ), professor of Hebrew studies and senior lecturer of Jewish thought at Ben Gurion University of the Negev, Israel, is a well known scholar and lecturer and the author of several books and numerous articles on Jewish thought and literature. He is also founder and director of the Abraham Joshua Heschel Institute and Shabbat Yachad Retreat Program in Jerusalem. During 1970–1971 he served as visiting professor at Yeshiva University where he became closely associated with the Rav, again in the

United States during 1979–1980 as visiting professor in theology at the University of Notre Dame. Since 1981 Professor Peli has occupied the Norbert Beechner Chair in Jewish Values at BGU of the Negev.

# FOREWORD

"No one in our own life time has expounded the authentic Torah concept of *teshuvah* (repentance) to so many students and scholars with such profound feeling, originality and depth, as the Rav has done it at our annual Rabbinical Council *teshuvah* convocations. These annual *teshuvah shiurim* have become an eagerly anticipated ritual and the Torah event of the year, attracting an incredible number of rabbis and lay scholars from New York and far beyond it. . . . These four-hour lectures are an intellectual experience without comparison in the entire Jewish community. . . . Zealously and consistently adhering to the tradition of his illustrious rabbinical Bet Harav ancestors, the Rav, with a few minor exceptions, refuses to publish his countless lectures and Talmud shiurim . . . therefore the publication in Jerusalem of the new volume *On Repentance* is virtually an extraordinary literary event for Jewish scholarship. . . . Although we, his students and disciples, are actually aware that the Rav's incomparable analytical methods, astonishing originality, unique gift of *hasbarah,* and clarification of the most complex and intricate issues of Talmudic law and Jewish theology are generously enhanced by the very presence of his luminous personality which invariably exudes genuine spirituality and intellectual restlessness and by his rare gift of articulation which electrifies his audience, yet, even in their written form, the teshuvah lectures of this volume constitute an inestimable treasure of great Jewish ideas and authentic Torah thought. . . . The central theme and objective of these teshuvah essays is neither academic nor a mere exercise of intellectual brilliance. It is rather relevant to the perennial and very timely human dilemma of narrowing down the agonizing gap between knowing and doing what is right. What some contemporary men of letters are endeavoring to achieve for human redemption through their fictitious protagonists in an improvised or imaginary human situation, the Rav most admirably achieves through the reverent and thorough analysis and application of the Biblical text, the Talmudic exposition, the Maimonidean ruling and the Kabbalistic exploration. . . . It is one's fervent hope that this remarkable volume . . . will some day in the not too far distant future find its way, after a proper translation, on the campus where it will serve as a guide for the perplexed."

The above is an excerpt from a lengthy article penned by one of the leading Orthodox rabbis in the United States, Rabbi Dr. Bernard A. Poupko, and published in the official Rabbinical Council Record (May 1975). It was one of many such enthusiastic responses to the publication in 1975, of *On Repentance*, which I wrote after listening to the Rav's teshuvah discourses during the years 1962–1974. Such responses came not only from the disciples and followers of the Rav in the Jewish orthodox camp in America, where he is considered to be the foremost teacher and spiritual leader, but also from academic and non-academic wide circles in Israel (penetrating articles on the book were written, among others, by Hebrew University professors, Nathan Rottenstreich, Eliezer Schweid and Joseph Dan), as well as from other branches of American Jewry. Thus writes Rabbi Dr. Theodore Friedman, a former president of the (Conservative) Rabbinical Assembly in the *Jewish Spectator* (Summer 1976): "Dr. Peli's book is based on a series of Rabbi Soloveitchik's lectures on the theme of teshuvah (the English 'repentance' hardly conveys the full import of the concept; a better equivalent is 'turn' or 'return'). Rabbi Soloveitchik does not speak from a prepared text. It was, therefore, no mean feat to transpose the lectures into written form and thus make available ideas and insights that might otherwise have been lost to our and subsequent generations. . . . A thought-provoking book, assuredly one of the most important volumes in contemporary Jewish thought published in recent years. . . . The volume is a must for anyone interested in the contemporary meaning of traditional Jewish concepts."

And Rabbi Arnold Jacob Wolf, of Yale University, a leading member of the Reform rabbinate, writes (*Sh'ma*, Sept. 9, 1975): "Rabbi Joseph Soloveitchik seems to me more and more obviously the teacher of the time. How paradoxical that this doggedly orthodox, European-born Talmudist should speak more clearly to our needs than the most sophisticated modernists from all the great universities of the West. These essays tell us about t'shuvah and what it really means to change. . . . In a time without leaders, without direction, without wisdom, this old wise man succeeds in teaching us something very precious. If I am not mistaken, people will still be reading him in a thousand years."

And to cite one more of the many responses to *On Repentance*, here is Curtis Arnson, chief librarian at the (Reform) Hebrew Union College (*Ariel*, Winter 1976): "In the continuing debate over how best to live as an observant Jew in Israel, and amidst the confusion caused by religion having become involved in politics, it is easy to overlook the theological and philosophic aspects of Judaism. Many of the works discussing purely spiritual aspects of Judaism tend to have an apologetic tone. It is, therefore, surprising how refreshing an unapologetic theological work of high standard can be, as is the case of *On Reptenance....* This book ought to be translated into English and made available to as many people as possible, if only to exemplify the pleasure that can be derived from immersion in the world of spirit."

The appearance of *On Repentance* was also welcomed by the Rav himself, who acclaimed it, saying that it "represents an authentic rendition of the concept of Teshuvah in all of its halakhic and philosophic ramifications."

This volume in English is a translation of the seven essays and Afterword of the Hebrew *Al Hateshuvah* (not included is the Foreword which contains an attempt at a literary evaluation of the style of the essays). It should be reiterated here that these essays were penned by the undersigned who is solely responsible for their content. In this impressionistic rendition every effort was made to emphasize not only the halakhic and philosophical value of the Rav's approach, but also its creative, poetic and artistic values. Rabbi Soloveitchik is no doubt one of the greatest contemporary masters of rhetoric, following the glorious tradition of the great masters of the midrash of old. While he pursues the "close reading" method of the Maimonidean texts in the dialectical tradition of his "Brisk" family, his own approach reflects wells of subtle humor, profound lyricism, clear thinking and brutal psychological incision into the innermost depth of the human personality. These are accompanied by unlimited, good-hearted understanding and sympathy for the human condition of vulnerability and helplessness. In order not to lose this individualistic and artistic impact, there appears in the text of the essays the use of the first-person pronoun "I". Those, to be sure, are not necessarily exact quotes from the Rav and the responsibility for them too rests solely with the writer of these lines. They are part of the effort to give authenticity to the unique midrashic genre as represented in our times by Rabbi Soloveitchik, whereby philosophical and psychological or sociological categories derive from "dry" legal-halakhic principles or structures. One has to be familiar with Talmudic dialects to fully appreciate and marvel at the creative intellectual ingenuity of the translation of Halakhah into independent epistemological and ontological categories without, at the same time, losing sight of the fact that the process of *teshuvah* is an event which takes place in the deepest recesses of the human mind and psyche.

The Rav's teshuvah discourses were always given in Yiddish, while this book was originally written in Hebrew. It was not an easy task to render it into an English understandable by people without prior acquaintance with rabbinic literature. This is the place to thank all those who helped make this possible: Dr. Benny Morris, Mr. Aaron Lewin, Rabbi Uri Kaplun, Mrs. Fay Tenzer and above all my dear wife Pnina Peli, herself a gifted student of Jewish thought and mysticism, who put in many hours to edit and prepare the English version of this book. Her able cooperation in this as in our other joint educational and literary efforts has been a source of inspiration, guidance and encouragement.

I cannot close this Foreword without expressing my profound gratefulness for the genuine friendship I was privileged to enjoy with the great teacher of our generation Rabbi Soloveitchik, as well as with his life's partner Dr. Tonya Lewit Soloveitchik of blessed memory, who graciously opened both heart and home to me, coming from afar. A visit to the Rav while Mrs. Soloveitchik was still alive was always "a lesson" in Judaism and kindness, imparted by her sheer presence, personality and wisdom. Looking back now at those unforgettable encounters one comes to realize again the full meaning of the words said about her by her husband, the Rav (*Tradition,*

Summer 1965): "A woman of great courage, sublime dignity, total commitment and uncompromising truthfulness."

*Pinchas Hacohen Peli*

Ben Gurion University of the Negev
Beer Sheva, Israel

# INTRODUCTION

[1]

Man stands at the center of Rabbi Joseph Dov (Baer) Halevi Soloveitchik's religious thought. His study of man is not comprehensive, nor does it attempt to encompass the totality of human experience with the aim of identifying and establishing a typology of man and of human society.[1] According to this approach, man must be studied and judged in the light of essentially human criteria. Thus, the Rav[2] solidly established the typological characteristics of "Halakhic Man"[3] by contrasting him with"Religious Man" and "Rational Man";[4] thus, too, he anchored his "Lonely Man of Faith"[5] in the prototypes of "Adam the First" and "Adam the Second" as these emerge,

1. On the typological categories and their problematics in the writings of Rabbi Soloveitchik, see Eugune B. Borowitz, *A New Jewish Theology in the Making* (Westminster Press, Philadelphia), pp. 164–70. Compare Rabbi Soloveitchik's view on this matter in notes 5 and 6 below. See also Lawrence Kaplan, "The Religious Philosophy of Rabbi Joseph Soloveitchik," *Tradition* (A Journal of Orthodox Jewish Thought), Fall 1973, Vol. XIV, No. 2.

2. Soloveitchik is generally referred to among his many followers as "the Rav," meaning "the teacher."

3. Rabbi Joseph B. Soloveitchik, "Ish Halakhah" ((Halakhic Man) in *Besod ha-Yahid ve-ha-Yahad* (In Aloneness, In Togetherness), A Selection of Hebrew Writings (henceforth IAIT), ed. Pinchas Peli, Orot, Jerusalem, 1976, pp. 37–188.

4. *Ibid.*, p. 45.

5. Soloveitchik, "The Lonely Man of Faith" (henceforth LMF), *Tradition*, Summer 1965, Vol. VII, No. 2, pp. 5–67.

according to him, from the two versions of the creation of man in the Torah.

The lines of demarcation between one type and another are not always clear or sharply drawn. Often, characteristics of one type will be shared by another, and though the types portrayed in the Rav's typological system are ideas such as are often used in theoretical philosophy, he was aware that in reality the types—rarely simple, often complex—at most approximated their ideal counterparts. That he was aware of this is apparent in his comparison between the ideal "Halakhic Man" and the real "Halakhic Man."[6] Similarly, he occasionally noted the congruence between the different types (by way of shared traits).[7]

The publication of Rabbi Soloveitchik's reflections on repentance seems to compel the addition to his typological categories of another type definable along the lines of the Rabbi's terminology, as "Repentant Man." Unfortunately, Rabbi Soloveitchik has not yet given a final or systematic presentation of his thought in this matter. We have at our disposal only fragmentary and disjointed evidence upon which to build our analysis. Nonetheless, it appears that "Repentant Man" may be legitimately viewed as inhabiting the highest rung of this typological ladder. To judge from the evidence, "Repentant Man" enjoys an abundance of the positive traits identified by the rabbi in the other established types, as these endeavor to express their humanity as creatures created in the Divine Image. They are at the same time possessed of independent creative powers coupled with a powerful compulsion to draw near to their Creator. In the person of "Repentant Man" these two ontological tendencies converge and become a unified perfec-

6. "Halakhic Man," IAIT, p. 39, n. 1, where the Rabbi deals with the typological system formulated by Edward Sprenger in his book *Lebensformen*.

7. LMF, p. 48, n. 38: "In reality there are no pure typological structures." See also note 66 below.

tion which propels man toward his ultimate destination—salvation.

Moreover, the depth of the personality of Rabbi Soloveitchik's other types is measured according to criteria of the torments of duality, contradiction, doubts and struggles which issue in the "emergence of a personality shrouded in sanctity whose soul was purified in the smithy of perplexity and contradiction and refined in the fires of spiritual conflict." From the spiritual struggle which is the lot of "Repentant Man," there emerges a perfection of personality "of incomparable splendor and glory unknown among those, whole and simple, who have never undergone the tribulations of internal spiritual conflict."[8] As Rabbi Soloveitchik asserts: "According to the trouble, so the wage; according to the tear, so the patch." In the rabbi's conception of human ontology which rests, according to his own testimony,[9] on the dialectical philosophies of Heraclitus and Hegel concerning the general process of being, and on the views of Kierkegaard, Karl Barth and Rudolph Otto concerning the religious experience and religious awareness, immense creative power is vested in the antithesis, "Inconsistency enriches existence, contradiction renews Creation, negation builds worlds and denial deepens and expands consciousness."[10] The portrait of "Repentant Man" rests mainly upon these foundations. Should one seek a parallel in the Rav's typological framework, it would be found in the type defined as the "Man of God," about whom the Rav intimates that "his stature is established in the pangs of redemption and appearance crystallizes in the pains of salvation."[11]

8. "Halakhic Man," IAIT, p. 40.

9. *Ibid.*

10. *Ibid.*

11. *Ibid.*, p. 41, n. 4. Soloveitchik offers exegesis on the Biblical passages: "Out of my straits I called upon the Lord . . ." (Ps 118:5) and "From the depths have I cried unto Thee, O Lord" (Ps 130:1). Out of the straits of contradiction and internal tur-

[2]

If suffering creates, ennobles and toughens, and brings the soul nearer to the object of its yearning, then "Repentant Man" is the type which comes closest to attaining man's goal, for his conception and maturation owe everything to suffering.

Four characteristic traits identify "Repentant Man" as seen by Rabbi Soloveitchik: profundity of suffering, a depth of experience, the ability to make decisions in the light of free choice, and the capacity to create.

The rabbi's conception of ontology is directed to four traits which are to be found, in some measure, in the other types established and described by Rabbi Soloveitchik, but never in so concentrated a form as in his thought on repentance. It comprises man's freedom, his drives, his existence as a repository of the *Shekhinah,* his investiture with free choice (which allows him to adopt a new law of causation) and his penchant for salvation. God created man free. This liberty, however, does not represent an abandonment on His part. Rather man, born in the image of God, always remains, as it were, in the Divine Presence. He can never completely free himself from the religious attraction which draws him to God, which is akin to an unseverable umbilical cord.[12] Man cannot flee from God because God chose the human soul as a dwelling place much like a temple. "The House of God of Old—where is God's house? 'Behold, the heaven and heaven of heavens cannot contain thee, how much less this House that I have built?' (1 Kgs 8:27). Where lives the Almighty and where lives God the Eternal? The Almighty resides in man, in his

---

moil, spiritual doubts and perplexities, from the depths of the soul riven with antinomianism and negation, from the furthest recesses of the spirit, perplexed and suffering, I called unto God, I called You, O Lord.

12. See below, p. 83. Compare with Rudolf Otto, *The Idea of the Holy,* translated by John W. Harvey (Oxford University Press, N.Y. 1958), pp. iff., on man's "creature feeling."

heart and soul, and He never departs from there even if man sins and defiles the sacred abode. God, as it were, inhabits the deepest recesses of the sinning soul . . . 'that dwelleth with them in the midst of their uncleanliness' (Lev 16:16)."[13]

"The Almighty has two dwelling places in man, two temples. One is the temple of the emotions, a holy of holies from which issue human sentiments such as sympathy, astonishment, mercy, goodness, reverence, happiness, sadness, amazement. The other temple is that of the mind. In man's thoughts, as he studies the Torah and refines and sanctifies his intellect, there resides the Almighty. One house of the God of Old is in the heart of man, and the other is in the human brain; one is in the emotions, the other in the mind."[14]

The permanent religious affinity, the "living together" of God and man in one house, does not produce a calming or tranquilizing effect. On the contrary, "the religious act is essentially one of suffering. When man and God meet, man is called upon by the Divine to embark on a course of self-sacrifice which is manifested in a struggle against his primitive instincts, in a breaking of the individual will, in the acceptance of a 'transcendental burden,' in an occasional dissociation from the pleasant and attractive, and in an addiction to the bitter and the strange. . . . 'Make sacrifices'—that is the command governing the religious man."[15]

The lot of the religious man is a constant, difficult and tiring struggle, not tranquility. "The beauty of religion, with its grandiose vistas, reveals itself to man not in solutions, but in problems; not in harmony, but in the constant conflict of di-

13. *Ibid.*, p. 207.

14. *Ibid.*, p. 208.

15. Rabbi J. B. Soloveitchik, "On the Love of the Torah and the Redemption of the Soul of the Generation," an answer to an interlocutor, in IAIT, pp. 403–32. Cf. Pinchas H. Peli, "On Suffering in the Thought of Rabbi J.B. Soloveitchik," in *Da'at, A Journal of Jewish Philosophy and Kabbalah,* No. 12, Winter 1984, pp. 48-62.

versified forces and trends."[16] The attainment of sanctity, according to Rabbi Soloveitchik, does not lead man to paradise, but rather to paradox.

The suffering to which man is condemned is not necessarily a punishment; rather, "suffering is there to uplift man, to cleanse his spirit and sanctify him, to purify his thought and to rid it of all manner of superficial dross and vulgar chaff, to ennoble his soul and to expand his life's vision. In short, the function of suffering is to set right that which is distorted and defective in the human character. . . . Suffering appears in the world in order to enhance man. . . . It is a time of distress for Jacob and he shall be saved out of it (Jer 30:7)—i.e., out of misfortune will spring forth eternal salvation. [Man will be] uplifted to a degree incomparably above that possible in a world devoid of suffering."[17] Man's existence in the presence of God involves suffering; man's affinity to God is expressed in constant sacrifice. Only through sacrifice and total subservience to God can man achieve complete freedom and salvation.

Man's subservience to God must be complete and unconditional. This decisive subordination is tantamount to total freedom in relation to the other enslavements to which man is prone. The enslavement to God—which is all-embracing—releases man from a long list of other bondages. Only when a man has one sovereign, to whom he owes unreserved allegiance, is he truly liberated and free. When a man is subservient to more than one being, he is then "taking a hand in some form of idolatry." What then of positive ties of loyalty, such as to children and family? The Torah instructs us to love our children with a great passion. "As a father pities his son" is a

---

16. Rabbi J.B. Soloveitchik, "Sacred and Profane: Kodesh and Hol in World Perspectives," *Gesher*, published by Yeshiva University, Sivan 1966, Vol. 2, No. 1, p. 7.

17. Rabbi J.B. Soloveitchik, "Kol Dodi Dofek" (The Voice of My Love Calls), in IAIT, p. 339.

common simile of compassion and love in our liturgy. Nonetheless, Rabbi Soloveitchik suggests the daring proposition that the narrative of the sacrifice of Isaac was related only in order to teach later generations that parental love must not be allowed to deteriorate into complete enslavement, i.e., into a form of idolatry.[18]

Man attains liberty through self-sacrifice. "Total and unreserved offering of soul and body—that is the foundation of Judaism," asserts Rabbi Soloveitchik.[19] Moreover, he hazards that, in essence, "Judaism does not prohibit the sacrifice of humans"; i.e., he explains, though the Torah forbids human sacrifice and regards the phenomenon as an example of the obscene in idolatry, it does not ban the notion of self-sacrifice. In the words of the Rav, "God demands not tribute from man, but man himself."[20] Rabbi Soloveitchik sees the central philosophical idea underlying the act of sacrifice explained in Mai-

---

18. See below p. 224. The Rav deals with this point at greater length in his essay "On the Love of the Torah and the Redemption of the Soul of the Generation" (IAIT, p. 428). "God said to Abraham: 'Take now thy son, thine only son, Isaac, whom thou lovest' . . . (Gen 22:2). In other words, I demand of you the greatest sacrifice possible. I want your beloved and only son in sacrifice. Do not delude yourself that after obeying my command and offering up your son, I shall give you another in his place. From the moment Isaac is slaughtered upon the altar, you will remain alone and childless. No other will be born unto you. Your existence will be governed by an incomparable isolation. I want your only son, for whom no substitute exists or shall exist. Similarly, do not imagine that you will succeed in forgetting Isaac or putting him out of mind. For the rest of your days you shall brood upon his fate. I demand that son whom you love and will love forever. Your life will turn into one long epic of suffering. Nonetheless, this is the sacrifice that I demand. Of course, at the end of the experience, whose essence is dread and pain, is endless joy. At the moment Abraham removed his son from atop the altar at the behest of the angel, the suffering changed into boundless joy and the dread into eternal happiness. At the beginning of the religious experience lies the sacrifice of essence; at its end, the discovery of essence. Indeed, man cannot discover himself without the sacrifice. For man can find only that which has been lost, and none can retrieve a thing unless it has first left his keeping."

19. *Ibid.*

20. See below, p. 245. Compare with Soloveitchik, "Five Sermons," translated by David Telsner (Tal Orot, Jerusalem 1974, pp. 14–15). Soloveitchik here explains Deuteronomy 20:29, i.e., the means by which a Jew achieves purchase on the Almighty is through his "whole being," be-khol nafshekha, as explained in Rabbi Akiva's ser-

monides' assertion that man is the property of the Creator. Man and all his belongings, his body and soul, ideas, actions, achievements and possessions, even his wife and children—all belong not to man, but to his Creator. And if man is "the property of the Almighty, then he has no choice when the Voice of God calls out to him to 'take now thy son, thine only son,' and sacrifice him, but to arise and set out to obey the command." Abraham has no rights in the disposal of his son, Isaac; Isaac has no claim over Abraham. Man is free; he attains that freedom through exercising his right to self-sacrifice in the service of his Creator.

Were it allowed, the Law would call for human sacrifices, but the dispensation of grace precludes this, asserting: "Ye shall bring your offering of the cattle, even of the herd, and of the flock" (Lev 1:2). Animal sacrifice is allowed as a substitute for human sacrifice, but the meaningfulness of the sacrifice remains, as it were, undiminished; so in the sacrifice of Isaac, and so in all other sacrificial offerings. "As the sacrifice is burnt upon the altar, so we burn, in the act of confession over the sacrifice, our entrenched tranquility, our well-nurtured pride, our artificial lives. Through the sacrifice, or through the suffering which stands in its stead, we repeatedly feel ourselves 'in the presence of God.' "[21]

Man's existential condition, in fact, means suffering, doubt, struggles with the world and within oneself. Only "Repentant Man" can attain that highest plateau to which suffer-

---

mon (*Ber. 63a*): "Even if it costs one's life." The Almighty can be reached through suffering and obstinate devotion: "in short, one reaches the Almighty through sacrifice."

21. See below, pp. 95, 246. Compare with Rabbi A.I. Kook, *The Lights of Repentance* (Jerusalem 1970), pp. 46–52. In general, there are many points of convergence between the thinking on repentance of the "poet of repentance," Rabbi Kook, and the "philosopher of repentance," Rabbi Soloveitchik, as, for example, on the problem of time, suffering, the individual and the community, etc. A comparative study of the two might prove enlightening.

ing can introduce man, for the very emergence of "Repentant Man" into this world involves conscious and severe birth pangs.

[3]

In order to understand the concept of repentance, it is necessary to fathom the concept of sin as it emerges from Rabbi Soloveitchik's reflections on the subject of repentance. The two concepts—sin and repentance—are interlocked and bound together in a single, dialectical system, and both constitute stages through which "Repentant Man" must pass on his way to salvation.

Yom Kippur has two aspects: the experience of that day results first in atonement and, secondly, in purification; as it is written (Lev 16:30): "For on that day shall atonement be made for you to purify you." Both these elements—atonement and purification—according to Rabbi Soloveitchik, are a direct consequence of sin. For in sin both elements are to be found: (a) sin binds; atonement or pardon provides a counterweight; (b) sin defiles; purification or forgiveness restores the sinner to his original state.

The sin that binds does so, much like obligation and subjection in the juridical sense. There is no sin without punishment, which in a terrestrial or in a heavenly court means pardon (*meḥilah*), a word originating in laws of property. As a man foreswears (*moḥel*) a sum owed to him by a friend, so God forgoes (*moḥel*) and erases (*mekhaper*) the punishment which sin entails. However, the sin that defiles is of another order—the metaphysical one. It exists in the domain of man-God relations. Sin deforms and damages the innermost part of man—his soul, wherein dwells the *Shekhinah.*[22]

Judicial sin, the sin that binds, is revealed to man by his

---

22. See below, p. 60.

intellect. Repentance of such a sin is generally undergone through calculation, through a desire to erase an obligation, or through fear of the impending punishment. Metaphysical sin, on the other hand, becomes part of man's existential experience, and the deeper the sin, the deeper the experience of repentance which follows.

Sin causes man's remoteness from God. The sinner becomes, in the words of Maimonides—whom Rabbi Soloveitchik is wont to quote—"Separate from the God of Israel, for it is written that your sins separate you from God." To be sure, God remains in man also after he sins, but He is so remote that the sinner does not feel His presence at all. Only afterward he begins, sooner or later, to feel God's absence and, as a result, is beset by existential dread and fear.

Before the stage of "recognition of sin," which is already an integral part of the act of repentance itself, Rabbi Soloveitchik distinguishes a prior stage defined as a "feeling of sin," which is similar to a man's feeling of an encroaching illness. *Ḥet, Ḥoli* (sin, illness) is a parallel concept employed by medieval Jewish philosophers, and already hinted at in the Bible (Ps 103:3): "Who forgiveth all thine iniquities; Who healeth all thy diseases." It was expanded by Rabbi Soloveitchik[23] to explain the feeling of sin, which is the initial experience and precondition for all repentance or purification. Sin constitutes a kind of spiritual pathology. As there are pathological, physical illnesses in which the tissues cease to function normally and the cells begin to grow wild, so sin is a sign of a spiritual pathology whose outcome is the disintegration of the whole personality. As in physical disease, so in the spiritual disease of sin. Sometimes a man attempts to erase, to belittle or to deny pain, because of overt or covert fear. Pains begin to engender dread, but man's first reaction is to dismiss them or to belittle

23. *Ibid.,* pp. 192ff.

their significance. But belittling them will not diminish their importance; on the contrary, had he taken immediate action and had them treated, it is possible that a cure for his spreading illness could have been found.

The comparison between sin and pathological illness is complemented by the comparison between sin and mourning. The Torah says of the sin of the golden calf: "And when the people heard these evil tidings, they mourned; and no man did put on him his ornaments" (Ex 33:4). In the wake of this sin there descended upon the people a strong sense of mourning. Likewise, in the episode of the spies, a sense of mourning overcame the people after the sin (Num 14:39). Mourning is a reaction to loss; it descends upon man like a vague, almost primitive, sense of loss, of awful incapacity, and develops into a strong feeling of nostalgia, of pining after something, of retrospective memories. The power of mourning, its brutality and loneliness, is centered in the human memory. Were man able to forget, to erase memory, there would be no mourning. The mourner mourns a kindred and loved person who was once and is no more, while the sinner mourns that which has been lost. What has been lost is man's soul, which is like losing everything, for he has lost his closeness to his Creator, that proximity which allowed him access to purity and sanctity, to perfection and spiritual richness; he has lost the inherence of the holy spirit in man and that which gives meaning and the significance of life to human existence.

"Repentant Man" in excelsis reaches repentance not through calculation and fear of punishment, but through the *via dolorosa* of a sense of sin which fills him with powerful longing and sharp feelings of mourning. The experience of sin completely fills man with boundless fear and a wild, vague dread; the more deeply these are felt, the closer man comes to the possibility of overcoming them through the power of repentance.

[4]

This dread-filled sense of remoteness from God, isolation, longing and mourning is in the main a powerful aesthetic (or anti-aesthetic) experience. Mourning always contains an element of masochism. The mourner tortures and chastises himself; indeed, he hates himself. This applies equally to the "mourning of sin." The sinner begins to feel contempt and abomination of self, and masochistic self-hatred. In his eyes the sin turns into something abominable, loathsome, nauseating.

"The feeling of sin," says Rabbi Soloveitchik, "is not a moral experience." Man's ethical sense is not a very potent factor. This feeling of sin, which draws man toward repentance, is an aesthetic experience, or rather, a negative aesthetic experience. The sinner senses that which is abominable and corrupting in sin. "The pangs of sin lie in the nausea caused by its obnoxious taint."[24] This sense of abomination (wonderfully described in the story of Amnon and Tamar [2 Sam 13], as interpreted by Rabbi Soloveitchik),[25] is also connected to a sense of shame—shame about one's own acts. The sense of abomination intermingles with the sense of shame and opprobrium. The sin appears to the sinner like a terrible monster; he is filled with shame through having come into contact with the "bestial"; and out of the shame, the sense of abomination, of mourning, and of the other emotions which comprise the sense of sin, he begins to ascend the ladder of "Repentant Man," at last attaining repentance itself. This transition from sin to repentance does not occur on the intellectual plane: "The human intellect takes practically no part [in the process]"; it transpires rather on the emotional, experiential and instinctive planes.

---

24. *Ibid.*, p. 195.
25. *Ibid.*, p. 198.

Through all the stages of the ascent of "Repentant Man," Rabbi Soloveitchik lays strong emphasis upon the experiential-emotional element which leads the penitent to the feeling of sin in contrast with the intellectual-cognitive element; the latter leads man to repentance by way of "knowledge of sin" of "consciousness of sin," but not to a "repentance through love"—*Teshuvah me-Ahavah*—the "higher repentance through love"—*Teshuvah me-ulah*—which is the peak attained by "Repentant Man."

This stress on the experiential-emotional element, side by side with the intellectual-cognitive element, runs like a motif through all Rabbi Soloveitchik's descriptions of the essence of the religious phenomenon in general. Thus, for instance,[26] he distinguishes between the *mitzvah* of "belief in the Divine" (in Maimonides' *Sefer ha-Mitzvot*) and "the foundation of foundations and the mainstay of wisdom, to know that there exists a First Being" (with which Maimonides' *Mishneh Torah* opens).

He discerns here two different aspects of the principles of faith and he adds that "this double employment of the *mitzvah* of the existence of God in the sense of 'believing' and in the sense of 'knowing' is not confined to this issue only, but has implications which extend to all the other *mitzvot*, as this *mitzvah* lies at the root and source of all the *mitzvot*."[27] Rabbi Soloveitchik applies this "knowing" to all the *mitzvot* and not

26. *Ibid.*, p. 129.

27. *Ibid.*, pp. 130, 200. Compare with Aaron Lichtenstein, "Rabbi Joseph Soloveitchik, in *Great Jewish Thinkers of the 20th Century*, ed. Simon Novecek (Clinton, Mass., 1964). Lichtenstein's assertion (p. 296) that Rabbi Soloveitchik's emphasis upon religious experience is reflected only in some of his "recent writings" dealing with the relation of intellect and emotion, is worth re-examining because, as it seems to us, the value of the religious experience is primary in all of the Rav's published works from "The Halakhic Man" (1944) until today. Compare also Jacob B. Agus, *Guideposts in Modern Judaism* (New York 1954), pp. 38–43. Agus argues that one cannot regard Soloveitchik's thought as entirely bound by the confines of the *halakhah* and that inevitably it ventures beyond these into the realms of the Kabbalah and philosophy.

merely to the belief in the existence of God, and he interprets it in such a way that the belief in the existence of God will become a continuous and constant awareness of God's reality, a consciousness that never wavers or suffers from absent-mindedness. While the phrase "to believe" contains no prohibition against forgetfulness—for it is possible to believe and yet turn one's mind away from the object of that belief—the phrase "to know" implies "that the belief in God shall be constant in man, a permanent orientation, a living reality from which man cannot divert his attention even for a moment. This awareness of the reality of God must be the basis of our thought, ideas, feelings under all conditions and in all circumstances; all must turn upon this faith."[28]

At this point Rabbi Soloveitchik draws near to the Ba'al Shem Tov's *ḥasidic* concept of faith which incorporates this interpretation of faith under the heading of *devekut* (communion).[29] Like the Ba'al Shem Tov, Rabbi Soloveitchik links his interpretation[30] to the biblical corroboration of Proverbs 3:6: "In all thy ways know Him," which already in the Talmud (*Ber.* 53a) was considered "a small matter upon which the whole body of the Torah hangs," and which explains the passage in a manner almost identical with that presented in the name of the Ba'al Shem Tov which states: "In all thy ways 'know Him'—that is a great rule, 'know Him' in the sense of a coming together. . . . In all His deeds, even in things terrestrial, it is necessary that his work be done only for a higher purpose and let nothing, even the smallest thing, be done for any purpose other than a heavenly one" (*Zava'at ha-Ribash,* Jerusalem 1969, p. 230). In the words of Rabbi Soloveitchik, " 'In

28. See below, p. 132.

29. On the concept of "Devekut" in *ḥasidism,* see Gershom Scholem, *The Messianic Idea in Judaism* (Schocken Books, N.Y. 1971), "Devekut or Communion with God," pp. 203–27.

30. See below, p. 131.

all thy ways'—in everything thou doest, in every path thou takest, in all situations, under all conditions—'know Him,' retain this awareness of the existence of God."

As is his wont, Rabbi Soloveitchik splendidly and at length describes all the places, situations and circumstances in human life in which man can and should "know" God. "To believe is necessary, but it is not enough; one must also feel and sense the existence of God. The presence of the Almighty must be a personal, intimate experience. And if this experience is not common, and if it proves impossible to achieve that *devekut* in Him, blessed be He, and if one feels not the touch of His hand, one cannot be a complete Jew."[31]

This insistence upon experience (which is so close to *ḥasidic* thought) is rooted in Soloveitchik's thought, in *halakhic* categories, based on Maimonides' halakhic code, the *Mishneh Torah.* Rabbi Lichtenstein has already noted[32] that Rabbi Soloveitchik has added a new category to the customary division of the *mitzvot* into *ḥovot ha'evarim* (the duties of the limbs) and *ḥovot halevavot* (the duties of the heart)—the physical and spiritual duties. Soloveitchik's innovation lies in the identification of a category of *mitzvot* which are of a dual character; they are compounded of both "fulfillable" and "enactable" elements, in which ḥovot haevarim and ḥovot halevavot come together as one. There are *mitzvot* in which the fulfillment and the enactment cannot be separated, the *mitzvah* being fulfilled and enacted at the same time. This, for example, occurs in the *mitzvah* of the *lulav* (palm branch). The Torah states: "And you shall take unto you." When one "takes the *lulav,*" one both fulfills and enacts the *mitzvah.* Similarly, with regard to eating *maẓah* and "counting the *omer.*" In contrast, there are

31. *Ibid.,* p. 133. Here and elsewhere Rabbi Soloveitchik reaches unusually intimate and moving confessions, rare in Jewish tradition, of nearness to God.

32. In his splendid biographical essay on Rabbi Soloveitchik (note 27, above), p. 295.

*mitzvot* wherein the enactment and the fulfillment are distinct (occurring, as it were, on different planes and, perhaps, at different points in time). This happens, for instance, in *mitzvot* where the enactment is by hand or through speech, while the fulfillment takes place, perforce, within the heart. Thus a *mitzvah* may be enacted but not, in fact, fulfilled, since the fulfillment depends upon a certain feeling or state of mind. Among such *mitzvot* one may count those of mourning. Acts, such as the removal of sandals, are called for, but without a concomitant fulfillment of the *mitzvah* in the heart of the mourner; the *mitzvah* cannot be said to have been consummated (see *Mishneh Sanh.* 6:6). Other outstanding examples of this distinction between the enactment and the fulfillment of *mitzvot* are the reading of the *shema*; the enactment is in speech, but the fulfillment lies in the acceptance of Divine Sovereignty. Even more so is this the case with regard to prayer and repentance. Prayer is called *avodah she-belev* (worship of the heart) and the *mitzvah* involved is consummated not on the plane of enactment (speech), but on the plane of fulfillment (in the heart), in the experiential happening. The same applies to repentance which is similarly a "silent" or "heart"-centered form of worship.

Rabbi Soloveitchik's teachings about repentance focus on the description of that experiential happening, which he transmits in concepts drawn from the world of *halakhah.* From these teachings emerges the character of "Repentant Man"; he embodies the experience which begins with a feeling of sin and ends in the redemption of a wondrous proximity to God. Between these two points stands man as a creator of worlds, as he shapes the greatest of his works—himself.

[5]

All that is tragic in man, his sense of nothingness and non-being, is manifest in the feeling of sin. Man scrutinizes himself in shame and says: How remote [from God] am I; how abominable and unclean. He sees that his life is a cul-de-sac, that his whole existence is flat and meaningless. He is completely enveloped by Ecclesiastes' cry: "Vanity of vanities, all is vanity." This is a terrible feeling; it leads man to total despair, to a burdensome sense of guilt and to self-destruction.[33]

The sinner feels himself an exile, homeless, marooned on remote shores; his is a schizophrenic personality.[34] His spiritual powers, his feelings and thoughts are bereft of internal cohesion and his character lacks any single focus or center of gravity. When a man begins to feel this way he is at the starting point of the process of repentance. This is the initial stage. The next stage, though the antithesis of the former, is also contained in it and is a part of it. This second stage is fashioned out of the capacity for faith in man's spiritual make-up. This faith posits that, though today a man may be unclean and abominable, he can transcend and escape the constraint of his desperate condition. According to Rabbi Soloveitchik, Maimonides already asserted this when he emphasized again and again in *Hilkhot Teshuvah* that man can shape himself, free himself from deterministic causation and adopt a new system of causality according to his preference. Great is man's power.

It is by virtue of this power that man feels and knows that though all paths are *prima facie* barred to him, yet there remains a narrow and mysterious route somewhere, which meanders and twists between hills and mountains, climbs and descends, turns upward and downward and proceeds backward and forward. And if a man chooses this route, none can stop him. On more public pathways, man will immediately encounter obstacles: "Who are you, and what seek you here?" The "king's way" is barred to the sinner. Neither will the an-

---

33. See below, p. 239.
34. *Ibid.*, p. 307.

gels of mercy allow him passage, for none can pass through the royal gate wearing the sackcloth of sin and iniquity. But though the king's way be barred, yet one may pass along the secret path in the undergrowth; if the main gate is locked, there yet remains a small wicket through which man may enter. The way to reach the goal is not by the public highway, but along the solitary route—and each man has a route of his own.

And as a man feels and knows that he has at least one further path to traverse, so must he believe that, in the depths of his heart, there still subsists, among the piles of burnt-out cinders, one glowing ember, one flickering spark—and from this spark it is possible to rekindle a new flame.

Here is the whole dialectic of the process of repentance. Repentance implies that there are powers in man which allow him to leap from that sense of sin, which profoundly oppresses him and casts him far away, to a different feeling of *ḥazarti lefanekha'* (I am again in Your presence). "Yester-eve he was unclean and abominable . . . and today, beloved and precious"—a gigantic leap within mere minutes. Here is revealed that complete polarity which pervades the soul of man.

This leap lies at the heart of the act of sacrifice, which is at the core of the worship on the Day of Atonement (Yom Kippur). "When a Jew brings a sacrifice for atonement, how are his sins expiated? Is it by virtue of a two-shekel lamb? Certainly not! Atonement comes to him through the recognition and confession of sin embodied in the act of sacrifice. This confession means abnegation and annihilation of self, total submission and subservience, sacrifice of self, of all one's being and possession . . . as though one were oneself laid upon the altar."[34a]

---

34a. *Ibid.*, p. 247; compare *Sefer Ha-Ḥinnukh,* 91 based on Naḥmanides' explanation for the sacrifices.

As a sacrifice upon the altar, so is the man in the whirlpool of purification. A man goes down and takes a dip, and when he emerges, he is a new man, "Repentant Man."

This leap from sin to repentance, from exile and separation back to the Divine, is anchored in the principle of free choice. Rabbi Soloveitchik sees this not as a voluntary option wherein a man can choose to do as he pleases, but as a clear exological imperative, as an existential commitment from which one cannot escape. In free choice man discovers his "self." The assumption that man is free and unconstrained, empowered with the courage of free choice and with the ability to do everything to determine the destiny of his religious and moral life—this assumption cannot be satisfied by faith alone; it requires awareness as well ("knowing," in the sense used by Maimonides), a feeling which will fill his whole being with the tension of that God-given "free choice." Choice should implant a feeling of self-esteem and responsibility in man. As Hillel put it (Avot 1:6): "If I am here, everything is here." Hillel the Elder was the most humble of men, yet it was he who stressed the "I," for "without a recognition of the self the feeling of free choice would not arise in man; without awareness of the 'I', man cannot decide and determine."[35] This possibility of choice is necessary and man cannot evade it.

Seen in this light, man must look upon himself as a guardian of the fate of the world. As the Talmud puts it (*Kid. 40b*): "Man must always regard himself as though he were half guilty and half meritorious"; the world, too, should be viewed as if it is half guilty and half innocent. When performing one *mitzvah,* man is blessed for tilting his own and the world's scales to the side of merit; when committing one transgression, man is damned for tilting his own and the world's scales to the

35. *Ibid.,* pp. 142–144.

side of guilt. Choice is a perpetual feeling of maximum responsibility which permits no absentmindedness even for a moment; "choice demands of man commitment, courage, valor and bravery."[36] Thus Rabbi Soloveitchik paraphrases Maimonides' reflection on faith, saying: "It is a positive commandment to know that there is free choice and that man is responsible for his actions."[37]

Man's existence, according to Rabbi Soloveitchik, has two dimensions: fate and destiny. Destiny-directed existence is "an active existence" in which man stands up to the environment into which he has been cast, and defends his individuality and uniqueness, his freedom and his ability not to deprive himself of his essence and independence in his struggle with the external world. The motto of the destiny-directed "self" is: "Against your will you are born and against your will you die, but by the existence of free will you live." Man is born an object, dies an object, but can live as a subject, as an innovator and as creator, who impresses upon his life an individual stamp.[38]

Salvation, the very possibility of a Messiah, according to Rabbi Soloveitchik, is contingent upon the acceptance of the idea of free choice, which confers upon man a power of transcendence and a capacity to rise above himself and to reach the infinite and eternal.[39]

"Judaism asserts," wrote Rabbi Soloveitchik in "Halakhic Man,"[40] "that man stands [forever] at a crossroads and wonders which way to proceed. Confronting him is a terrible choice: between the image of God or a beast of prey; the glory

---

36. *Ibid.*, p. 143.
37. *Ibid.*
38. "Kol Dodi Dofek." IAIT, p. 337.
39. "On the Love of the Torah," etc., IAIT, p. 405.
40. "Halakhic Man," IAIT, p. 157.

of nobility or the monster of the universe; the choicest of creatures or a corrupt creature; the image of a man of God or the portrait of a Nietzschean *übermensch.* Man must always, always determine and decide."

Free choice, which is part of man's being, means that man can create himself at will and, as it were, be born anew. Rabbi Soloveitchik does not completely reject the law of causation which governs mankind, but the distance is great between this and a subscription to total determinism. Following Kant, Rabbi Soloveitchik accepts the dualism of human existence—life unfolding in a mathematical, scientific world governed by physical laws of causation, and the life of the spirit, the internal existence, which is characterized by extreme freedom.[41] But, employing the principle of free choice, Soloveitchik demonstrates that man can fashion for himself a new law of causation which will take effect from a specific moment onward, i.e., the moment of repentance-salvation, when a complete transformation occurs from within.

Indeed, years before voicing his reflections on repentance, Rabbi Soloveitchik asserted that "the acme of moral and religious perfection, which Judaism aspires to, is 'man as a creator.' "[42] He wrote: "The Almighty, when He created the world, left room for His creature—man—to participate in His creation. It was as if the Creator spoiled reality so that mortals might set it right and modify it. God transmitted the mystery of Creation—the Book of Creation—to man not only that he might read it, but in order that he might carry on the act of Creation. God left an area of evil and chaos in the world so that man might make it good . . . the abyss breeds misfortune and trouble and chaos lie in ambush in the dark alleys of reali-

41. Compare Borowitz, *op. cit.,* p. 163.
42. "Halakhic Man," p. 146.

ty desiring to undermine the Absolute Being and to subvert the radiance of Creation."[42a] All this was determined early by the Creator Who, on purpose, "diminished the character and stature of Creation in order to leave room for [improvement] by His own creature and to crown man with the laurels of 'improver' and 'creator.' "[43] Nothing serves better than the act of repentance "to create a new essence in man; the act of repentance is achieved through the complete application of will and a determined decision of the intellect." These were engraved in man from the commencement of his creation. "From here onward, he was compelled to become a chooser and was obliged to participate in the renewal of Creation; and most important of all is the obligation that man create himself: This is a conception which Judaism gave to the world."[44]

[6]

In the end, the answer lies in the concept of grace. "The very phenomenon of repentance, the fact that man can transcend his baseness and ascend the mountain of God, is one of the great acts of Grace conferred by God on His creations."[45] In justice, sin should have caused man's extinction; man's divorce from the seedbed of his existence should have spelled the end of his life. Thus was sin perceived also by the Sages ("the sinning soul shall die") and by the Prophets ("sins will follow evil"). From a metaphysical standpoint, the possibility of repentance is an act of Grace on the part of the Creator, but this Grace becomes explicable through an understanding of the concept of time.

The problem of repentance is tied up with the concept of

---

42a. *Ibid.,* p. 148.
43. *Ibid.,* p. 154.
44. *Ibid.,* p. 157.
45. See below, p. 207.

time, for it involves a future correction of something in the past. According to the definition of time offered by one of the Jewish Sages of the Middle Ages, Rabbi Yedaiah Ha-Pnini in his famous epigram, "the past is not; the future—still not; and the present—like batting an eyelid." Man's existence is not rooted in time. For time itself, in the case of the past, appears as "was"—"is not," and as future, as "will be"—"still not." From this perspective the concept of repentance is meaningless and hollow. . . . One cannot feel remorse about a past which is already dead and has sunk into the abyss of oblivion, and one cannot decide about a future which is as yet unborn. . . . In this sense Spinoza and Nietzsche did well to deride the idea of repentance."[46] However, according to Rabbi Soloveitchik, whose thought is based upon the different classifications, one may apply time in line with the thinking of Bergson and Heidegger,[47] and especially with Max Scheler's essay on repentance,[48] there is time which is actually "nothing"; i.e., quantified time, which flows according to the mechanistic law of causation (in which moment "A" fades and is replaced by moment "B," which gives way to moment "C"). This time is continuous and follows the order of past-present-future; each point evolves from a previous one and is—or is not—self-sufficient. This is physical or technical-quantitative time; it passes and expires at the moment it gives birth to the subsequent point in time. In contrast there exists qualitative time, a dynamic continuity, in which the "Past is continuous and stable, does not pass or slip away through one's fingers, but re-

46. "Halakhic Man," IAIT, p. 162.

47. Hebrew Encyclopedia, Vol. IX, p. 448; V Vol. XIV, p.52.

48. Max Scheler. "Repentance and Rebirth," in his book, *On the Eternal in Man*, translated by Bernard Noble (SCM Press Ltd., London 1960), pp. 35–65, and in greater detail and length in a dissertation by Johann Schindler, *Gott und Mensch in ihrer gegenseitigen Zuordnung in der philosophischen Konzeption Max Schelers* (Augsburg 1968).

mains static. This past obtrudes and enters the domain of the present which intermingles with the future."[49] In this conception of time, the future is not of the "still not" variety, is not "hidden beyond the mists, but is revealed in the here-and-now in all its splendor and beauty. . . . Such a future infuses from its hidden resources power and potency, vitality and freshness into the vessels of the past. . . . Both past and future are alive, act and create in the hub of the present and determine the appearance of existence." In this perspective the order of time is not past-present-future; rather all three intermingle and interpenetrate, and the conception of threefold time erupts and rises forth beshrouded in the glory of unity—until the principle of "one after another" often no longer serves as a clear indication of time. Rather, "man lives in the shadow of the past, future and present simultaneously," and then "the future determines the direction and indicates the way. . . . There exists a phenomenon whose beginning is sin and iniquity and whose end is *mitzvot* and good deeds, and vice versa. The future transforms the trends and tendencies of the past."[50]

This intermingling of tenses occurs within man, who lives and acts not as if from one evolving moment to the next, but lives entirely at once.[51] Thus it is that "man, as he returns to his Creator, shapes himself out of the living and extant past as he looks to the future which offers up a happy visage." This leads us to the conclusion reached by Rabbi Soloveitchik[52] that "the fundamental principle of the essence of repentance is that the future will rule and govern the past unrestrictedly." For repentance, he believes, means nothing other than (a) retrospective contemplation of the past and the distinction be-

---

49. "Halakhic Man," p. 162.

50. *Ibid.*, p. 163.

51. Scheler, *op. cit.*, pp. 40–41. In "Halakhic Man," p. 72, the Rav refers to his reliance on Scheler's thinking; compare also Kaplan, *op. cit.*

52. "Halakhic Man," p. 187.

tween the living and the dead in it; and (b) the vision of the future and its utilization according to the free determination of man.

Man's very existence, according to Rabbi Soloveitchik,[53] is contingent upon these two realms of activity: (a) in the memory of those situations and experiences undergone by man in the past and which, in many senses, have not died or been erased, but rather continue to exist in the inner recesses of his heart; and (b) in his expectations of the future, in his plans and hopes for the morrow and for the day following. In these two realms man responds to the question: Who am I? Memory and expectation come together and focus on the character of man and give significance to the whole of his life, above and beyond the flow of meaningless time, whose flux is devoid of significance and purpose.

Repentance creates and shapes time—in all its tenses—and gives it an image and character in the order of future-past-present. The past returns to life in the light of the future. Occasionally, life is short—as in the case of the dry bones resurrected by Ezekiel in the Valley of Dura who, according to one opinion among the Sages (*Sanh.* 92, b), stood on their feet, sang for a short while and immediately returned to the dead. In this case, though the penitent revisits the sinful past, in his confrontation with it he immediately uproots and destroys it, thoroughly erasing it from his personality. While fully conscious, he divorces himself from his past. Among the signs of *teshuvah gemurah* (complete repentance) enumerated by Mai-

53. See below, pp. 249–253. Rabbi Soloveitchik here develops the idea that the old have more memories and less expectations, and the young less memories and more expectations; the two constitute the elements of the "self" in man. Compare with a similar idea developed in Ahad Ha-Am's essay, "*Avar ve-Atid*" (Past and Future) in *Al Parashat Derakhim*, Vol. I, p. 150, which begins: "A great philosopher inadvertently was Adam, the first person who expressed the word I . . . the self of each person is the product of the combination of his memory with his will, of the past with the future."

monides appears the following: "And he changes his name, meaning, 'I am different and no longer the same person who did these deeds.' " Nevertheless, true "Repentant Man" is characterized by a creative power which enables him to forgo uprooting the past. He can, on the contrary, take up the past and exalt it, and shape it so that it can be molded with the future to create the present himself.

Here lies revealed, in all its forcefulness, the whole creative potency of repentance. It issues from the dialectical dynamic of sin, the very thing which severs man from God, which makes him abominable and unclean, the very thing which leads him—after repentance—to that high peak unattainable even by the "completely righteous."

[7]

"Repentant Man," if he wishes to attain this high peak, does not forget his sin or tear out or erase the pages of iniquity from the book of his life. Rather he exists on the spirit of "my sin is ever before me" (Ps 51:3). Instead of uprooting the past and erasing the sin, he carries them up with him to heights he could never have dreamed of had he not sinned.

The force of the sin and the feelings of guilt and shame engendered in man are transmuted in the penitent's heart into an irresistible force propelling him toward the Creator. "The energy of sin pulls, as it were, upward."[54]

Thus said the Sages (*Ber.* 34, b): "Where penitents stand the completely righteous cannot." How can it be that the penitent will draw nearer to God than the completely righteous? How can sins turn into a dynamic force propelling toward sanctity? Here, to Rabbi Soloveitchik's mind, is above all a mystery, a manifestation of God's grace, as is repentance in

---

54. See below, p. 256. Compare with Max Scheler, *op. cit.,* p. 42, which speaks of repentance as revealing in man's soul hidden, untainted corners of youthfulness.

general. The Ruler and Creator of the world was He Who created the possibility that purity might be born out of abomination ("Who can bring a clean thing out of an unclean?" [the only One Who can]:Jb 14:4). It is also possible that the idea of raising sin to the level of sanctity is contained in this mystery.

Rabbi Soloveitchik does not content himself with indicating the mysterious in this phenomenon. He attempts also to reveal the spiritual, ontological motives underlying the dynamics of sin.

There is a tragic aspect to man's essence: it lies in the fact that people and the things closest to his heart are not properly appreciated so long as they are alive and present. Man begins to accord them appropriate recognition only after they have moved away and have become distant and inaccessible. "From afar they now entice him like the stars in heaven; he appreciates their value, but cannot touch them."[55] The yearning after one who is gone and no longer lives is extremely difficult to bear, and occasionally the soul actually becomes deranged through nostalgia and a craving to return to that original, vanished state. In his lifetime every man confronts this situation of yearning for one who was recently about and is now remote to the point of inaccessibility. Such yearnings are usually accompanied by a strong sense of guilt, which haunts man and may drive him to madness.

In a similar fashion, this phenomenon occurs in the penitent. When a man sins he expels the Almighty from his presence.[56] God's departure is like that of a dearly beloved soul. After some time, following the initial shock, a man suddenly feels that his life has been impoverished, that his house has collapsed about him, that he has lost that thing most intimate and precious. As it is in the life of the individual, in the disap-

---

55. See below, p. 257.
56. Compare Zohar on Genesis 3:24.

pearance of a beloved soul, so is it in man's spiritual life, in God's departure from man's bosom in the wake of sin. "Mourning the withdrawal, as it were, of the Almighty from the sinner is like the mourning over a beloved father and mother." Sooner or later the cloud of mourning will inevitably descend, and then will come fear and loneliness, estrangement, alienation, remoteness and separation; sadness will grow and emptiness will spread in the soul, and man will begin to yearn for the Almighty, and when he apparently sights God's Image from afar, he will begin to run toward it rapidly with all his strength. The power of the unleashed nostalgia in man's bosom, after such protracted incarceration, propels him onward; he will run more quickly now than was his wont before growing apart from God. Through this nostalgic drive the penitent surpasses the completely righteous, who has never sinned, who does not know sin or recognize it.

Moreover, the Sages of the Kabbalah (and of psychology) assert that in the soul there are two sets of forces: constructive and destructive. Love is a constructive force; it is opposed by the destructive forces of jealousy and hatred. The positive-constructive forces are by and large static and passive, while the negative forces are dynamic and aggressive. Hatred is more emotional and fiercer than love; the destructive forces are more powerful than the constructive forces. The completely righteous person, who has never tasted sin, is not swayed by hatred and jealousy; he excels in love, charity and mercy, which are by nature tranquil and restrained drives. In contrast with him, the man who has sinned and repented can conjure up the dynamic energy of the destructive forces which once prevailed in his soul, and can channel it into his newly-adopted good ways. The future takes from the energy developed by the sinner and refashions it into a gigantic force for good. The same passion exhibited by the sinner in his thirst for iniquity can now be displayed in the fulfillment of *mitzvot.*[57] The same appetite and commitment previously invested in theft and illegal earning can now be funnelled into acts of charity and mercy.

"Through sin man discovered in himself new spiritual forces, a reservoir of energy, of cupidity and obstinacy unknown to him before indulging in sin. Now he can sanctify all these drives and can direct them heavenward. The aggressiveness within him now will not let him make do with his previous, wonted measure of do-gooding, but will propel him ever closer toward the heavenly throne."[58] In support of this point, Rabbi Soloveitchik elucidates the following passage (Ps 29:9): "The Voice of the Lord maketh the hinds to calve, and discovereth the forests . . ." and explains:[59] on the Day of Atonement the Almighty demands that man become "a discoverer of forests"; that he endanger himself and enter the "jungle" of his soul, that place where hides the beast that is in man. The Almighty does not ask man to cut down the trees of the forest, nor that he uproot the jungle completely. For as men need fields for grazing and beds in which to raise flowers, so they need giant forests. These contain a great deal of animality and vivacity, a lot of healthy aggressiveness subsists in the depths of the forest. But woe to the forest which is impenetrable to the Voice of God, which maketh hinds calve and discovers forests.

Our aim is not to kill off the hinds, nor do we wish to burn down the dark forests, but rather to turn them into receptacles of the Voice of God. And after this is achieved, as

---

57. Here, too, is felt the influence of *ḥasidic* thought. Compare with "The Book of the Ba'al Shem Tov," Gen. pp. 158–161. On the influence of *ḥasidic* thought upon Rabbi Soloveitchik even from his childhood, compare Lichtenstein, *op. cit.,* p. 282.

58. See below, p. 263.

59. *Ibid.,* p. 264.

the verse continues: "And in His Temple doth everyone speak of His glory." The rabbis say that the ingredients of incense of the Day of Atonement are alluded to here. In incense there is an admixture of resin and components of perfume. Why must one place resin, whose smell is unpleasant, among the perfumes? In order to show us that one may take the bad and blend it with the perfumes, in order that it may be exalted and enter the Holy of Holies. The exaltation of evil and not its mere purgation, the past itself and not only its eradication—these are the goals of "Repentant Man."

[8]

The path of repentance is a lonely road. Alone and solitary, man feels the pain of the sense of sin, and in the inner recesses of his being, he makes his way to repentance. "On the Day of Atonement," writes Rabbi Soloveitchik,[60] "we unite with Moses on top of the Mount (to receive the second set of Tablets) as he listened intently to the fine silence which was shattered by the eruption of the wonder of repentance and the Grace of God." The latter presentation of the Law on Mount Sinai, in which the second set of Tablets were bestowed, does not resemble the first, in which the Tablets were given and broken. On this occasion "no public revelation, in the sight of all, occurred. The primal creatures did not tremble; the sound of the shofar was not heard in the camp; nor did thunder and lightning disturb the sleep of the hosts of Israel," who were still in a profound slumber at this early hour of the morning. Total silence enveloped the mountain and the half-light of a wondrous and secret dawn shrouded it. Moses alone, unaccompanied by friend or disciple, climbed the cold and steep cliffs of the Mount. Even Joshua, who had never left his side,

---

60. "Ma Dodekh Mi-dod," in IAIT, pp. 189–254.

did not join Moses this time. Thus God commanded (Ex 34:3): "And no man shall come up with thee, neither let any man be seen throughout all the Mount." As God revealed Himself to Moses on the mountain, he underwent spiritual suffering, out of a sense of aloneness, out of a silence of a man whose life is at a standstill and without foundation; in fear, the fear of a creature when he is for a fleeting moment cut off from his Creator.

The Day of Atonement is the day of "Repentant Man," and "the appearance of the Day of Remembrance (Rosh ha-Shanah), is not that of the Day of Atonement. On the first of the seventh month, God sets out toward man; on the tenth of the month man sets forth toward God. In the public setting-forth of God toward the community is hidden the secret of sovereignty and judgment; in the secret setting forth of the individual toward God, Who sits hidden in the shadows, is concealed the secret of repentance."[61]

Such is the way of "Repentant Man": alone, in secret, unaccompanied. Repentance buds and transpires in the heart of the individual. However, "Repentant Man" will not reach his goal and the completion of his mission—salvation—as a lonely man of faith, but only as a part of the community of Israel. His whole endeavor as an individual is worthless to him until he renews his connection with the covenantal community and reintegrates in it. This integration does not abolish his loneliness or isolation,[62] nor does it help to ease his suffering or diminish his pain, but it gives him a certain status that is a prerequisite to salvation.

The individual Jew constitutes an integral part of *Knesset Israel* (the community of Israel). This is not a free and volun-

61. *Ibid.,* p. 198.
62. Soloveitchik, "The Lonely Man of Faith," *op. cit.,* pp. 22ff.

tary association; it is an ontological-essential one. As *Knesset Israel* is not a sum total or arithmetic combination of such and such individuals, but a metaphysical personality of singular essence and possessing an individual judicial personality, so the individual Jew does not have an independent existence but is a limb of *Knesset Israel*—unless he commits such sins as cut him off from the congregation and uproot him from the community of Israel.[63] In this manner the way to repentance is sealed off completely. However, remaining tied to *Knesset Israel* through loyalty to that body and its goals,[64] and enjoying the special attitude which such membership elicits offers no protection, as it were, except in the one sense of the two compelled by his existential reality as an individual and as part of the community. He still has need of private confession, private spiritual stock-taking, individual purification. In this dialectic of individual and community, Rabbi Soloveitchik sees one of the foundations of Judaism.

"A Jew who has lost his faith in *Knesset Israel* even though he may, in his own little corner, sanctify and purify himself through severities and restrictions—this Jew remains incorrigible and totally unequipped to partake of the Day of Atonement which encompasses the whole of *Knesset Israel* in all its parts and in all its generations. . . . Only a Jew who believes in *Knesset Israel* will be privileged to partake of the sanctity of the day and of atonement as part of the community of Israel. . . . A Jew who lives as part of *Knesset Israel* and is ready to lay down his life for it, who is pained by its hurt and is happy at its joy, wages its battles, groans at its failures, and celebrates its victories. . . . A Jew who believes in *Knesset Israel* is a Jew who binds himself with an indissoluble bond not only to the People of Israel of his generation, but to *Knesset Israel* through all the

63. See below, p. 108.
64. *Ibid.*, pp. 120–121.

generations."[65] This necessary loyalty to *Knesset Israel* is not, according to Rabbi Soloveitchik's explanation, a matter of mysticism or metaphysics; it is rooted and embodied in the *halakhic* categories which assert, in reference to the sanctity of Israel, that "this sanctity has two roots: first, the sanctity of the Fathers, which reaches us as an inheritance transmitted from generation to generation, from the Patriarch Abraham down to the present day; second, the sanctity of self. In addition to the sanctity vouchsafed each person of Israel as an inheritance from his forefathers, there is in him a portion of sanctity which the Almighty invests in every one of Israel in every generation." The roots of these two portions of sanctity, explains Rabbi Soloveitchik, lie in the two Covenants between God and His people Israel (in fact there were three but two of these can be counted as one): the Covenant at Horeb with those who received the Torah, and the Covenant of the Wilderness of Moab with those who entered the land. In these covenants, Israel was sanctified, and that sanctity passes down to us from generation to generation. That is the sanctity of the Fathers. These two covenants are joined by a third—the covenant in Deuteronomy. That covenant was not concluded with that generation only, but with all the generations and with all children of Israel down to the end of time, as it is written (Dt 29:14, 15): "Neither with you only do I make this covenant and this oath, but with him that standeth here with us this day before the Lord our God and also with him that is not here with us this day." From here springs an original sanctity of self, of every generation, and every individual in every age. Before us, therefore, is a double bond between Israel and the Lord, both as individuals and as a people, seed of Abraham.

"The origin of the sanctity is in the making of a covenant, i.e., in a contract entailing mutual obligations. Sin means that

---

65. *Ibid.,* p. 125.

if one party to the agreement fails to meet the conditions of the contract, the agreement becomes null and void."[66] The sanctity that was conferred by virtue of the contract lapses. This applies also when the sinner has sinned through error or under external compulsion. The reference here is to that personal sanctity of the self. With regard to the sanctity of the Fathers, the sanctity passes down as an inheritance and it does not lie in the power of a sinner to breach or break the contract; the covenant is the inheritance of the whole people of Israel and no power exists which can revoke it. Nevertheless, though the covenant with Israel exists, the sinner, as it were, cuts himself off from it until he repents. Once repentant, "not only does the repentance cleanse the sinner of the filth of iniquity, but it contains a kind of fresh act of covenant-making between the individual and the Almighty. . . . Repentance is not merely the purification of the personality, but a special sanctification of the individual, making him ready once more to conclude a covenant."

The renewal of the personal covenant ("there are no delegates in covenant-making, and if repentance is a renewed acceptance of personal sanctity, then there is no escape from direct confrontation with God") leads the individual back to the framework of the complete agreement, the double one, which rests upon the dual connection between God and the people of Israel and God and each individual in Israel.

The prophet Elisha was privileged to enter into just such a renewed covenant, as Rabbi Soloveitchik describes him at the end of his essay "The Lonely Man of Faith."[67] In the depths of his soul Elisha remains the lonely man of faith, but in obedience to God's command he returns to participate in the drama of the covenant and to take part in "the great and

---

66. *Ibid.*, p. 216.
67. *Ibid.*, p. 222.

festive dialogue" between the God and the People of the Covenant.

The ways of repentance are many and varied. Repentance, it is true, is not restricted merely to the ideal "Repentant Man." There are penitents whose repentance is efficacious and perhaps excellent, who yet remain remote from the concept of the typological "Repentant Man." There are also penitents who are not true penitents like the usurer who leaves debt-pledges in his drawer in case he has "need" of them again, and like that sinner who retains the address of the woman with whom he had sinned, in case he "desire" her again. These stand on the borderline of repentance and are light years away from resembling "Repentant Man" who, after deep spiritual torment and personal decisiveness, achieved a total and radical transformation of character "until the One Who knows all mysteries will testify that he [the penitent] will not revert to this sin ever after,"[68] without, in any way, damaging the power of free choice that is in man. "Repentant Man" reaches that rung which is above and beyond the momentary, transient choice that determines the nature of the immediate act; he propels himself, as it were, into a state of permanent, standing sanctity, of "sanctity for the moment and sanctity for the future," insofar as he has placed the whole future in his present life which illuminates afresh his past life as well. Moreover, "Repentant Man" does not live with the past, but with the future of which the past has become a part.

---

68. Maimonides, *Laws of Repentance,* Chapter 2, Section 2, explicated by Soloveitchik pp. 157ff. below.

# *Soloveitchik*
# ON REPENTANCE

# ACQUITTAL AND PURIFICATION

Yom Kippur—the Day of Atonement—has a double function. The first is *kapparah*—acquittal from sin or atonement: "For the virtue of this very day shall acquit you of sin" (Lev 16:30). This was expressed in the prayer recited by the High Priest in the Holy Temple: "Please grant acquittal for sins."

The second aspect of Yom Kippur is *taharah*—catharsis or purification. As it is written: "For the virtue of this very day shall acquit you of sin, to cleanse you. . . ." This, too, was brought out in the Yom Kippur Temple service. The High Priest pronounced to the assembled people: "Before God, be you cleansed."

These two motifs recur repeatedly in all the prayers said on Yom Kippur. "Acquit us . . . pour cleansing waters upon us. . . ."

Both of these elements, acquittal and purification, are a direct response and remedy for the ontological effects of sin. This is because sin places man under the burden of culpable liability and it defiles him as well.

In order to understand the concepts of *kapparah* (acquittal) and *taharah* (purification), one must find out what is meant by liability and defilement which are brought about by sin.

Sin and its punishment are born together. No sin goes without its retribution, whether it be meted out by a terrestrial or a celestial court. The belief in reward and punishment is fundamental to Jewish belief: "A man who says that the Holy One, blessed be He, is lax in the execution of justice, shall be disemboweled for it is stated, He is the Rock, His work is perfect; for all His ways are judgment" (T.B., Baba Kama 50a). And in the Torah it is written: "Know therefore that the Lord thy God is the faithful God Who keeps covenant and shows mercy to those that love Him and keep His commandments to a thousand generations, and repays those that hate Him . . . to destroy them" (Deuteronomy 7:9). Jewish creed is based on the belief in reward and punishment and on the conviction that sin is by no means a transitory phenomenon that passes by, leaving no trace and incurring no liability. Sin and punishment are always linked together. If you will, the very definition of sin is that it is an act that entails paying a penalty. If punishment exists, it is because sin does too.

*Kapparah* means forgiveness or withdrawal of claim. This is a legal concept, borrowed from the laws of property. Just as one may release his fellow man of a debt owed to him, so may God absolve one of penalty to which he is liable due to sin. *Kapparah* removes the need for punishment.

We find the first instance of *kapparah* in the story of the sin of Cain (Genesis 4:7). "If you shall do better," God admonishes Cain, "the punishment will be carried over," and if you do not, "sin (punishment) crouches at the opening." The punishment is linked, understandably, to the sinful act. The Bible also speaks of the removal of sin. The prophet Nathan said to King David (2 Samuel 12:4): "The Lord has also removed your sin, you shall not die." The medieval Bible commentator, Rashi, while explaining the verse in Genesis 32:21, observed that "whenever the term *kapparah* is used in connection with a matter of trespass and sin . . . it has the connotation of wiping away and removal." That is to say, a barrier is set up through which punishment may not pass. By means of *teshuvah* (repentance) and *kapparah* (acquittal) man puts a protective covering between himself and the punishment for his sin. According to Rashi, the words "*kapparah*" (acquittal) and "*kofer*" (indemnity payment) are derived from the same Hebrew root ["*kfr*"] and have a common signification. Punishment is not a self-negating phenomenon; an indemnity must be offered and paid in order to withdraw the liability claim. That indemnity payment is made through *teshuvah* (repentance) itself. *Kapparah* (acquittal) is the result of the payment of this "ransom" which releases and redeems man from punishment.

All this concerns the liability incurred by the sinner. The moment acquittal is granted and punishment wiped from the books, man's liability is terminated.

However, sin also has a polluting quality. The Jewish view recognizes a state of "impurity of sin" (*tum'at ha-ḥet*). The entire Bible abounds in references to this idea of self-pollution, contamination, rolling about in the mire of sin. This impurity makes its mark on the sinner's personality. Sin, as it were, removes the divine halo from man's head, impairing his spiritual integrity. In addition to the frequent appearance of this idea in Scripture and in the homiletical teachings of the Aggadah, we also find many concrete references to the "impurity of sin" in the Halakha (Jewish Law).

An Israelite who has transgressed suffers a reversal in his legal status. Should a man commit a prohibited act and be charged with stripes or capital punishment, not only does he have to pay the penalty for his sins, he is also discredited as a witness in a court of Jewish Law. This does not constitute further punishment but is rather indicative of a change in his personal status. As a result of sin, man is not the same person he was before. Every man is presumed acceptable as a credible witness. Natural truthfulness is, to my way of thinking, an integral part of man's character. The moment a person sins he lessens his own worth, brings himself down and becomes spiritually defective, thus foregoing his former status. Sin deprives man of his natural privileges and unique human attributes. He is subjected to a complete transformation as his original personality departs, and another one replaces it. This is not a form of punishment, or a fine, and is not imposed in a spirit of anger, wrath or vindictiveness. It is a "metaphysical" corruption of the human personality, of the divine image of man.

The communists speak of the commission of "error" and of "deviation," but have no concept of sin. Error carries no implication of metaphysical impurity or of psychic pollution. An "error" is a legal, rational term which must be distinguished from "sin" which harms the inner quality of man and has a deep and far-reaching effect on his being.

Indeed true *teshuvah* (repentance) not only achieves *kapparah* (acquittal and erasure of penalty), it should also bring about *taharah* (purification) from *tum'ah* (spiritual pollution), liberating man from his hard-hearted ignorance and insensitivity. Such *teshuvah* restores man's spiritual viability and rehabilitates him to his original state.

And sometimes it makes man rise to heights he never dreamed he could reach.

### *Purification Impossible by Proxy*

According to Rabbi Judah Hanassi, the Day of Atonement procures acquittal of sin even for those who have not repented individually (T.B., Yoma 84b). The question arises: May a Jew who has sinned, and, as a result, been discredited as a witness in a court of law, be accepted as a qualified witness on the day after Yom Kippur, even if he has not personally repented? The emphatic answer is: No. *Kapparah* (acquittal) affects the removal of punishment. The "indemnity payment" shields man from divine anger and wrath. However, his personality remains contaminated, and this condition may be remedied only through ritual "immersion," that is, by wholehearted repentance. *Kapparah* (acquittal of punishment) is possible even when an individual has not repented: but without personal repentance *taharah* (purification) is unthinkable.

*Kapparah* is principally connected to the bringing of sacrifices, and in the Holy Temple the prescribed time for offerings were the daylight hours. Ritual purification, in contrast, begins with nightfall, at the "sanctification of the day"—that time when, according to Jewish law, a new day is born.

Purification is conditional upon our drawing near and standing directly "before God," and as such it is a spiritually uplifting experience.

There are two forms of confession on Yom Kippur: a communal, public confession and personal, private one. After the destruction of the Temple, the communal recitation of confession by the synagogue reader was substituted for that of the High Priest. However, the intimate, personal type of confession of a broken man, directed inward to himself, remained exclusively in the area of individual responsibility. This is the confession that brings about purification. The communal confession, which is for *kapparah* (acquittal), should be said together with the synagogue reader. However, it is impossible to appoint an intermediary in order to achieve self-purification as it is by definition clearly a personal obligation. It is absurd from the point of view of Jewish Law for a ritually impure person to send an appointed agent to immerse himself in the former's behalf. No one can grant another power of attorney to deliver him from a state of impurity and restore him to a state of holiness.

This is the way it was in the time of the Temple where the High Priest would "direct his attention to those who were assembled" and say, in effect: "We, the Temple priests, are engaged in the performance of those precepts which concern the sacrificial service of the day of Yom Kippur whereby acquittal of sin, *kapparah*, is granted. However, the act of purification is something you must perform by yourselves, each man in his own heart." And he would then say: "Be you cleansed!"

For this reason, the confession of the *Minha* (afternoon) service on the eve of Yom Kippur, whose purpose is purification, is not recited by the synagogue reader, for "one cannot appoint an intermediary for purification." Every Jew must enter within the "holiness of the day" as an individual and stand as he is "before God." As the nightfall of Yom Kippur approaches, each person listens to the inner voice that calls on him to "be cleansed."

The Mishna teaches us: "Rabbi Akiba said: Fortunate are you, Israel! Who is it before Whom you become clean? And Who is it that makes you clean? Your Father Who is in heaven" (Yoma 8:9).

It seems certain that Rabbi Akiba said this soon after the fall of the second Temple. To understand the full meaning of his words, we must try to picture the mentality and broken spirit of the Jews in that first year after the destruction of the Temple. Yom Kippur had arrived and suddenly the people realized that there would be no sacrificial service, the High Priest could not enter the Holy of Holies, there was no incense, no public celebration for the High Priest as he emerged from the holy place. They were deprived of the entire sacred service which took place on Yom Kippur when the Temple was standing. They felt that all they cherished was lost and that there was no hope of repairing the damage. It seemed as though they would remain plunged forever within the deep darkness enclosing them. It was then that Rabbi Akiba declared: "Fortunate are you, O Israel, before Whom do you cleanse yourselves?" You may achieve a state of spiritual cleanliness even without the sacrificial service of the High Priest. Comply with the directive "*Be cleansed before God*" and this will suffice. Come and stand "before God." Sense His nearness and you will be cleansed.

"Who cleanses you? Your Father in heaven. For just as a ritual immersion purifies the unclean, so does the Holy One, Blessed be He, cleanse Israel. . . ." Man must come before God and enter into the sanctity of Yom Kippur in the same manner that he immerses himself in a ritual bath. He must enter wholly without any interposition, not excluding any part of his being.

"Before God be cleansed!" "For the virtue of this day shall acquit you of sin to cleanse you." In Hebrew the syntax of the phrase "will acquit you of sin *to cleanse you*" has the same implication as the verse in Genesis which says: "which God created *to do,*" meaning that which God created and made; so, too, in this case, it may be read as saying: "He will acquit you of sin and cleanse you."

## *The Path of Sinners and the Path of Sin*

The main feature of repentance is confession. There are, as stated before, two categories of confession: one, whose purpose is *kapparah* (acquittal of sin) and the other which has as its goal *taharah* (purification). Although their liturgical formulation is identical, repentance of acquittal is actually quite different from repentance of purification.

The Talmud lists those who are disqualified as credible witnesses and mentions dice players (including checker players), usurers and gamblers on pigeon races among them. The

Talmud then poses the question: "Dice players . . . when are they considered to have repented? When they break up their checkers and undergo a complete reformation, to the extent that they will not play even as a pastime. . . . And a usurer? . . . When he tears up his credit slips and undergoes a complete reformation refusing to lend on interest, even to an idol worshiper. Pigeon trainers: that is those who race pigeons. . . . When may they be reinstated? When they break up their pegmas (pigeon traps) and undergo a complete reformation to the extent that they will not practice their vice, even in the wilderness" (T.B., Sanhedrin 25b: cf. Maimonides' formulation, Laws of Testimony, Chapter 1, sections 5–8).

The above violations center on the prohibition of theft and robbery. Why, then, is not repentance considered an accomplished fact as soon as the sinner regrets his wrongdoings and ceases to engage in those fraudulent, thieving practices? Playing dice for free, lending money with interest to an idol worshiper and setting up a pigeon trap in the desert are not forbidden by law. Why is not the repentance of these sinners a "complete return" until they literally break their dice, tear up their loan contracts and dismantle their pigeon traps?

It is interesting to note that Maimonides did not deal with this issue under the Laws of Repentance, but rather within the Laws of Testimony. This is because readmissibility as a witness depends upon the achievement of purification from sin which involves much more than repentance which brings acquittal, dealt with in the chapter on the Laws of Repentance. All that is required for acquittal is the sinner's regret of past actions and his resolution not to return to his folly.

However, repentance of purification necessitates a complete breaking away from the environment, the contributing factors and all the forces which created the atmosphere of sin. For repentance of purification, which restores man to his primary condition of integrity, man is required to break the dice, tear up the deeds and burn all the bridges leading to the world of sin which he has left behind him.

Thus we see that there are two levels of separation—the first, from sin and the second, divergence from the path leading to sin. Sin is not created *ex nihilo nihil.* Evildoing is the product of a certain atmosphere, of favorable conditions—flattery of men in positions of power, indolence, imagined or real fear, weakness or spinelessness; such is "the path of sin."

Even when we do not actually commit a wrongdoing, we often find ourselves on the "path of sin." Along the sides of this road, sin is permitted to bud, flower, bear fruit and take root. Like any other organic creation, sin requires an environment in which it can flourish, absorb nourishment, and thrive under the warm rays shining down upon it, as does a sprouting tree.

For acquittal of sin (*kapparah*), remorse is sufficient. Only a person who actually commits a transgression needs to seek *kapparah.* However, in regard to purification, abandoning the act of sin is only a partial remedy. Refraining from sin in accordance with what is specifically forbidden in the law is necessary, but more than that is demanded. One must turn away from any temptation to walk in the "path of sin"—"Let the wicked man leave off his way and the man of evil deed his thoughts. . . ."

The reference here is not to refrain from sin itself, but to avoid the path leading toward it and away from it. The verse does not speak of "sinful thoughts" but just of "thoughts" which means man's entire way of thinking, his world concept, the intellectual obscurity and emotional ambivalence which combine to create sin and then cast man within it as though into a dungeon.

"A new heart and a new spirit" come about only by means

of departure from the path of sin, which is considered complete return, while separation from sinful acts is all that is necessary in order to achieve *kapparah,* acquittal.

### *Abundant Loving-Kindness and Truth*

In the teachings of the Kabbala there is a discussion whether, when a man repents and has his sin retroactively erased, it is derived from the divine attribute of loving-kindness or that of judgment, is it due to the divine attribute of mercy or that of truth and justice?

Scripture and the teachings of our sages contain statements which support both sides of the argument. An example of repentance being accepted due to the quality of loving-kindness is demonstrated in the case of Menashe, King of Israel, "for whom the Holy Blessed One tunneled an underpass beneath the throne of glory," though he did not meet the criterion of strict judgment. And in the Jerusalem Talmud the very possibility of repentance is attributed directly to the Holy One. For God is good and upright, therefore He instructs sinners in the right path (Psalm 25:8). They inquired of Wisdom, "What is the punishment of a sinner?" Wisdom said, "Evil pursues the wicked." They asked Prophecy, "What is the punishment of the sinner?" Prophecy said to them, "The sinful soul shall die." They asked the Holy One, and He said, "Let him return and be forgiven" (T.J., Makkot 2:6).

In the Torah repentance appears several times, but it is mainly elaborated on in the incident of the Golden Calf, where we find the thirteen divine attributes which are recited in the prayers of Yom Kippur, the day of divine compassion. They include "abundant loving-kindness and truth" from which we may infer that repentance not only is due to loving-kindness but is also related to the divine attribute of truth.

As a matter of fact, repentance encompasses both of these principles. The repentance of acquittal emanates from *ḥesed*, abundant loving-kindness. If a man regrets his sin but does not yet abandon the path of sin, he is not considered cleansed of the pollution within him. His decision not to sin was probably motivated by the fear of punishment. Even so, the Holy Blessed One accepts his repentance and acquits him. Certainly, this may be considered the work of the attribute of loving-kindness.

In contradistinction, repentance which fills the qualifications of the attribute of strict judgment and truth can only be achieved through complete purification. This repentance is acceptable, for the sin which polluted man disappears as though it never existed, since man has proven himself to be, what is considered in the words of Maimonides, "another person." It is as though he has undergone a complete transformation. How, then, can sins committed by someone else be counted against him? Through repentance of purification man is reborn and he gains a new heart, a renewed spirit, another outlook on life and different horizons. One man enters the bath of ritual immersion and another emerges from the water. The sinful person emerges as a pure one. And, indeed, our sages have pointed out that changing one's name is especially beneficial for penitents.

## *A Time To Speak and a Time To Be Silent*

If one visits the home of a penitent and sees that the dice are still on the table, the dovecotes still standing in a corner and the usurious loan deeds still lying in a drawer, then it is obvious that he has not as yet broken his will so as to allow for rehabilitation. He has not as yet reordered his environment or changed his habits. Even so, one may ask what brought about his return to God in the first place? Why doesn't he sin and lapse into his folly again?

It seems certain that his return was not promoted by his conscience. Had he given a full account of his deeds and faced all the implications of his behavior, he would undoubtedly have reached the spiritual level of repentance of purification. However, it is evident we are speaking of someone who attained only repentance of acquittal. What led him to that? It would seem that a certain awakening and awareness came upon him, shocked him out of his complacency and unwittingly brought about a change of heart. His repentance was not the result of soul searching, but of a sudden realization. This psychic experience is narrated in the story of Abigail and Nabal:

> And Abigail came to Nabal; and behold, he held a feast in his house, like the feast of a king; and Nabal's heart was merry within him, for he was very drunken; wherefore she told him nothing, less or more, until the morning light. And it came to pass in the morning, when the wine was gone out of Nabal, that his wife told him these things, and his heart died within him, and he became as a stone (1 Samuel 25:36–37).

This has been the way of sin since the beginning of time. It overtakes man while indulging in a night of iniquity. Mist and fog conceal the inner light of the soul of a man who is immersed in the blinding, obsessive night of his passions and is plunged within the oblivion of his lust. At the very hour when "Nabal's heart was merry within him," he was in such a state of intoxication that he did not notice the flashing blade of the sword hanging over his very door. At that moment of orgiastic excitement, Abigail cautiously enters, bearing with her the bitter news of his impending doom which she has been told by David. While Nabal was enjoying his lavish feast, "fit for a king," Abigail had already been informed of the end. "And Abigail came . . . [and] she told him nothing, less or more, until the morning light." She kept it to herself, for "there is a time to speak and a time to remain silent." There is a time when moral criticism is effective and a time when any discussion with the inebriate sinner is impossible and nothing anyone says can penetrate his hearing or enter his heart.

Oftentimes rabbis feel the same way as Abigail who came upon Nabal in the midst of a drinking party. They feel that their moralizing will fall on an impenetrable surface. The people they address are drunk with the pursuit of luxuries, trying to imitate foreign lifestyles and currying favor with their neighbors. There is simply no one with whom to talk, and at this stage the rabbi "tells nothing less or more." However, a state of intoxication always ends in a sobering up and it is an inflexible law of nature that night is followed by dawn. And then: "And it came to pass in the morning, when the wine was gone out . . . his heart died within him."

### *An Abigail Follows Every Sinner*

The rabbi, the one who does the reproving, must be able to discern the exact moment when the "wine has gone out of Nabal" and only then should he say "these things." Then there is a chance that the words will have an effect even on a heart of stone.

Rest assured: an Abigail watches over every sinner. Close on the trail of each sin is its punishment, its final reckoning. The sinner doesn't always give Abigail a chance to tell him the bitter truth about himself. It often happens that during the night of revelry, while the drunken party is still in full swing, Nabal is incapable of understanding what she is saying. It is even possible that, should Abigail start talking to Nabal during the wine party, she would not live to see "the morning light." However, if Abigail knows how to recognize the right moment "when the wine has gone out of Nabal" then she may say her painful words concerning "these things," and she knows how to say them, for then, as it is written, "his heart died within him." Suddenly the sinner feels Abigail clasping his hand, and, following upon his heels, she cries out from his own heart, grips his being, giving him no peace. For her message is a terrible one, and he is utterly shaken, trembles with fear and returns to God. He does not always grasp the meaning of Abigail's message, but he is frightened and regrets his past deeds. He resolves to change his ways and requests absolution.

Even then, however, he does not smash the dice or tear up the promissory notes. It seems that he is, as yet, uncertain whether he wants to radically change his way of life. Why should he abandon his life of hedonistic pleasure? Why should he give up a growing bank account? Why should he forego the festivities "fit for a king"? "Meanwhile," he says to himself, "let the dice and promissory notes lie in a safe deposit box!"

Many Jews are overwhelmed by the fearful awe of Yom Kippur, the day of judgment, and come to the synagogue only because they are frightened by the approach of "the morning light." They come because from afar they hear the whisper of Abigail urging them on. Withal, they achieve a certain degree of return to God, a certain degree of *kapparah* (acquittal), but they still have far to go before attaining the exalted level of self-purification, of *taharah.*

## *Two Immersions*

How does one arrive at repentance of purification? This repentance does not come about as the result of fear of punishment. Abigail and her message of warning may bring Jews to the synagogue but not to the ritual act of purification. To submerge oneself in these waters, it is necessary to bend one's head, and it is not within the power of Abigail to demand this of any man. Fear of punishment is not enough to bring repentance of purification; only ritual immersion may achieve this end. We are referring to a double baptism—of water and of fire. Immersion in water represents an analytical plunge into the sea of knowledge which is done through intense self-contemplation and profound soul searching. The baptism of fire, in contrast, represents the great act of breaking one's own will, passing through the fire of one's passion. This is proof of man's self-transcendence, when he succeeds in subjugating his animal will to the supernal will. These two immersions are what bring man to the stage of repentance of purification.

What is meant by regret of the past? It is not what Nabal experienced when Abigail told him that David was about to launch an attack. Such news only causes a momentary shock. However, remorse which issues from a penetrating analysis, from sharp self-criticism and facing one's spiritual and psychological situation, results in true self-recognition. This manner of regret is related to the sin and its *meaning.* At the moment when man sobers up from the drinking party, he grasps the implications of his sin. They are: failure, despair and spiritual bankruptcy. To sin [ḥata] actually means "to miss [le-haḥti] the target."

When man is tempted to sin, he is led to think that it will get him everything he wants, and he will have his fill of pleasures. What in effect happens? Sin misleads him and he finds himself in a state of despondency and despair.

"Return, Israel, to the Lord, your God, for you have stumbled in your sins" (Hosea 14:2). The prophet's admonition concerns the causal nexus of sin. "It is not your sins, Israel, which led to your fall. Rather, the sins in which you were caught up became your stumbling block, they threw you off your course. And when you examine yourself you see where you have failed, that you have achieved nothing, or, perhaps, that you have even regressed."

A Jew desecrates the Sabbath, hoping it will make him rich. What happens? "You have stumbled in your sin." He remains the same small-time businessman he was before.

A rabbi flatters men of power in the community. And the result? They become his worst enemies and undermine him—"for you have stumbled in your sin."

Sin itself becomes a stumbling block. ". . . lest you serve other gods . . . and He shut up the heaven that there be no rain . . ." (Deuteronomy 11:16–17). Sin cannot be separated from its punishment. It is no use abstaining from sin to evade its penalty because sin is its own true punishment. Whenever I see a man collecting and hoarding more and more wealth, I am reminded of the following story told in the tractate Shabbat [119a]: "Joseph-who-honors-the-Sabbaths had in his vicinity a certain gentile who owned much property. Soothsayers told him, 'Joseph-who-honors-the-Sabbaths will consume all your property.' [So] he went, sold all his property, and bought a precious pearl, which he sewed into his turban. As he was crossing a bridge the wind blew it off and cast it into the water, [and a fish swallowed it]. Subsequently it [the fish] was hauled up and brought to market on the Sabbath eve toward sunset. 'Who will buy now?' cried they. 'Go and take it to Joseph-who honors-the-Sabbaths,' they were told, 'as he is accustomed to buy.' So they took it to him. He bought it, opened it, found the jewel therein, and sold it for thirteen roomfuls of golden denarii. A certain old man met him and said, 'He who lends to the Sabbath, the Sabbath repays him'." Sooner or later, the hat into which the sinner has sewn a pearl will fall off his head and the right fish will be there to swallow the pearl.

The Hebrew verb, *ḥatati,* does not mean "I have sinned." It means "I stumbled, I missed my goal; sin has failed me; sin has brought me to despair and led me astray." This is what is meant by the term "regret of the past" which even the High Priest himself was not free of, and in his confession on Yom Kippur, he said: "O God, I beseech Thee, I have sinned!"

Every man has his own version of dice, loan contracts, dovecotes, and even when to all appearances he repents he does not give them up. This is evidence that he has not as yet entirely subdued his drives. Does he then deserve repentance of purification? "Making a resolution concerning future actions" necessitates a complete negation of one's selfish desires by undergoing a baptism of fire. Only fire can succeed in bending man's iron will which persists in dragging him down. Only fire can raise him upward in its leaping tongues of flame.

The Talmud tells a tale about a baptism of fire: "Certain [redeemed] captive women came to Nehardea. They were taken to the attic of the house of Rabbi Amram the pious, and the ladder was removed to prevent anyone from approaching them. As one passed by, a light fell on the skylights; [thereupon] Rabbi Amram seized the ladder, which ten men could not lift, and singlehandedly set it up through the power of his passions. When he had gone halfway up the ladder, he stayed his feet in order to conquer his lust and cried out, 'A fire at Rabbi Amram's!' The rabbis, hearing his cries for help, came running, and thus he was saved from sin."

The evil inclination burns within man as fire and it is only possible to overcome it with a greater flame as "fire consumes fire." Such baptism of fire leads to repentance of purification.

We make two requests in the prayers of Yom Kippur. "Pardon us our sins on this Day of Atonement," and also

"Erase and pass out of Your sight our transgressions and iniquities."

One of these requests corresponds to repentance of acquittal and the other to repentance of purification. The verse states "I have erased your sins as a haze and your transgressions as a vanished cloud; return to me for I have redeemed you" (Isaiah 44:22). The erasure of sin resembles the dissipation and disappearance of the clouds which obscure the shining sun. When a man achieves repentance of purification, all the clouds above disperse and he feels the pure rays of the sun shining upon him and his entire being is permeated with: "For I have redeemed you."

# THE POWER OF CONFESSION

Maimonides was very exact in his use of words as far as we know and did not indulge in flowery language. In light of this, we should be as scrupulous as possible when studying his code, the *Mishneh Torah,* in trying to learn the true significance of each word we read. Let us turn to Chapter I, Section I of the Laws of Repentance, keeping this in mind as we do so:

> With regard to all the precepts in the Torah, positive commands or negative ones, whenever a person transgresses one of them, either wilfully or unknowingly, and turns away from his sin, it is his duty to confess before God, blessed be He, as it is said, "When a man or woman shall commit any sin that men commit, to do a trespass against the Lord, and that person be guilty, then they shall confess their sin which they have done" (Numbers 5:6–7); this means confess in words; and this confession is an affirmative precept. How does one confess? One says, "I beseech Thee, O Lord, I have sinned, I have acted perversely, I have transgressed before Thee, and have done thus and thus, and lo, I repent and am ashamed of my deeds and will never do this again." This constitutes the essence of confession. The more one elaborates and the more de-

tailed the confession one makes, the more he is praiseworthy.

Some of the later commentators underscore Maimonides' careful choice of words—"when he repents and turns away from his sin, it is his duty to confess"—and infer from them that the obligatory precept is not the act of repentance but the latter stage of *confession.* Otherwise Maimonides would have written, "with regard to all the precepts . . . it is his duty to repent and to confess," and we would then have assumed that the obligatory precept is the act of repentance which is accompanied by a confession of sins.

The author of the *Minḥat Ḥinukh* and the author of the commentary on the *Mishneh Torah, Avodat haMelekh* are both in agreement that Maimonides did not see repentance as a precept, but rather as a self-understood deed, considering it inconceivable for a Jew to remain sunk in sin without wanting to repent. I find it hard to accept this supposition expounded by the author of the *Minḥat Ḥinukh,* and my father and teacher [Rabbi Moshe Soloveitchik] told me that my grandfather, the sage [Rabbi Joseph Ber of Brisk] rejected it outright, citing the fact that the Torah, in a number of places, explicitly refers to repentance as a precept. Take, for example, what is said in Deuteronomy (4:30) "In thy distress, when all these things have come upon thee, in the end of days, thou shalt return to the Lord thy God and hearken unto His voice. . . ." The Torah clearly refers to repentance in saying "thou shalt return"; confession is not mentioned.

We find another expression in this vein in the weekly portion of the Torah recited on the Sabbath preceding Rosh Hashana: "And it shall come to pass, when all these things are come upon thee, the blessing and the curse, which I have set before thee, and thou shalt bethink thyself among all the nations, whither the Lord thy God hath driven thee, and shalt return unto the Lord thy God and hearken to His voice, according to all that I command thee this day, thou and thy children, with all thy heart and with all thy soul; that then the Lord thy God will return thy captivity, and have compassion upon thee, and will gather thee again from all the peoples whither the Lord thy God hath scattered thee" (Deuteronomy 30:1–3). Maimonides interpreted these verses as a *promise,* according to what he wrote in Chapter 7 of the Laws of Repentance (Section 5):

> And the Torah has already promised that in the end Israel will do repentance at the conclusion of their exile and they will immediately be redeemed, as it is written, "And it shall come to pass, when all these things are come upon thee . . . and thou shalt return unto the Lord thy God . . . (and) the Lord thy God will return thy captivity. . . ."

The author of the *Avodat ha-Melekh* concluded that Maimonides' use of the phrase, "the Torah promised," in this context, is further proof of maintaining his conviction that repentance was not to be seen as a precept, but as a promise. This is, however, refuted by a statement Maimonides makes in that very same section: "All the prophets ordained repentance, and Israel will not be redeemed except [by doing] repentance." Moreover, in Chapter 2 of the Laws of Repentance, Section 7, when dealing with the Ten Days of Penitence, Maimonides wrote:

> The Day of Atonement is the time of repentance for everyone, for the individual as well as the multitude. It is the goal of the penitential season, appointed unto Israel for pardon and forgiveness. Hence, *all are under the obligation of repenting and making confession* on the Day of Atonement.

From this we may infer that it was Maimonides' opinion that there was a precept of repentance and confession which applied only to the Ten Days of Penitence. Thus, repentance on the Day of Atonement is according to a precept which relates to that day alone. Had Maimonides shared the view of Rabbi Jonah he-Ḥasid, formulated in his book *Sha'arei Teshuvah,* that confession and repentance were separate matters, he would have counted them as two separate commandments in his enumeration of the 613 precepts: one precept—confession—being applicable throughout the year, and a second—repentance—applicable only on the Day of Atonement, a day on which the Torah ordained that "You shall be clean before the Lord." Yet in Maimonides' enumeration of the 613 precepts, only one concerns repentance and confession.

Further proof of the fact that Maimonides considered repentance itself to be a precept is furnished by the heading to the Laws of Repentance, which states: "The Laws of Repentance [consisting of] one positive precept, namely, that the sinner shall repent of his sin before the Lord and confess."

But do we really need evidence of this sort? Can one really contemplate the possibility that confession be considered a precept while repentance is not? What would be the significance of confession without repentance?

It seems to me that this subject affords us another opportunity to focus our attention on Maimonides' unique method of classifying the 613 precepts, or, to be more exact, his way of defining them. According to his method there are two kinds of precepts, the first consisting of those whose *fulfillment* and *performance* are combined as for example, the precept of taking four species on the Feast of Tabernacles (Sukkot). The Torah ordained, "And ye shall take you" (the fruit of goodly trees, branches of palm trees etc.), so that when one actually takes the palm branch in hand, one performs the precept and fulfills it at the same time. The same is true, for example, of the precept of sacrificing the Paschal lamb or the precept of counting the Omer, the forty-nine-day period between Passover and the Feast of Weeks (Shavuot). But there are other precepts whose *performance* and fulfillment are not identical, for example when the *performance* of the precept is through specific action of some kind, or through a verbal utterance, but its *fulfillment* is up to the heart. The precept is, in fact, performed by means of an utterance or an external act, but fulfillment is dependent on attaining a certain degree of spiritual awareness.

Take, for example, the laws of mourning. According to the Mishna, "there is no mourning except in the heart" (Sanhedrin 6:6). Although there are specified acts related to mourning—not washing, not anointing oneself with oil, not wearing shoes, etc.—the precept can only be fulfilled within a person's heart.

The same is true of rejoicing, concerning which we have been commanded, "And thou shalt rejoice in thy feast." When the Temple in Jerusalem was in existence, the actual performance of this precept consisted of bringing sacrifices. Today it is performed by eating a festive meal with meats and wine, by wearing colorful clothes and by other deeds of this nature. But the precept cannot be fulfilled through performance of these external acts alone; its true fulfillment lies within the realm of the heart.

## *Service of the Heart*

An outstanding example of this distinction between the performance of a precept and its true fulfillment is the daily recitation of the "*Sh'ma.*" One performs the precept by means of a vocal recitation of the three passages, or at least the central one, beginning with "Hear, O Israel" but its real fulfillment depends upon the acceptance of the yoke of the heavenly

Kingdom. Yet, the most outstanding example of this type of commandment is afforded by the precept regarding prayer.

The Talmud associates the precept of prayer with the verse, "to serve Him with all your heart" (Deuteronomy 11:13). "What is service of the heart? It is prayer" (T.B., Ta'anit 2a). But what is meant by service of the heart? How does one fulfill this requirement?

In the final chapers of the *Guide to the Perplexed* (the philosophers and historians who have written about Maimonides generally do not deal with these chapters, though it is in them—and not in the "Aristotelian" chapters—that the real Maimonides is revealed), Maimonides offers us an explanation of this concept. And in the *Mishneh Torah*, under the Laws of Repentance, he sets forth a similar explanation:

> And what is the love [with which the servant of God loves God]? That he loves God with a great and abundant and intense love so that his soul is bound up with the love of God to such an extent that he is constantly absorbed in his love, as a man who is love-sick for a woman and who is never free from his longing for that woman, whether awake or asleep, even while he eats and drinks—even greater than this is the love of God in the hearts of those who love Him and who are forever engrossed in Him as He has commanded "with all your heart and with all your soul" (Chapter 10, Sections 2, 3ff.).

Thus, for Maimonides, "service of the heart" encompasses man's whole being, and vocalizing the words of prayer is not enough. The heart must do its share. Of course, "service" involves external acts and performance. "Just as [the sacrificial] service at the [Temple] altar is called service, so may prayer be called service" (Sifre, Deuteronomy, 41).

Prayer—like the offering of sacrifices—cannot be fulfilled within the heart alone, without performing an external deed. But the act of prayer cannot in itself exhaust all that is implied in the concept of "service of the heart," which encompasses all of man's being, wherever he is and whatever opportunities are available to him, both his joys and sorrows, his grief as well as his rejoicing. Prayer can give expression to only a very small portion of the overwhelming totality that constitutes service of the heart. It surges forward from the immeasurable recesses of devotion felt within the heart. According to Maimonides, prayer was ordained by the Torah (and not by an enactment of the Sages). But the act of prayer is merely the *performance* of the precept while its fulfillment remains within the realm of the heart.

The best proof of this is the fact that even those Sages who argued that "intention" was not a necessary component in the observance of the commandments admitted that conscious intent is a prerequisite for prayer, for its very fulfillment must come from the heart.

Fulfillment of the precept of prayer embraces our entire existence. It signifies a personal encounter with the Master of the universe, who speaks to man, as He spoke with Moses, "mouth to mouth." This is the only interpretation of fulfilling the lofty precept of prayer which the Jew is obligated to do three times a day, every day. The act of prayer, verbalizing the words of the prayers, gives only partial expression of its purpose.

Maimonides very clearly distinguished between these two aspects of the precept of prayer. At the beginning of his directives on the Laws of Prayer, he wrote: "It is a positive precept to pray every day," that is, to recite prayers daily, "as it is said, 'And you shall serve the Lord your God' (Exodus 23:25), [and] tradition has taught us that this service is prayer. . . ." Following this, Maimonides details all the laws specific to the actual performance of every type of prayer and prayer service.

But we do not find in these chapters on the Laws of Prayer as much emphasis upon the concept of "service of the heart" as we find elsewhere. In vain will we search there for a world outlook or a philosophy of man based upon the idea of "service of the heart." Maimonides' Laws of Prayer deal exclusively with the acts and deeds which constitute the performance of the precept of prayer—prayer as a service of the heart is dealt with elsewhere. In these chapters, he is not concerned with man's spiritual condition, with what takes place deep inside him, but only in the function of the heart. However, in the heading to the Laws of Prayer, where he offers a *definition* of prayer, Maimonides clearly speaks of "*serving* the Lord every day [by means of] prayer." Here he does not use the same term found in his description of the laws themselves—"it is a positive precept to *pray*"—referring to the performance of the act of prayer. He uses a different term—"to *serve* the Lord"—which describes the fulfillment of "service of the heart," and one of the ways in which this finds expression is in prayer. The true essence, the inner meaning of the precept, depends on the service of the heart and prayer is its means of communication.

The differing terminology used in the heading and in the laws themselves is not accidental. Throughout the *Mishneh Torah,* whenever Maimonides dealt with a precept whose fulfillment is within the heart and whose performance is by external deed, he intentionally used different terms in the heading than those he used in the laws themselves. In describing the laws, he deals with the *performance* of the precepts, while in the headings, which contain definitions and introductory statements to the laws, he deals with all that is involved in carrying out the mitzvah fully.

### *Repentance—as Service of the Heart*

The same method is used in describing the Laws of Repentance. Maimonides considers repentance as a form of service of the heart. It is a precept whose essence is not in the performance of certain acts or deeds, but rather in a process that at times extends over a whole lifetime, a process that begins with remorse, with a sense of guilt, with man's increasing awareness that there is no purpose to his life, with a feeling of isolation, of being lost and adrift in a vacuum, of spiritual bankruptcy, of frustration and failure—and the road one travels is very long, until the goal of repentance is actually achieved. Repentance is not a function of a single, decisive act, but grows and gains in size slowly and gradually, until the penitent undergoes a complete metamorphosis, and then, after becoming a new person, and only then, does repentance take place. And what is the concluding act of repentance? It is confession.

"When he repents and turns away from his sin, he is under a duty to confess . . ."—here Maimonides is being consistent with his overall approach. Within the context of the laws themselves, he only deals with the object of repentance, with the deed: "How does one confess? One says . . ." But in the heading, in defining the precept, he emphasizes the internalized experience that is the essence of repentance, the painstaking process and the soul-searching which bring man "to repent of his sin before God." And when repentance has ripened and reached its full maturity, when he actually does repentance—"he shall confess." Maimonides emphasizes that "this act of confession is a positive precept." This is how repentance is indeed *performed*, but the fulfillment of inner repentance is a *sine qua non* which must precede it, for otherwise confession is not valid.

Thus, repentance in itself is seen as a fundamental precept, although it is an obligation of the soul and not of the body. Many other precepts are of a similar nature—prayer, which we have already mentioned and other precepts such as "love thy neighbor as thyself." This precept, too, entails a long list of deeds—of loving-kindness, of help to another—but its very essence is in love felt within the heart.

### *"I Beseech Thee, O Lord"*

Let us now return to the text with which we began—Chapter 1, Section 1 of the Laws of Repentance: ". . . when one repents and turns away from his sin, he is under a duty to confess before God, blessed be He." We have already noted that Maimonides was not one to waste words for their poetic effect. What, then, was his intention when he wrote of confessing "before God, blessed be He"? Would it not have been sufficient to have written, "he is under a duty to confess," without specifying "before God"? Is there any other alternative?

However, with these words Maimonides gave expression to three distinct ideas, three separate laws.

The public confession of the High Priest on the Day of Atonement began with the formula, "I beseech Thee, O Lord." The Talmud explains the significance of this formula, and cites scriptural support for the need to use both the ineffable name of God (here indicated by the term "Lord") and the phrase "*ana*" = "Oh, I beseech Thee"). According to Maimonides, the use of this formula was not restricted to the High Priest. It was, rather, the paradigm for all confessionals, all of which were to be formulated on the model of that employed by the High Priest. Thus, in Section 1, Maimonides writes: "How does one confess? One says: I beseech thee, O Lord, I have sinned, I have acted perversely, I have transgressed before Thee and have done thus and thus. . . ."

We may infer from this that Maimonides was of the opinion that the Halakhah did not permit everyone to confess in any manner he saw fit, but that a set formula was to be used in making confession, and it began with the word "*ana*" ("Oh, I beseech Thee").

What is meant by saying, "I beseech Thee, O Lord, I have sinned . . ."? The phrase is understandable in the formula used by the High Priest—"I beseech Thee, O Lord, forgive your people . . ."—but what is meant by a person pleading "I beseech Thee—I have sinned"?

"Oh, I beseech Thee"—what for? What is being petitioned here? "[that] I have sinned"?

In fact, the phrase "Oh, I beseech Thee" gives expression to the very *possibility* of repentance. If we listen attentively, we can actually discern in these pleading words a heart-rending cry—"Oh, I beseech Thee," do not slam the door in my face, do not close the gates . . . allow me to speak . . . I beseech Thee, accept our prayers and ignore not our supplications!

If the Holy One, blessed be He, does not "open the gates for those who come knocking in repentance," they remain closed and locked.

"Oh, I beseech Thee" is a clarion call that the gates be unlocked, that our confession be allowed to enter within and be heard, though we know it is forbidden to approach the King while clothed in the sackcloth of sin and transgression.

Repentance cannot be comprehended rationally; it does not really make sense. Even the angels do not understand what repentance is. They shut the gates. But the Holy One, blessed be He, "undercuts" as it were, the work of the angels (see T.B., Sanhedrin 103c) so as to receive those who repent of their sins. That is the significance of the cry "Oh, I beseech

Thee" which precedes confession. "Oh, I beseech Thee" finds a way to open the gates on our behalf.

Confession must be preceded by prayer. "Oh, I beseech Thee, accept our prayers and ignore not our supplications." It is not enough for a man to come and say, "I have sinned." God is not, so to say, compelled thereby to keep the gates open for him. That is not what repentance is. He must sense and realize that the gates are locked, for the sins have already been committed; and now if he wishes to repent of his ways he must cry out and beat incessantly at the gates so that they allow him and his confession to enter within. God is referred to as "He who opens the gate for those who *come knocking* in repentance"—and not for those who *do* repentance or *come* to repent. Unless one knocks on the gates loudly and continuously, repentance and confession are impossible.

The entire liturgy for Yom Kippur, from beginning to end, is geared to this one goal: knocking upon the gates, again and again, crying out over and over again: "Oh, I beseech Thee!" Only at the concluding *Ne'ilah* service do we say: "The day has come and gone, the sun is setting, let us enter into Your gate . . ."—only after twenty-four consecutive hours of fasting and prayer, of knocking at the gate, only then is it possible to enter the gates that have been opened—for if not now, when?

This, then, is the meaning of the phrase, "it is his duty to confess *before God, blessed be He.*" It is the language of *prayer,* whose purpose is best defined as being an acknowledgment that one "know[s] before whom one is standing." In prayer, man stands before the *Shekhinah,* before the Holy Presence. Confession is not a declaration for anybody to hear but first, and foremost, *prayer,* "for as paupers have we come knocking at your gate."

The chief task of confession is knocking upon the locked gates. At times they do open up before those who confess, and at times, alas! they remain locked and sealed. And so, when man is about to confess "before God, blessed be He"—confession which is really prayer—he begins by saying, "I have sinned, I have acted perversely, I have transgressed"; he bursts out with the cry, "Oh, I beseech Thee!" "Oh, I beseech Thee, accept our prayers!"

## *Confession Before God Alone*

As we have already noted, two additional ideas are embodied in the phrase, "before God, blessed be He." In Chapter 2, Section 5 of the Laws of Repentance Maimonides writes:

> Great praise is accorded the penitent who confesses in public and who announces his wrong-doings to the public, revealing to others the sins he has committed against his fellow-men. And he says to them: In truth, I have sinned against such and such a person and have done such and such to him, but today I do penitence and console myself.... In what matters is this so? With regard to sins between man and his fellow-man. But sins between man and God should not be made public, and he is brazen-faced if he does so. Rather, he should repent before God, blessed be He, and declare his sins before Him and confess to them...."

In this context, Maimonides again used the phrase "before God, blessed be He," and he did so to emphasize the contrast between confession of sins between man and his fellow-man—which one is obligated to do in public—and confession of sins between man and God—which need not be said in public.

Why is this distinction necessary? Because, at times, a man may confess and declare his sins as a means of winning public approval, so that others will admire him and say, "What a righteous man he is!" That is why Maimonides emphasizes here that confession must be "before God, blessed be He"—the penitent must have only one thing in mind: the account that is between him and God. What the public thinks of him cannot matter when he stands "before God, blessed be He."

Ecclesiastes, in his time, berated man for making "numerous calculations." "God has made man upright, but *they* make numerous calculations." Man rightly has to give only one account of himself in the straight reckoning that is between him and God. Man cannot be considered upright and trustworthy if he is subject to the sways of public opinion, if he seeks to find favor with some, to please others and to be popular everywhere. When man repents, he has to settle one account only, and when he comes to confess he must have in mind only that he is standing "before God, blessed be He."

This is not the case regarding sins committed against one's fellow-man. Here man is obligated to make public confession. It is not enough to feel remorseful or to beg forgiveness from another in private, after one has either fought with his fellow-man, spread gossip about him or cast aspersions on his good name. He must make his apologies in public in order to clear the name of his fellow-man that has been muddied, and effectively remove the stigma he applied to him. "And he says to them: In truth, I have sinned against such and such a person and have done such and such to him. . . ." When he says, "In truth," he admits that the other—not he—was right and confesses that he has caused him harm. It is only by means of public pronouncement of this sort that he can undo the damage that he has caused.

"In what matters is this so? With regard to sins between man and his fellow-man, but with regard to sins between man and God . . . he should repent before God, blessed be He, and declare his sins before Him"—before God and not before people.

The third idea embodied in the phrase, "before God, blessed be He," is that not only confession, but also repentance itself must be made before the Holy One, blessed be He. In Chapter 1, Section 1, of the Laws of Repentance Maimonides writes that a man "is under a duty to *confess* before God, blessed be He," while in Section 5 of Chapter 2 he emphasizes that man "*repents* before God, blessed be He." At first glance, it would seem to be totally extraneous to speak of repentance "before God." If the phrase is employed with regard to confession, as a means of associating it with prayer, could it be otherwise regarding repentance of the heart? Before whom does man repent of his ways, if not before God? Why, then, does Maimonides emphasize that a "man must repent before God"?

The formula of confession used by the High Priest in the Temple—which, as we have seen, is also the formula to be used in all other confessions, according to Maimonides—begins with these words: "I beseech Thee, O Lord, I have sinned, I have acted perversely, I have transgressed *before* Thee. . . ." The Talmud accounts for each and every word used in this formula and cites scriptural support for all of them. It becomes apparent that the formula of confession actually originates in the Torah, and not in the Talmud. Therefore, we must pay particular attention to its terminology and try to figure out the exact meaning of the word "before."

In Hebrew, it is equally possible to say "I have sinned *before* Thee" and "I have sinned *against* Thee" (using the dative preposition, "to"). An example of the latter usage can be found in Judah's pledge to his father Jacob, "If I bring him not unto thee . . . then will I have sinned against (to) thee forever" (Genesis 43:9). In Chapter 2, Section 11 of the Laws of Repentance, Maimonides sets forth the formula of confession to be used by one who has sinned against his fellow-man and (that man has) died: "And he says before them, I have sinned against (to) the Lord, God of Israel and against (to) this man." From this, we may infer that there is a distinction in the grammatical usage of the prepositions "before" and "against" ("to"): "Before" is used only with regard to God, while "against" ("to") is used regarding both God and man.

What is the difference between them? "I have sinned against (to) you" means I have injured you, I have caused you damage, I owe you something, as Judah declared to Jacob. This expression is appropriate for relations between people, and according to the Jewish perspective it is also appropriate for the relationship between man and the Master of the universe. When man sins, he undermines the *Shekhinah* and inflicts harm and damage, as it were, on the Divinity itself. Men cannot harm the "Infinite, blessed be He," who is "above and beyond all reckoning," just as he cannot benefit Him: "If he is righteous, what can he give Thee?" (cf. Job 35:7). Nevertheless, when one views God as "our Father who art in heaven" and relates to Him as "my shade upon my right hand" (cf. Psalm 121:5) whenever one seeks His presence to draw comfort and support from Him—then, when one sins, one drives away the hapless *Shekhinah* who suffers when a Jew sins. It is as if the sinner actually harms the *Shekhinah* and inflicts a loss on her. This allows him to say, "I have sinned against (to) the Lord God of Israel and against (to) you."

What, then, is the meaning of this combination of words, "I have sinned before Thee"? In order to understand this expression, the text of the confession should be read as if it said "I have sinned, I have acted perversely, I have transgressed *while* standing before Thee. . . ."

For Judaism views man as standing before God always—it does not accept a division between the two worlds, one in which man stands before God and the other in which man flees from Him. Man is always standing before God—whether he be in the study-hall, the office, the synagogue or the bedroom. At all times wherever he may be, man is standing *before Him,* before the Holy One, blessed be He.

And yet, when man sins he creates a distance between himself and God. To sin means to remove oneself from the presence of the Master of the Universe. I was standing before You and sin came and estranged me from You and I no longer feel that I am "before You." The whole essence of the precept of repentance is longing, yearning, pining to return again to being "before You." Longing develops only when one has lost something precious. "From afar the Lord appeared unto me" (Jeremiah 31:3). Sin pushes man far away and stimulates his longing to return, so that when man comes to the point of confessing he must say, "I have sinned, I have acted perversely, I have transgressed before Thee," that is to say, free me from the tangling web of my sins and allow me to return and stand "before Thee." Restore me to where I was before.

This is what Maimonides wrote in Chapter 7, Section 6 of the Laws of Repentance: "How powerful is repentance, for it brings man closer to the presence of God, as it is said, 'Return, O Israel, unto the Lord thy God' (Hosea 14:2) . . . that is, if you repent, you will cleave unto me. Repentance brings close those who have strayed afar. One day man may be despised of the Lord, abhorred and loathed and cast far away, and the next day be loved and desired and close at hand, a friend."

The very term "repentance" (literally: "return") signifies that this is so. Repentance is not "remorse" or "acknowledgment" and does not depend upon depression or a sense of despair. Repentance is "return," "restoration." To whom does one return? According to the prophets: "Return, O Israel, unto the Lord thy God," and God Himself declared: "Return unto Me and I shall return unto you." And the sages found a homiletical reference to the Ten Days of Penitence in the verse: "Seek the Lord while He may be found, call upon Him while he is *near*" (Isaiah 55:6). Thus, Maimonides correctly emphasized that repentance shall be "*before* God."

### *God Before Man Sins, God After Man Sins*

"How does one confess?" asks Maimonides, in Chapter 1, Section 1 of the Laws of Repentance, and he replies: "One says, I beseech Thee, O Lord, I have sinned, I have acted perversely. I have transgressed before Thee and have done thus and thus. . . ." In the Talmud, in the context of a discussion of the thirteen qualities of divine mercy enumerated in the Torah (Exodus 34:6), the following homily is attributed to Rabbi Johanan: "This teaches us that the Holy One, blessed be He, enwrapped Himself as one who leads the congregation in prayer and taught Moses the liturgy. He said to him: 'Whenever Israel sins and comes before Me with this liturgy, I shall forgive them.' 'The Lord, the Lord' [why does it say 'the Lord' twice?]—I am He who is there before man sins and I am He who is there after man sins and repents, 'God, merciful and gracious' " (T.B., Rosh Hashanah 176). Rabbeinu Tam (Tosafot, *ad loc.*) interpreted this to mean two separate qualities, the first "Lord" indicating God who is there before man sins, and the second "Lord" indicating God who is there after man sins (Rabbeinu Nissim Gaon, in his *Megilat Starim,* has a different method of enumerating the thirteen qualities. He counts "Lord, Lord" as only one divine quality, but this method was not accepted by the early medieval commentators. See Tosafot and Rosh, *ad loc.*) What is meant by two qualities? What was the significance of the double repetition of the term "Lord"—before man sins, and after?

When man sins, he creates a distance between himself and God and becomes, in Maimonides' words (Chapter 7, Section 7), "separated from the Lord, God of Israel," as it is written, "Your iniquities have separated between you and your God" (Isaiah 59:2). The end result of sinning is the driving out, as it were, of the Holy Presence. But who, then, will take care of the sinner after the Holy One removes Himself and the sinner is left alone? Who will help him to cut himself off from his sins and escape from their contamination? Who will lead him back home to his heavenly Father? Who will extend a helping hand to rescue him from the quicksand into which he has sunk?

"Thou extendest a hand to sinners and Thy right arm stretches forth to receive the penitent." The sinner begins to struggle and twists and turns but lacks the strength to extricate himself. He must be assisted. Someone must give him a hand. And then "Thou extendest a hand to sinners"—as one extends a hand to a child, helping him as he takes his first steps. "Thy right arm stretches forth to receive the penitent." When the sinner has already begun to walk and run by himself, how many obstacles are strewn in the path before him, how easy it is for him to stumble and fall! And here arms are stretched forth to receive him, just as one holds out one's arms to embrace a running child lest he fall.

Who is it that extends a hand to the sinner and stretches forth his right arm to receive penitents? What is the internal voice that seizes hold of the sinner and draws him away from sin? From whence the voice within his conscience that calls him to "Return!"—if the Holy One, blessed be He, has rejected him and is far removed from him as a result of his sins? Who will read the soul of the evildoer? "The wicked are like the troubled sea" (Isaiah 57:20). Why does the evildoer in vain seek peace and quiet? Who is it that disturbs his tranquility?

"The Lord, the Lord": two times the Ineffable Name is

mentioned—the first removes Himself from the sinner, abandons him, but the second, the Lord who is there after man sins, remains. The "Holy King," what the Kabbalah refers to as the sphere of "Glory" or "Foundation," departs for it can have no part with the world of sin. But the *Shekhinah* as "Kingdom" still remains.

"And he shall make atonement for that which is holy, because of the impurity of the children of Israel . . . that dwelleth with them in the midst of their impurity" (Leviticus 16:16). "That which is holy"—that is, the Holy One, blessed be He, who becomes impure, as it were, from the iniquities of the children of Israel. Sin is contaminating, and even the Holy One, blessed be He, as it were, becomes contaminated. But the *Shekhinah* never departs completely from any Jew, no matter how far he has gone or how deep he has immersed himself in sin. God is there *after* man sins, He remains hidden in the inner recesses of the heart of even the worst evildoer until the moment arrives when he remembers his Maker and renounces his ways and repents. Rabbi Meir ran after his master, Elisha ben Avuya, and called upon him to repent. But Elisha did not respond because he heard a voice calling "Return, Israel, unto the Lord your God"—all except "Aḥer" (a term of derision for Elisha ben Avuya). Only Elisha, whose sins bore down so heavily upon him and cast him so far away heard such a voice which does not really exist (T.B., Hagiga 15a). There are no "excepts" to repentance. And, indeed, the Jerusalem Talmud records that "Aḥer" confessed before he died and that Rabbi Meir said: "My master died, while crying."

Even "Aḥer," who forsook his past and gave up his world, whose senses were dimmed and whose feelings became petrified, reached the moment when he broke down and cried, when he recalled his youthful years as a disciple of Rabbi Joshua. Who was it that brought tears to "Aḥer's" eyes?

The God who is there after man sins! The God who did

not remove himself even from the heart of "Aḥer"! The God who is there before man sins closes the gates after man has sinned! The sinner becomes cut off, he is cast far away. What does he do then? Is he cut off forevermore? Definitely not! He can still cry out to God who is there after man sins. The second Holy Name is ready to listen even after the first has shut the gates of "Glory" through which man passes to stand before his Maker.

When someone reaches the closed gates he has to cry out: "Oh, I beseech Thee!" "Open the gates for those who come knocking in repentance!" "Allow us to repent and to enter!"

On the Day of Atonement, the High Priest would shout out the Ineffable Name of God three times. Why was this so? So as to arouse the sinners to repent and confess—which can occur only in the wake of the "Name" (of God) who is there after man sins, the divine quality that swells within man even during his impurity. Man is sunk up to his neck in the quicksand of his sins, he is abandoned and cut off and all his friends have deserted him, his strength has left him—everyone except God has abandoned him! "O Lord!"—open the gates a little to let me come before You. "O Lord, I beseech Thee!"—forgive me, purify me, cleanse me of all my filth, for I am soiled and full of defects! And then: "For the virtue of this very day shall acquit you of sin, to cleanse you; you shall be clean before the Lord!" When the Ineffable Name was proclaimed for the third time, after the cleansing, man could again find himself "before the Lord," as he is allowed once again to approach God who is there before man has sinned.

"And he [the High Priest] prolonged the intoning of the Divine Name . . . and said to them: Be you cleansed." After the cleansing, the quality of "Glory" once again shines in all its splendor, and whoever has sinned and has been cleansed glows alongside it in refined purity. In Maimonides' words, he is now "loved and desired and close at hand, a friend."

It was for this reason that Maimonides considered it indispensable that the Ineffable Name be incorporated within the formula of confession. Without the Name of God who is there after man sins, man would be ground into the dust and oppressed by darkness and death. Only the Name signifying the God who does not abandon man after he sins can lead him back, and extricate him from the dark dungeon of iniquity.*

### *"For There Was His Home"*

What is the meaning of the word "*teshuvah*"? What is the exact etymological significance of the term? In the Bible, the word bears a specific connotation, "at the return of the year" (2 Samuel 2:1; 1 Kings 20:22; 1 Chronicles 20:1 and elsewhere), that is at the termination of the year's cycle. The word also appears in the following context (1 Samuel 7:15–17): "And Samuel judged Israel all the days of his life. And he went from year to year in circuit to Beth-el and Gilgal and Mizpah; and he judged Israel in all those places. *And his return (u-teshuvato) was to Ramah, for there was his home* and there he

---

*Allow me, please, to make a "private confession" concerning a matter that has caused me much loss of sleep. I am not so very old, yet I remember a time when ninety percent of world Jewry were observant and the secularists were a small minority at the fringes of the camp. I still remember—it was not so long ago—when Jews were still close to God and lived in an atmosphere pervaded with holiness. But, today, what do we see? The profane and the secular are in control wherever we turn. Even in those neighborhoods made up predominantly of religious Jews one can no longer talk of the "sanctity of the Sabbath day." True, there are Jews in America who observe the Sabbath. The label "Sabbath observer" has come to be used as a title of honor in our circles, just like "Harav HaGaon"—neither really indicates anything and both testify to the lowly state of our generation. But, it is not for the Sabbath that my heart aches, it is for the forgotten "eve of the Sabbath." There are Sabbath-observing Jews in America, but there are not "eve-of-the-Sabbath" Jews who go out to greet the Sabbath with beating hearts and pulsating souls. There are many who observe the precepts with their hands, with their feet and/or with their mouths—but there are few,

judged Israel; and he built there an altar unto the Lord." Here, too, the word *teshuvah* bears the connotation of completing a circle; after Samuel would make a circuit throughout Israel he would return to Ramah, for there was his home.

*Teshuvah,* repentance, signifies circular motion. When one finds oneself on the circumference of a large circle, it sometimes seems that the starting point is becoming farther and farther removed, but actually it is getting closer and closer. "At the return of the year," on Rosh Hashana, a new calendar year begins, and with every passing day one gets farther and farther away from the starting point, the New Year. But every passing day is also a return, a drawing near to the completion of the year's cycle, the Rosh Hashana of the next year. "And his return was to Ramah." Samuel went in circuit. The moment he left Ramah, with the goal of making a full circuit of Beth-el, Gilgal and Mizpah, he was already returning to Ramah, for it was there that he made his home; there, in Ramatayim Zofim, lived his mother Hannah; there he had spent his childhood; there were his roots. Samuel was a leader and a judge for all Israel; he made a circuit of all of Israel's scattered living places, but everywhere he went, he was heading for

---

indeed, who truly know the meaning of service of the heart! What is the percentage of religious Jews today in contrast to the ninety percent only two generations ago? It seems to me that religious Jewry survives today solely by force of the Name of God who is there after man sins. Otherwise we should have utterly despaired and given in to the feeling, with which I am often overcome as I lie awake at night, that we are building castles of sand, and any moment a wave will come and wipe out everything. But God who is there after man sins does not allow us to despair. He whispers in our ears that "Jerusalem is surrounded by mountains"—one must do much climbing and work hard, grasp every hand-hold and out-cropping, slide backward and try again to climb the mountain so as to be able to reach Jerusalem. "Who shall climb the mountain unto the Lord?" I do not believe that it is easy to return and repent. The path of repentance, for the individual, as well as the community, is arduous and many boulders are strewn about which can be overcome only with supreme effort. The road is long and tortuous until one arrives at the stage of: "Be cleansed before the Lord," the cleansing of the Name of God who is there before man sins.

home. He belonged to all of Israel, for the land of Israel was his home, but his true home was only in one place, in Ramah, as it is written, "for there was his home." Only there could he construct the altar of his life to God. "And Samuel judged Israel all the days of his life." Samuel served as leader and judge in many different places, but the force of his leadership and judgment stemmed from Ramah, from his home: "*there* he judged Israel." No matter how great a man may be, he cannot leave his ancestral home. All of his judgments are derived from there.

This is the secret source of *teshuvah*, repentance. An individual Jew cannot sever himself completely from the Holy One. The community of Israel cannot travel on a straight path away from God. It is always on the path to return and repentance—of going away from God and coming back to Him. "In your distress when all these things are come upon you . . . you will return to the Lord your God." The circle may be very large, it may have an immense radius, but those who follow its path always move in a circular direction. The community of Israel simply cannot escape from this circular route. God who is there after man sins bars them from doing so.

Man may wander about in circles and become entangled in all sorts of vain causes and pursue empty ideas. He may believe that he has found the true goal in his life's fight for socialism, for "civil rights," for communism, or any of the other "isms." He makes a circuit of Beth-el, Gilgal and Mizpah, he searches for gods, overturns worlds, and it may appear to him that he can see ahead and is heralding a new and better future—but always and ever "his return is to Ramah, for there is his home." God who is there after man sins gives him no peace. Soon his world will be overturned upon him, he will be banished from Beth-el, from Gilgal and Mizpah, and people will cry out after him: Dirty Jew! Traitor! Exploiter! Cosmopolitan! Then, willingly or not, he will return to Ramah, to his home, where his mother Hannah welcomed him with her longing and supplication, where he lay in his cradle and absorbed the affectionate dulcet melodies sung to him by his mother.

"And his return was to Ramah"—traveling a circuit, he had to find his way back to his starting point; coming from afar, he made his way back home.

### *Confession, Sacrifice, Remorse and Shame*

"What is repentance?" asks Maimonides in Chapter 2, Section 2 of the Laws of Repentance. And he answers: "It consists of this: that the sinner abandon his sin, remove it from his thoughts and resolve in his heart never to repeat it again . . . that he call Him who knows all hidden things to witness that he will never return to this sin again. . . . And he must confess in words, with his lips, and give voice to these matters which he has resolved in his heart." In this chapter, Maimonides speaks of a process of *remorse (ḥaratah),* while in Chapter 1 he speaks of an additional element—*shame*: "How does one confess? . . . I repent and am ashamed of my deeds and I will never do this again." These two elements—remorse and shame—give us the right perspective of the value of confession. For at first glance, confession would seem to be superfluous, if man is truly penitent and has undergone the long and tortuous process of return. Yet Maimonides ruled that even after man has truly repented spiritually, and even after he has brought a sacrifice of atonement, and even after he has died, his repentance remains incomplete if confession has not taken place.

Why is this so? It seems that there are two reasons why the Torah obligated the penitent to make confession.

Feelings, emotions, thoughts and ideas become clear, and are grasped only after they are expressed in sentences bearing a logical and grammatical structure. As long as one's thoughts remain repressed, as long as one has not brought them out into the open, no matter how sublime or exalted they may be, they are not truly yours; they are foreign and elusive. "The heart is deceitful above all things, and it is exceedingly weak—who can know it?" (Jeremiah 17:9). Jeremiah did not mean that one cannot know what is in the heart of others and others cannot know what is in your heart, but that man does not know for sure what is in his own heart until his feelings and thoughts become crystalized and are given shape and form in the usual modes of expression. Repentance contemplated, and not verbalized, is valueless. In Chapter 2, Maimonides states that the sinner must "confess in words, *with his lips,* and give voice to those matters which he has resolved in his heart." And in the *Neilah* service, at the conclusion of the Day of Atonement, we say, "Thou extendest a hand to sinners . . . and hast taught us to confess all our iniquities before Thee." Confession completes the process of repentance—"So that we may desist from the violence of our hands"—and then: "Accept us [as we stand] fully repentant before Thee."

But confession has still another dimension, and not only as the ultimate act in the process of repentance. It also goes above and beyond repentance itself—for confession is the act which brings man acquittal. In the Temple service, on the Day of Atonement, the High Priest would "make acquittal for himself and his household" (Leviticus 16:6). With regard to this, the Talmudic Sages asked: "Was this acquittal in words or acquittal in blood [by means of a sacrifice]? Scripture says, 'And Aaron shall present the bullock of the sin-offering which is for himself and make acquittal . . .' [when he made acquittal] the bullock had not yet been sacrificed." The High Priest confessed for the sins of all Israel and his confession atoned for all of their sins. Could he, then, do repentance for all of Israel? It seems to me that this confession of the High Priest was transformed, so to say, into a sacrifice. Confession which is not merely a perfunctory verbalization of a set formula, but is bound up with tribulations of the soul and pangs of conscience, shall be deemed a sacrifice.

There are many things a man knows and thinks about which he does not dare to bring to his lips. Man is stubborn by nature and builds fences within himself, sometimes refusing to acknowledge facts and denying harsh reality. We instinctively reject facts that are unfavorable and unpleasant to us. The Talmud records that after Rabbi Judah Hanassi died, his disciples declared: "Whosoever says that Rabbi ["Our Master" = Rabbi Judah] is dead shall be pierced with a sword!" (T.B., Ktubot 104a). They knew that Rabbi Judah Hanassi was dead, but it was difficult for them to believe that anyone could actually give expression in words to the bitter fact that their master, symbol of life and the leadership of Torah and personal greatness, could actually be dead. To know is one thing, but to confirm it through verbal expression was something else. They refused to listen to the bitter truth. God instilled in man a mechanism of self-defense which enables him to ignore facts, to flee from reality, to deny its existence and to avoid seeing things as they are.

A man may know, without a shadow of a doubt, that he has sinned and is diverted from his life's goal, having betrayed all his values. He even knows why—but is not ready to say so openly or to hear it from others. "Whosoever says . . . shall be pierced with a sword." He lies awake at night and thinks about it; his soul cries out in the darkness; but in the light of day, in the eyes of others, he seems happy and content. In order to hide the truth that is eating away inside of him, he continues to sin, picks up speed and rushes madly toward the brink of the abyss.

There is another idea that emerges from a careful reading of Maimonides' choice of words: "How does one confess? One says, 'I beseech Thee, O Lord, I have sinned, I have acted perversely, I have transgressed before Thee, and have done thus and thus.' " This formula is appropriate for the confession of the High Priest who confesses on behalf of all of Israel and who therefore makes reference to both willful and unwillful sins and all types of transgressions. But when the individual comes to confess his sin, or specific sins, and itemizes them and says, "I have done thus and thus"—why should he also make a general declaration that he has "sinned, acted perversely and transgressed"? However, the principle that is operative here is the principle of "dissolving oaths"—when a man is required to take an oath for a specific purpose, the court uses the opportunity to devolve upon him other oaths as well. Here, too, even when man comes to confess specific sins, he must also say: "I have sinned, I have acted perversely, I have transgressed." These three phrases refer to the basic classes of sin, and when man comes to confess he must confess to all of them. For does man really know when he has sinned, whether intentionally or unwillfully? When a man confesses, he turns to God and says: "Master of the Universe, I do not know the difference between 'sin,' 'transgression' or 'iniquity.' I do know that I have gone far away from You. . . . How I came to be what I am, I know not. There were times that I thought I acted thoughtlessly—but in truth what I did was willful and intentional. . . ." Take, for example, the case of a man who came and told me that he wanted to send his daughter to a prestigious college frequented by the children of the wealthy. She would board in the college dormitory, he told me. I warned him of the risk that he would be taking, but he was "sure" that his daughter would not go astray. It was difficult for him to withstand the temptation of having his daughter attend such a prestigious institution, of which only the select few were found to be worthy. A year later he came back—in tears—to tell me that his daughter was about to marry a gentile whom she had met at the college. Was his initial act of sending her to the college an unwitting sin or was it willful? Had he known that this would be the outcome, he swore to me, he would have done all in his power to stop her from attending that college. What he did was a mistake, but was it really an unwitting mistake?

This is only one example of the many situations we face in life when we have to make crucial decisions. Do we really know when we err unwittingly and when willfully? Master of the Universe, we do not know. Only You know. That is why we also say: "I have sinned, I have acted perversely, I have transgressed. You determine to which of these categories my sin belongs. It is like what the simple Jew did in the well-known Hassidic story; he called out the letters of the alphabet before God, and said: 'O Master of the Universe, take You these letters and join letter to letter to create acceptable prayers!' "

Confession compels man—in a state of terrible torment—to admit facts as they really are, to give clear expression to the truth. This, indeed, is a sacrifice, a breaking of the will, a tortuous negation of human nature. Both remorse and shame are involved in this process. "And teach us, O Lord, our God, *to confess before Thee* all of our sins"—to look inward at the truth, to look ourselves straight in the eye, to overcome our mechanism of self-defense, to smash asunder the artificial barriers, to go against our natural inclination to run and hide, to tear down the screen, to put into words what our hearts have already determined—"so that we may desist from the violence of our hands." And then "Accept us [as we come before Thee] in full repentance as burnt offerings and sweet-smelling incense."

Just as the sacrifice is burnt upon the altar so do we burn down, by our act of confession, our well-barricaded complacency, our overblown pride, our artificial existence. Then, and only then: "Be you cleansed before the Lord." "Happy are you, Israel! Who is it before whom you become clean? And who is it that makes you clean? Your Father who is in heaven." Only then, after the purifying catharsis of confession, does one return, in circular motion, to God who is there before man sins, to our Father who is in heaven, who cleanses us whenever we approach Him for purification.

# THE INDIVIDUAL AND THE COMMUNITY

In previous essays the subject of our discourse was Chapter 1, Section 1, of Maimonides' Laws of Repentance. This essay will continue to deal with the same chapter, continuing with Section 2:

> Since the Se'ir Hamishtaleach (the scapegoat) brings acquittal for all of Israel, the High Priest confesses over it in the name of all Israel, as it is written (Leviticus 16:21), 'And he shall confess over it all the iniquities of the children of Israel.' The Se'ir Hamishtaleach brings acquittal for all the sins mentioned in the Torah, the venial and the grave, those committed with premeditation and those done inadvertently, those which become known to their doer and those which do not—all are granted acquittal by means of the Se'ir Hamishtaleach, provided only that the sinner has repented. If, however, he has not repented, the scapegoat can bring acquittal only for the lighter sins. And which are the light ones and which are the grave? The grave ones are those punishable by the judicial death sentence or the divinely inflicted death penalty (*Karet*). Bearing false witness and perjury are also among the grave iniquities. All the other negative and positive command-

> ments which do not involve the divinely inflicted punishment of death are light transgressions.

Anyone familiar with Maimonides' language and style will be struck by the difficulties posed by the phraseology of this section. Its initial passage appears, *prima facie,* to be utterly superfluous; does he, in fact, introduce any innovation here? Is it the idea that the *scapegoat* is a communal sacrifice? But this is something we know from the fact that the scapegoat is taken from the offering of the Tabernacle (*trumat hamishkan*) as is explicitly written in Leviticus (16:5): "... and he shall take of the *congregation of the children of Israel* two kids of the goats for a sin offering (*chatat*) and one ram for a burnt offering (*olah*)." Two kids for the sin offering—one is the scapegoat and the other is for internal use. What Maimonides tells us at the start of Section 2 not only adds nothing to our knowledge but unnecessarily veers from the train of thought he developed until now and from the manner of presentation he employed up to this point. At the end of Section 1 he had stated: "Likewise, he who injures another person or causes him monetary loss, even after he has paid damages—his sin is not expiated until he confesses and resolves never to commit the same offense again, as it is written regarding it (Numbers 5:6), '... any sin that men commit.' " In this section Maimonides took into account all the types of expiatory sacrifices and stressed that they were meaningless unless accompanied by repentance. He should then have proceeded to state that the sacrifice of the scapegoat expiates all the sins mentioned in the Torah, the venial as well as the grave (and he who repented ... but if he did not repent, etc.)—such phraseology would have been natural and consistent with what was said before. But the phrase used here, stating that the Se'ir Hamishtaleach brings acquittal for all of Israel, etc., is a repetition of a verse in the Pentateuch which is out of context here.

However, not only the difficulties posed by the wording of this section should be noted; its content is also puzzling. In this section Maimonides declares the necessity of repentance (in the context of the acquittal brought by the *se'ir hamishtaleach*) only in the case of grave sins which incur the divine death penalty (*karet*) such as the desecration of the Sabbath, idolatry and incest. With regard to venial sins, those positive and negative transgressions which do not involve such severe punishment, the temple ritual of the scapegoat provides acquittal even when not accompanied by repentance. (Maimonides' source for this is the first *mishna* of Tractate Shavuot and Talmud 22, 2 following it, and it has already been established that he ruled here in accordance with the Jerusalem Talmud.) Yet in the neighboring Section 1, Maimonides gives a long list of means of atonement: sacrificial offerings, punishment, suffering, judicial death sentences, blows, financial restitution, etc., none of which are effective without repentance, as it is written, "any sin that men commit." Thus, according to Maimonides, expiation is never effective without repentance. Yet, in Section 2 we unexpectedly find that the scapegoat is so powerful a means of atonement that it provides acquittal for all transgressions of positive and negative commandments (except the grave ones) even when unaccompanied by repentance. In what way is the scapegoat unlike all the other means of atonement?

Moreover, the ritual of the scapegoat is part of the rites of the Day of Atonement concerning which there is a specific principle that "the day itself brings acquittal" (*itzumo shel yom mekhaper*). Indeed, today, when there are no sacrifices, what is it that brings atonement? *Itzumo shel yom.* It is the holiness of the day itself (*kedushat hayom*). On this point there is a difference of opinion between Rabi and the Rabbis (*rabanan*) (Shavuot XIII:1; Yoma 86b) whether or not the Day of Atonement provides expiation only when accompanied by repentance. Maimonides' ruling is apparently in line with that of the Rabbis. He explicitly states (*Hilkhot Teshuvah*, Chapter I, end of *Section C*): "The essence of the Day of Atonement (*itzumo shel Yom Ha-Kippurim*) provides acquittal for penitents, as it is written: 'For on that day shall ye be atoned.' " From a precise scrutiny of the way each word is used, "for penitents" (*lashavim*), we learn that the Day of Atonement affords expiation only when accompanied by repentance.

Furthermore, it appears that the degree of acquittal afforded by the *se'ir hamishtaleach*, which is the expiatory sacrifice of the Day of Atonement, is linked to the outcome of the controversy between Rabi and the Rabbis concerning the effect of the essence of the day (*itzumo shel yom*). If one accepts Rabi's contention that the Day of Atonement brings acquittal even without repentance, then the *se'ir hamishtaleach* brings about acquittal in the same way. And if one goes according to the opinion of the Rabbis, that the Day of Atonement can bring acquittal only when accompanied by repentance, then this holds true for the *se'ir hamishtaleach* as well. As to the extent of acquittal granted on that Day, no distinction has been made between light and grave sins. Why then does Maimonides rule that the essence of the day (*itzumo shel yom*) only brings acquittal for light or grave sins when repentance takes place? And when it comes to the *se'ir hamishtaleach*, he makes a distinction between "grave sins" (which require repentance, as well) and the "light sins," for which expiation is granted even without repentance through the sacrifice of the *se'ir hamishtaleach*. On what basis is this distinction made?

And still another question is raised by this section: The Talmud mentions the distinction between "light" and "grave" precepts (Yoma 85b) in connection with another matter contained in Maimonides' Section 4 (Chapter I): "Though repentance brings acquittal for all [sins] and the essence of the Day of Atonement grants acquittal, there are transgressions which can be atoned for immediately and there are those for which a period of time must elapse. How so? If a man transgresses against a positive commandment (that does not involve the divine death penalty) and repents, he does not budge from where he is until he is forgiven, as it is written (Jeremiah 3:22): 'Return, ye backsliding children, and I will heal your backslidings.' Here the expiation is effective *immediately*. If a man transgresses against a negative commandment which does not carry the divine or judicial death penalty and he repents, he receives a suspension [of sentence], and the Day of Atonement brings acquittal, as it is written (Leviticus 16:30): '*For the virtue of that day shall acquit you*' (meaning that full expiation is not effected *until* that Day). If a man commits sins involving either the divine or the judicial death penalty, repentance and the Day of Atonement achieve suspension [of sentence]; and the suffering he undergoes completes the process of expiation, etc." Thus the following emerges: For transgressions against minor commandments, repentance by itself suffices to bring acquittal; for grave offenses, the Day of Atonement in addition to repentance brings about acquittal; and for offenses involving the divine or judicial death penalty, expiation is effective only after the sinner receives his punishment. The Talmud (Yoma, *ibid.*) raises the problem of whether repentance achieves immediate acquittal (as in venial sins) for transgressions of negative commandments, or whether they are considered as being in the same category as grave transgressions which are deferred until the Day of Atonement when the Day, together with repentance, affords expiation. In Section 4 Maimonides rules that if one transgresses a negative commandment, then repentance alone is inadequate and the attainment of acquittal must be delayed until the Day of Atonement. This means that Maimonides rules that transgressions of negative commandments (which carry neither the divine nor judicial death penalty) must nonetheless be treated as "grave" offenses; and yet he then rules that the *se'ir hamishtaleach* (Section 2) suffices for expiation without need of repentance in the case of "light" transgressions. He then asks: "And which are the light ones? . . . all the rest of the negative commandments."

The contradiction in Maimonides' thinking is clear: With regard to the Day of Atonement (Section 4) he rules that violations of negative commandments are viewed as grave transgressions; yet concerning the *se'ir hamishtaleach* he rules (Section 2) that violations of negative commandments should be seen as light transgressions.

And, finally, one last question: If the *se'ir hamishtaleach* is powerful enough to bring expiation even without repentance—why distinguish in this connection between "light" transgressions which include, as we have seen, some very serious offenses, and the grave transgressions which carry the divine or judicial death penalty? Why should it not bring acquittal in these cases as well?

## *Communal Sacrifice and Joint Sacrifice*

Let us return to the opening passage of Maimonides' Section 2, "Since the *se'ir hamishtaleach* serves to bring acquittal for the whole of Israel . . ."—that is, the *scapegoat* is a "communal sacrifice." And it is not the only one; all the daily offerings and all the "additional" ones made for festive occasions are also communal sacrifices. What is the correct definition of a "communal sacrifice"? It does not mean a sacrifice brought by several people (for every sacrifice has an "owner" called *ba'al ha'korban*). This could define not a "communal sacrifice" but a "jointly-owned sacrifice." The Ramban states that if, for example, money was collected from all the Jews in the world and an offering was made from this money, it would still not be considered a "communal sacrifice" but a "jointly-owned sacrifice." And, as we know, there are different laws for each of these kinds of offering. Completely contrary to the jointly-owned sacrifice, which may have many owners—two or two thousand or two million, according to how many people are participating in it—a "communal sacrifice" has one sole owner, exactly as does an individual offering. Who is its owner? It is the entire community of Israel, which according to the law is not the sum total or arithmetic aggregate of such and so many individuals but a single, composite personality in its own right. *Knesset Israel* (the community of Israel)—and I employ the phrase in its practical connotation and not as it is used in the *Kabbala* or in mystical thought—constitutes an indivisible and separate legal body in the same way as any individual is a single, legal personality. Neither "Reuven" nor "Shimon" nor "Levi," not all of them together, nor all of those who contributed a half-shekel toward the purchase of the offering, are regarded as the owners of the "communal sacrifice." It is *Knesset Israel* as an independent body in its own right and not as the cumulative total of such and so many individuals.

Another example of something mistakenly regarded as a "communal sacrifice" is the Passover offering. Actually, it is an individual offering, even though it is offered up simultaneously by the whole of Israel. A communal sacrifice is bought from the Temple fund (*terumat ha-lishkah*), and its owners are not individual contributors even if they comprise all of Israel; it is made by one personality, a single body known as *Knesset Israel*.

The same line of thought applies regarding other matters such as "the Land of Israel which we possess by virtue of our forefathers" (T.B., Baba Batra 119a). Does this mean that every Jew shares individually in the ownership of the Land of Israel? It does not. The Land of Israel is not the individual property of any Jew by himself; rather, it belongs to the whole of Israel as an independent entity. In the division of the land (between the tribes) by Joshua, son of Nun, the rights of ownership were transferred from the collective whole to the individual tribes; public property became, by this act of division, individual possession. However, prior to the division of the land, and nowadays again when the tribal divisions no longer hold, the right of the Jewish People to the Land of Israel is not of an individual nature; it is a right accruing to the Jewish People as a whole. I, as an individual, can make no claims to the land. My personal share derives from my membership in *Knesset Israel.* Since the land belongs to *Knesset Israel,* I have a share in it as well. The individual Jew's right to the Land of Israel is derived from the communal prerogative of *Knesset Israel* as a metaphysical entity. Though each one of us has a right to the Land of Israel, it stems solely from our unequivocal and total identification with *Knesset Israel.* The individual Jew who is detached from the main body of Israel can make no claims to rights in the Land of Israel.

The same principle applies in communal sacrifice. The community as a whole owns the offering and the individual is represented by it insofar as he identifies himself wholly, without any reservations, to the main body of Israel. This definition of *Knesset Israel* as an independent entity has no relationship to the *Kabbala* where it is represented by *sephirat 'malchut'* nor with Hassidism (which focuses upon the special sanctity of *Knesset Israel*); we are referring to straightforward halakhic application, which has implications in several other areas where it is necessary to distinguish between the community of Israel as an aggregate of individuals and *Knesset Israel* as an independent, integral entity.

## *Individual Atonement and Communal Atonement*

Now we have to define the nature of acquittal afforded by the Day of Atonement. Is it personal acquittal bestowed upon each and every person who comes before God, as it is written (Leviticus 16:30): "For on that day shall ye be expiated and cleansed, that ye may be clean from all your sins before the Lord," where every individual is atoned for separately and taken together from a multitide which comprises the community of Israel? Or is the nature of acquittal afforded by the Day of Atonement not intended for the individual as such—for how does an individual enter into the presence of God?—but is rather directed to the totality of *Knesset Israel* as a collective "self," a mystical entity in which case the individual enjoys personal acquittal via the pipelines of *Knesset Israel*. Through our identity with *Knesset Israel*, into which we have been integrated and smelted together into one body, are we able to benefit from the acquittal granted it.

Which of these corresponds to the acquittal brought about by the Day of Atonement: that of the individual or that of *Knesset Israel* from which the individual receives his portion of expiation? The answer to this question is to be found in the prayers of the Day of Atonement, in the Blessing of the Sanctity of the Day: "Blessed is the Lord, Who pardons and forgives our transgressions and the transgressions of His people, the House of Israel, Who removes our guilt year by year, King over all the earth, Who sanctifies Israel and the Day of Atonement."

It says: " . . . Who pardons and forgives our transgressions," which indicates our transgressions as individuals, and also "the transgressions of His people, the House of Israel." Since it already stated "our transgressions" what is added by the words: "and the transgressions of His people, the House of

Israel"? From this one may infer that on the Day of Atonement there are two types of acquittal. One is individual expiation, bestowed upon each and every Jew. Every Jew can receive it if he possesses a sufficient amount of spiritual strength and can be purified of transgressions on the Day of Atonement, and of the contamination of sin and enter "into the presence of God." Secondly, *Knesset Israel*, in its entirety and as a separate mystical kind of self, as an independent entity in its own right, is also purified in the presence of the Almighty on that Day.

The dual phraseology, referring to "our transgressions" and then to "the transgressions of His people, the House of Israel" is therefore understandable. However, this dualism is not carried through the rest of the blessing where it says: "Who removes our guilt"—Why does it not also say "and the guilt of His people, the House of Israel"?

Naḥmanides, in his commentary on the Pentateuch, states (Leviticus 5:19) that the word *ashma* (guilt) is used only when a transgression is so grave that it results in the annihilation of the sinner. According to him, *ashma* and *shmama* (desolation) are derived from the same linguistic root. For a sin of *ashma* the only punishment is annihilation and death. An individual person is capable of committing a sin of *ashma* which brings in its wake desolation, *shmama*; but *Knesset Israel* cannot do so. *Knesset Israel* can sin, transgress or commit crimes but it cannot reach the point of engendering *ashma*. Therefore, in regard to transgression we speak of double expiation: for the individual and for *Knesset Israel*. However, in connection with *ashma*, only *ashmatenu* (our guilt) is mentioned—for as individuals we are capable of descent to the pit of destruction and death, but not when taken as *Knesset Israel*, which is why the blessing does not mention their collective sins.

And thus writes Maimonides (*Hilkhot Teshuvah*, Chapter II, Section 7): "The Day of Atonement is a time of repentance for all, for individuals and for multitudes, and is the moment of pardon and forgiveness for Israel." There are clearly two elements here: first, "a time of repentance for all, for individuals and for multitudes," meaning many individuals, perhaps very many, even to the point of equaling the number of the whole of Jewry, and, second, "the moment of pardon and forgiveness for Israel"—not for the individual, or for many individuals, but for *Knesset Israel* as a single entity.

This double acquittal is effected by the Day of Atonement's "essence of the Day" (*itzumo shel yom*). Is this also true of the scapegoat offering? The answer to this is: Definitely not! The acquittal afforded by the *se'ir hamishtaleach* does not apply to the individual. The sins expiated through sacrifice are those of the owner and in this case it is not made by any individuals but by the whole of Israel. The acquittal afforded by the "essence of the Day," the manner of expiation we have been dealing with—"for the virtue of this very day shall acquit you"—is effective both for the individual and for the community; it is an atonement for each person and for the whole of *Knesset Israel.* However, the acquittal afforded by the scapegoat when the Temple existed was not meant for the individual. The individual derived no benefit from this sacrifice. Atonement was for the owner of the offering only, in this case the community as a whole. Indeed, if we read carefully, we shall see that regarding sacrifices it is written: "and it expiated for him . . . and for the entire community of Israel," meaning for *Knesset Israel* as a single entity; whereas regarding the essence of the Day it is written "to atone for you"—meaning for each and every individual among you and not for the community of Israel as a whole.

This is what Maimonides wished to point out in his opening passage on the scapegoat as quoted: "Since the *se'ir hamishtaleach* is destined to serve as an atonement for the whole of Israel, it is confessed over by the High Priest in the name of the whole of Israel." He wanted to stress here that it was not the confession of the individual or of many individuals that was made, but that of the entire community of Israel. For what is it he recites? "Please, God, your people Israel have sinned, transgressed and committed crimes in Your presence. Please, God, forgive the crimes and sins they have committed in Your presence, Your people Israel." This confession is for the sins of the community. The High Priest was not the delegate of any individual, not even of millions of individuals. He acted in the name of all of Israel. So the atonement afforded by the *se'ir hamishtaleach* is not for individuals as such; they can only derive benefit from it via the pipelines of the community.

Now we can also understand why Maimonides ruled that the *se'ir hamishtaleach* affords acquittal even without repentance. When the offering is personal and private and when the one who brings the sacrifice is wicked and unremorseful, then it is of the order of "the sacrifice of the wicked is an abomination" (Proverbs 21:27), and it is worthless regarding acquittal. In the case of the *se'ir hamishtaleach,* the owner of the offering is not any particular person but the community, *Knesset Israel,* which possesses its own independent personality and can never be considered so corrupt as to cause it to be termed an "offering of the wicked." Therefore, the sacrifice of the scapegoat atones for the sins of each member of the people of Israel who adheres to *Knesset Israel* and remains inseparably linked to it by an unseverable bond. For the individual offering, acquittal is not possible without repentance, while for the communal offering the individual does not play any role and receives atonement only in his capacity as a member of the community, and the community does not require repentance.

It is here that one must seek the basis of Maimonides' distinction between "light sins" and "grave sins" in relation to the atonement afforded by the *se'ir hamishtaleach.* Apparently, if acquittal is communal, then there is no need here to distinguish between light sins and grave sins or between positive and negative commandments such as we discerned in studying the atonement offered by the essence of the day (*itzumo shel yom*) conundrum. Why, then, did Maimonides exclude from acquittal by the *se'ir hamishtaleach*, which does not require repentance, those deserving the divinely ordained '*Karet*'? Probably because concerning such people it is written: "this soul shall be cut off from its people" (Numbers 19:13) and "that soul shall be cut away from the congregation" (Numbers 19:20). In other words, these people have done *something which banishes them from the community of Israel;* still more does this pertain to those sentenced to the judicial death penalty which is far graver. Their severance from the rest of the community is what determines that the communal atonement, though uncontingent upon repentance, will have no effect on them.

Thus we see that there is no contradiction in Maimonides' presentation where in one place, concerning atonement afforded by the essence of the day, he rules that transgressions of the negative commandments were grave offenses while here, in the section dealing with the *se'ir hamishtaleach*, he included them among the light transgressions. The classification of light and grave transgressions varies in accordance with the kind of acquittal in question, as we have noted.

### *Itzumo Shel Yom* *(Essence of the Day) Without Repentance*

We must now examine the *Halakha* postulated by Rabi (T.B., Yoma 85b, Shavuot 13a): "for all transgressions mentioned in the Torah whether or not the sinner has repented—the Day of Atonement atones." According to this, even if one desecrated the Sabbath and persists in violating the commandments, the Day of Atonement brings him atonement.

The acquittal granted by the Day of Atonement is understandable when linked to repentance. The awareness of sin, remorse over the past, resolution not to sin anymore—these prepare man for acquittal. There is a certain logic to this. But how can we fathom Rabi's conception of the Day of Atonement? The Day of Atonement without repentance or confession, without fasting or prayer, with the sinner still refusing to abide by the law and even violating the Day of Atonement itself—why should such a person be granted acquittal by the Day?

In fact, this paradox already presented itself inadvertently, in *Tosafot Yeshanim* (Yoma, *ibid.*): If, according to Rabi, the Day of Atonement can bring acquittal without repentance or fasting or prayer, why do we, nonetheless, still recite in our prayer: "Because of our sins were we exiled from our Land"? For according to him, the Day of Atonement already eradicated our sins, even if it was against our will. So why do we say that the Temple was destroyed because of our transgressions? The answer supplied by the *Tosafot* is that the Day of Atonement, for Rabi as well, affords only partial acquittal. What in fact is meant by "partial acquittal"—for either acquittal is granted or it is not! It seems to me therefore that when Rabi says that the Day of Atonement brings acquittal even without repentance he is referring to *only one* of the two types which are obtained by virtue of that Day (namely the individual and the communal atonement). Rabi meant to say that *itzumo shel yom* (the essence of the day) suffices for the provision of communal expiation. But, regarding individual atonement, it can never be possible without repentance. No manner of acquittal—neither the Day itself, nor sacrifices, can bring the individual complete acquittal unless he repents. "Peace, peace, said God to him who is far and to him who is near"—but so long as he who is far takes no move toward repentance, he cannot have peace. "There is no peace for the wicked," says

God. Where there is no repentance, there can be no expiation, nor forgiveness, nor pardon.

Rabbi Judah Hanassi, Rabi, however, thought that since communal acquittal was an integral component of the Day of Atonement, the individual also shares in this, just as each person was represented by the *se'ir hamishtaleach.* True, Rabi thought the individual was required to fast and confess on the Day of Atonement, but this was necessary for personal acquittal, which cannot be attained without repentance. Nonetheless, since the individual was part of the community and communal acquittal was granted to all, the individual likewise achieved "partial acquittal" even though he had failed to do repentance. In other words, if the individual failed to achieve personal atonement for his sins, he still achieved it in part as a member of the community.

If a person has repented and the Day of Atonement arrives, he is eligible for two kinds of acquittal, for he stands before God both as an individual and as a member of the community. However, if he continues to commit violations and is impenitent, as an individual he will remain in a state of alienation from the Almighty, and he will not benefit from acquittal. He benefits only from the shadow reflected on him by communal atonement which falls upon him as a member of the community. This is Rabi's opinion.

What are the arguments brought by the Sages who take issue with Rabi? If the acquittal afforded by the Day of Atonement were only of a communal nature as in the case of the *se'ir hamishtaleach,* then the individual would have no obligation of repentance, for he does not in this context have any status as an "interested party." However, in reference to the "essence of the Day" [of Atonement] (*itzumo shel Yom ha-Kippurim*), individual acquittal does appear side by side with communal atonement. As Maimonides phrased it (Chapter II, Section 7): "The Day of Atonement is a time of repentance for all, for the individual and for the multitude." Since individual acquittal is contingent upon repentance, a person who appears as part of the community without having repented will not benefit from the communal atonement afforded by the "essence of the day" (*itzumo shel yom*). That acquittal, which covers both the community and the individual, is indivisible. On the Day of Atonement either a person enjoys dual acquittal, both as an individual who comes to be purified and to stand before God, and as a member of the community which is worthy of the forgiveness of "the transgressions of His people, the House of Israel," or he receives no acquittal at all. He who has no part in "a King Who pardons and forgives *our* transgressions" has no part in "and of the transgressions of His people, the House of Israel." Thus the Sages ruled, in contrast with Rabi, that the essence of the Day of Atonement affords no acquittal unless repentance has taken place.

### *The Individual in the Community*

The dual acquittal granted the individual and the community on the Day of Atonement is central to the entire outlook associated with the "Days of Awe" (the High Holy Days). Take, for example, the blowing of the shofar (*teki'at shofar*). "Though the blowing of the *shofar* on Rosh Hashana is ordained by the Torah with no reason given for it, Maimonides noted (*Hilkhot Teshuvah,* Chapter 3, Section 4) that "there is here an intimation, meaning: arise ye who sleep and awaken ye who slumber and search your souls and repent and remember your Creator!" Not only in the *blowing* of the shofar are there intimations of an awakening to repentance, but even the *shofar* itself is a reminder and a sign, and its shape, so to speak, affects the way we pray on the Days of Awe. Thus we find a controversy in the Talmud (Rosh Hashana, 26:6) about whether a bent (*kafuf*) shofar or a straight one (*pashut*) is preferable, for the shape of the shofar has an effect on man's spiritual state in his prayers, one group arguing that the more bent (in spirit) one is the better, the other claiming that the more straight (proud) one is preferable. And so, in the blowing of the shofar (*teki'at hashofar*), which is one of the major features of the Days of Awe, we find laws relevant to this double aspect of individual influence and community impact.

The *tekiot* (blowings), as we know, divide into two parts—those which are sounded before the *Musaf* prayer and those which follow the order of the blessings within the *Musaf* prayer. A respectable number of medieval scholars hold that the blowings which follow the order of the blessings are ordained by the Torah while the preliminary shofar blowings are not a required community obligation and their fulfillment is the duty of the individual. If a man lies ill on Rosh Hashana and cannot come to the synagogue to hear the shofar blown, someone is brought to him to perform the preliminary blowings which it is incumbent upon the individual to hear. If a thousand Jews hear these first *tekiot* together in the synagogue, they listen not as a community but as separate individuals. As to the second group of *tekiot* the case is different. Here the ruling is that one who says the *Musaf* prayer alone is under no obligation to hear the accompanying blasts of the shofar. Thus ruled both Rabbi Yitzchak Alfasi and Maimonides: "The community must hear the *tekiot* which follow the order of the blessings" (Laws of the Shofar, Chapter 3, Section 7). This is not an individual but a communal obligation, and it may be fulfilled not individually, but only communally.

This distinction between the individual and the community is inherent in all that pertains to the Days of Awe. This emerges very clearly from the phraseology of the *Zichronot* section of the prayers: "You recall the *whole universe*, neither is all of creation concealed from You. All is revealed and known to You, our Lord, our God, Who watches and sees down to the end of time"—here, then, is a reference to the whole community. And immediately afterward: "For You invoke the law of remembrance *to count each soul and being*."

Such too is the acquittal afforded by the Day of Atonement—both individual and communal. Judaism has always viewed man from this dual perspective. It sees every person as an independent individual and also as a part of a community, a limb of the body of Israel. Jewish thinkers have conducted an on-going dialectic on this subject through the ages. The pivotal question is: Does the individual stand above the community which should serve his needs, or should the individual subordinate himself to the community's needs? In Judaism this question has been asked in relation to the individual who serves as a community leader. Who, in our history, was a greater leader than Moses, redeemer of Israel, the great rabbi and teacher, about whom our Sages wrote that his worth was equivalent to that of six hundred thousand men, meaning the total number of the male community in his time? Nonetheless, when the Children of Israel fashioned the Golden Calf, "God said to Moses, 'Go down—lower yourself down; for did I not grant you greatness only to benefit Israel? And now that Israel has sinned, what need have I of you?' " (Berakhot 32b). Even the greatness of an individual like Moses is dependent upon the community. It would seem that the community and the individual are placed in balance with each other and are interdependent. At times we find that the community must sacrifice itself on behalf of the individual; for example, when gentiles surround a town and say: "Give us one man" (as a hostage), the community must refuse and rather let all be killed than hand over one single Jew to them, And at times the individual must sacrifice himself for the good of the community.

Never is the individual's worth belittled when measured against the whole community; and never is the community undermined because of any individual or individuals. Each has its own position of strength.

### *Two Confessions*

If we look into the wording of the confession said on the Day of Atonement we will note that it actually consists of two kinds of confessions: one intended for the individual and one for the community.

The individual confession is recited by each person in the silent prayers of *arvit*, *shaharit*, *musah*, *minha* and *ne'ila*, while the communal confession, that of *Knesset Israel*, is recited only by the prayer leader in the public repetition of the silent prayer. There are a number of crucial differences in the content of these two confessions, the first of which lies in their placement. The individual makes his confession at the conclusion of the prayer while the prayer leader says it in the middle of the service. Furthermore, when the individual begins his confession, he does so without any introduction or preambles; he goes straight to the point: "Our God and God of our fathers, etc. . . . we have sinned and betrayed, etc."; the prayer leader, before he begins the confession, introduces it with the recitation of *selichot* (penitential prayers).

On close inspection, we find that the *selichot* are not merely liturgies that have found their way into the prayer book in some forgotten way. "Rabbi Yohanan declared that were this not written in Scripture (cf. Exodus 34:6), one could not have said it. This verse teaches us that the Almighty shrouded Himself in the *tallit* (prayer-shawl) of a prayer leader and showed Moses the order of prayer, saying: 'Whenever Israel sins, they should pray to Me in this order and I will pardon them' " (Rosh Hashana 17b).

The *selichot* have a special order, with a character of their own, in that they are a special privilege granted to the community. At the core of the *selichot* stands the declamation of the thirteen qualities of divine mercy—and these may not be recited by a person who prays alone, for it is not in the power of any individual to approach the Almighty on the Day of Atonement and ask acquittal for his sins. He is not qualified to utter words of placation to God such as "forgive us, pardon us, expiate our sins," or "for we are Thy People and Thou art our God, we are Thy sons and Thou art our Father," so long as he, the individual, is not filled with remorse and recognition of his own sinfulness. For what right has an individual to come before his Creator with words of appeasement so long as he has not confessed and repented of those sins which so thoroughly removed him from the presence of God? What the individual is supposed to say is: "I have sinned, I have transgressed, I have committed iniquities," etc., to recognize the gravity of his sin, and to admit that there is nothing to be said in defense: "What can we say in Thy presence . . . for Thou hast acted justly and we have sinned?" If the individual seeks to approach God he cannot come and declare, "We are righteous and have not sinned"—certainly not "righteous" in the simplest meaning of the term, for can such a thing be imagined? But not even "righteous" in the sense of a person seeking self-justification due to such extenuating circumstances or weakness of character or financial hardship which made him forget himself. For none of these things are in place when an individual comes to confess. All he is called upon to do is to make his confession: "We and our forefathers have sinned." As individuals, we can come before the Holy Seat of the All-knowing and the All-judging, bringing with us only the simple, naked truth.

When the individual recites the *vidui ha'katsar* (the short confession) beginning with "we have sinned, we have betrayed," etc., there is no room for a plea for acquittal. Here the awareness of sin, the penetrating pain of remorse, reign supreme. Only afterward, when one reaches the *vidui ha'arokh* (the long confession) of *al ḥet,* which contains a detailed reiteration of the awareness of sin included in the "short confession"—only then does a certain spark of pleading begin to flicker: "And for all [our sins], God of forgiveness, forgive us, pardon us, grant us acquittal."

These are the rules of individual confession. The individual cannot demand acquittal for such, as he has no claim upon his Creator, he has made no covenant with Him and nothing is owed him. As he stands before God as an individual, he is dominated by the conviction that he has sinned—"I have sinned." And he knows that sin entails punishment: "I have sinned and have been punished. We have turned away from Your beneficent precepts and from Your laws, and it has not profited us. We have gained nothing by it, our soul is empty and hollow. And as for what You have done to us in retribution for our sins, You are righteous in all that has befallen us. You have acted justly and we have acted wickedly." Sin, concludes the worshiper, can result only in punishment and there is no penalty severe enough for the sins I have committed. It is these sins that have brought upon me this misery and terrible isolation. "And You are just in all that has befallen us." Individual confession can lead to only one conclusion—justification of the sentence.

Communal confession, made by the prayer leader, is based upon completely different assumptions, and arises out of a totally different spiritual state from that of individual confession. These differences are well reflected in the introduction to the confession itself: "O Lord, remember Thy mercy and Thy kindness, for they are eternal. Mind not our former iniquities; may Thy mercy hasten to our aid, for we are brought very low." Even though we have not yet declared that "we have sinned," we proceed to approach God with our pleas: "Remember us, O Lord, when Thou findest favor with Thy People, and grant us Thy salvation. Remember Thy congregation which Thou hast gotten of old. . . . Remember, O Lord, the devotion of Jerusalem and never forget the love of Zion. . . . Remember Abraham, Isaac and Israel, Thy servants to whom Thou promised. . . . Yea, remember Thy servants. . . . Look not unto the stubbornness of this people, nor to their wickedness, nor to their sin." What is going on here? Even before the prayer leader has managed to assert whether or not he admits to his guilt, he goes ahead and asks not only for acquittal and pardon but for privileges and favors as well: "Remember . . . to whom Thou promised, saying, 'I will multiply your seed as the stars of heaven. . . .' Have mercy upon us and destroy us not." And then: "Give us a sign of good will and our enemies will take heed and will be struck by shame; do not desert us and do not abandon us and do not disgrace us and do not annul Your covenant with us"—and moreover: "For we are Thy People and Thou art our God, we are Thy sons and Thou art our Father . . . we are Thy beloved and Thou art our lover . . . we are Thy subjects and Thou art our King."

First, all this, and only afterward comes the prayer: "We have sinned, we have betrayed."

At first glance, this arrangement may strike one as being odd. It is, however, based upon our most fundamental conception of the Day of Atonement and the underlying relationship between the Almighty and *Knesset Israel* upon which we elaborated previously. The acquittal granted to *Knesset Israel* on that Day is given in this spirit. Only after confirmation of the love and close relationship prevailing between the flock and the shepherd, the vineyard and the guard, the woman and her lover—only then do we arrive at the stage of communal recognition of sin expressed in the short confession of "we have sinned." And immediately after this comes the following: "Our

God and God of our fathers, pardon and forgive our transgressions on this Day of Atonement and heed our prayers, efface and remove from Thy sight our transgressions and sins."

This is not a justification of sentence; it is a plea-request-claim for pardon and forgiveness that is made here.

The difference between individual and communal confession is tremendous. When the individual confesses he does so from a state of insecurity, depression and despair in the wake of sin. For what assurance has he that he will be acquitted of his sins? And who can promise him that his transgression will be forgotten and will not haunt him till the end of his days? In contrast, *Knesset Israel*—and each and every Jewish community is considered to be a microcosm of the whole of *Knesset Israel*—confesses out of a sense of confidence and even rejoicing, for it does so in the presence of a loyal ally, before its most beloved one. In fact, in certain Jewish communities (I myself heard this in Germany) it is customary for the whole congregation to sing the *al-ḥet* confession in heartwarming melodies.

The individual does not sing *al-ḥet*; he weeps. Not so the community, because it does not come to *plead* for atonement; it claims it as its right. Thus, immediately after the confession comes the following benediction: "Our God and God of our fathers, pardon our transgressions on this Day of Atonement, efface our iniquities and our sins, and remove them from Your sight; as it is written in Scripture, 'I, even I, am He that effaceth your transgressions for Mine own sake.' And it is said, 'I have blotted out your transgressions as a cloud, and your sins as a mist; return unto Me for I have redeemed you.' And it is said, 'For the virtue of this day shall acquit you (of sin), to cleanse you; from all your sins shall ye be cleansed before the Lord.' "

Concerning *Knesset Israel*, we have here a well-founded,

graduated legal argument, concluding with the claim that the "essence of the day" necessarily brings acquittal for the community as a whole.

Thus, almost the whole of the prayer-book for the High Holy Days is divided into two streams, one to be followed by the individual and one for the community. Both are to be kept in mind and presented before God simultaneously.

## *Faith—*
## *Belief in Knesset Israel*

In order to enjoy both types of acquittal he is eligible for on the Day of Atonement, the individual must fulfill two obligations. For the achievement of individual acquittal he has to repent, do spiritual stock-taking, confess, acknowledge his sins, experience regret, and purify himself. And in order to partake of the communal acquittal he must be bound to the community; the stronger his bond, the greater the degree of acquittal he will enjoy through the intermediation of the community. How does one qualify as a member of the community? How does one bind oneself to *Knesset Israel* to the point of being "purified before God" which includes the community composed of the whole of *Knesset Israel* throughout the generations?

It seems to me that in order to achieve this level of belonging and integration with *Knesset Israel* one must above all have faith in what it stands for. The kind of faith I have in mind is what Maimonides refers to in Chapter 7, Section 5 of the Laws of Repentance: "All the prophets without exception regarded repentance as imperative, and Israel cannot be redeemed except through repentance." Maimonides was referring here to the dispute between Rabbi Eliezer and Rabbi Yehoshua (Sanhedrin 97b). Rabbi Eliezer contended that "if Israel repents, they will be redeemed, and if not, they will not be redeemed." Rabbi Yehoshua differed with him and stated that redemption did not depend upon repentance. If we accept Rabbi Eliezer's view that redemption is conditional, then there is no certainty that the Messiah will ever come, for his advent depends upon the fulfillment of a certain condition; if it is not fulfilled, he will not come. Upon the resolution of this controversy hangs our unswerving belief in the coming of the Messiah. During the Babylonian exile God promised redemption to Israel, come what may; as to the second (Edomite) exile, He made no promises and it is up to Israel to repent.

This controversy illuminates a certain episode in the Scriptures. It is in connection with the *tochacha* (divine reproof) which appears twice in the Torah: once in the Book of Leviticus (Chapter 26) and again in the Book of Deuteronomy (Chapter 28). At the end of the chapter in Leviticus prophesying doom, the hope of fulfillment of the promise appears in the following form: "And yet for all that, when they be in the land of their enemies I will not cast them away, neither will I abhor them, to destroy them utterly, and to annul My Covenant with them; for I am the Lord their God. But I will for their sakes remember the Covenant of their ancestors" (Leviticus 26:44–45); and "Then I will remember My Covenant with Jacob and also My Covenant with Isaac and also My Covenant with Abraham will I remember; and I will remember the land" (*ibid.,* 42). We are promised here that after the period of exile and suffering, redemption will come. But in the reproof found in Deuteronomy where there is a proliferation of curses, no such promise is given, and the chapter ends thus: "These are the words of the Covenant, which the Lord commanded Moses to make with the children of Israel in the Land of Moab" (Deuteronomy 29:1). No words of solace are offered here. According to Naḥmanides' interpretation, the first reproof refers to the Babylonian exile, and the second refers to the present exile, in which redemption will come, according to Rabbi

Eliezer, "only if Israel repents." And, in fact, after the words of reproof in Deuteronomy, the following chapter has in place of the plain promise of redemption made in the Book of Leviticus, a promise of redemption that is conditional on repentance, as it is written (Deuteronomy 30:1–5): "And it shall come to pass, when all these things have come upon you, the blessing and the curse, which I have put before you, and you shall have a turn of heart while still among all the nations, whither the Lord your God has driven you. And you shall return unto the Lord your God and shalt obey Him . . . then the Lord your God will turn your captivity, and have compassion upon you, and will gather you from among the nations, whither the Lord your God has scattered you. If any of you be driven out to the ends of the horizon, from thence will the Lord your God gather you, and from thence will He fetch you" (Deuteronomy 30:1–4).

Maimonides supports Rabbi Eliezer in this controversy: "Israel cannot be redeemed without repentance" (Laws of Repentance, Chapter 7, Section 5). But it is not that simple, as this postulation threatens to topple our faith in the advent of the Messiah, which is one of the cornerstones of the Jewish belief, which Maimonides himself laid down as the final and concluding rule of his Thirteen Principles. If we accept Rabbi Yehoshua's opinion that both those who have and those who have not repented will be redeemed, the matter can rest. We would then have a basis for our belief that the Messiah will arrive whatever happens. It would then be possible to declare with assurance: "I believe with complete faith in the advent of the Messiah and though he may tarry I will await his coming every day." But if one accepts Maimonides' opinion and sides with Rabbi Eliezer who says that the coming of the Messiah is dependent upon repentance and that if it does not take place then there will be no redemption, how is it possible to declare, "I believe with complete faith in the advent of the Messiah and though he may tarry I will await his coming every day"; it is possible that he will tarry indefinitely if Israel does not repent; what sense is there in awaiting his coming daily?

Maimonides was not oblivious to this contradiction and he went on to say: "The Torah has already assured us that Israel will finally repent at the end of their exile and immediately be redeemed." Though this is not an unconditional promise regarding the advent of the Messiah there is an assurance that *Knesset Israel* as an entity will not be extinguished and will never be exterminated. This promise has dual significance: *Knesset Israel* will never be wiped out physically and will never terminate its existence through spiritual assimilation or contamination. True, there are countless numbers of Jews who have wandered afar and gone astray in alien pastures, but "in the end Israel will repent." It emerges from this that *faith in the coming of the Messiah is dependent upon our faith in Knesset Israel.* This implies that however far the Jewish people may go astray and become alienated from Judaism and fall prey to assimilation, in the end it will be restored. If we allow this faith to waver, then our entire belief in the coming of the Messiah is undermined! "The Torah has already promised that Israel will finally repent at the end of their exile and immediately be redeemed, as it is written, 'And it shall come to pass, when all these things are come upon thee, the blessing and the curse . . . and you shall return unto the Lord thy God' "; and then: "That when the Lord your God will turn thy captivity, and have compassion upon you, and will return and gather you from all the nations, whither the Lord thy God has scattered you."

The concluding and most difficult credo, "I believe in the coming of the Messiah" is thus based upon faith in *Knesset Israel.* It is not an easy faith.

Let me confess: sometimes, in bed at night, when I cannot sleep and my mind wanders, I am assailed by sober thoughts and overtaken by worry concerning the Jews in Eretz Israel and the fate of Diaspora Jewry. As far as the Diaspora is concerned, it seems to us that despite all of our great efforts, despite the growth of the yeshivas and the flowering of a wonderful religious youth, we are a very small portion of the Jewish population of America, a tiny percentage, lonely islands in a vast sea. And doubt gnaws away: will we not also be swept away by these strong waves of assimilation which rage around us in America? Thus, doubt gnaws away, but nonetheless I am very much distressed when Jews from Eretz Israel come and claim this as being so, and say that all hope is lost and that Jewish life in America is disappearing. Such a view, in my opinion, strikes a blow and wounds our faith in *Knesset Israel* which we are commanded to keep. This faith is not limited to the community in Eretz Israel, but to all Jews wherever they may be. For this is something we have been told: "If any of you be driven out unto the outmost ends of the horizon, *from thence* will the Lord thy God gather you." "If any of you be driven out" does not necessarily refer to the Jew living at a great geographical distance; the reference to those driven out "unto the outmost ends of the horizon" is to the spiritually estranged, to Jews who have deserted, assimilated and have become extremely alienated from other Jews and Judaism. Even regarding these we have a standing assurance that "if any of you be driven out unto the outmost ends of the horizon, from thence will the Lord thy God gather you." Every prediction about "spiritual extinction" and "complete assimilation" is contrary to faith in *Knesset Israel*, which is the same as faith in the advent of the Messiah, a foundation-stone of Judaism! And as has already been affirmed, "in the end Israel will repent."

Another problem, similar to the first but graver still (I even fear to express it!) is our anxiety about the Jews in the Land of Israel. Here the danger to Jewish existence is more physical then spiritual. The State of Israel is surrounded on all sides by enemies who seek its destruction. In this regard too, our only strength and security is our firm faith in *Knesset Israel*, in the spiritual sense in the Diaspora, and in the physical sense in Eretz Israel.

A Jew who has lost his faith in *Knesset Israel*, even though he may personally sanctify and purify himself by being strict in his observance of the precepts and by assuming prohibitions upon himself—such a Jew is incorrigible and totally unfit to join in the Day of Atonement which encompasses the whole of *Knesset Israel*, in all its components and all its generations. Only the Jew who believes in *Knesset Israel* may partake of the sanctity of the Day and the acquittal granted to him as part of the community of Israel. The Jew who believes in *Knesset Israel* is the Jew who lives as part of it wherever it is and is willing to give his life for it, feels its pain, rejoices with it, fights in its wars, groans at its defeats and celebrates its victories. The Jew who believes in *Knesset Israel* is a Jew who binds himself with unseverable bonds not only to the People of Israel of his own generation but to the community of Israel throughout the ages. How so? Through the Torah which embodies the spirit and the destiny of Israel from generation to generation unto eternity.

fession, the ways repentance is achieved and the kind of behavior appropriate to the penitent. Afterward he discusses the obligation all Jews have to repent and to make confession on the Day of Atonement. Maimonides devotes Chapter 3 to the account which each man will one day have to present to the Almighty, and to a discussion of Rosh Hashana (the Jewish New Year) as a day of judgment, and deals as well with the period known as the Ten Days of Repentance. In addition, he speaks of the punishments prescribed for various transgressions and enumerates those on account of which one is excluded from any place in the World to Come. In Chapter 4 Maimonides deals with those things which stand in the way of repentance, demonstrated in cases where a man says "I will sin but the Day of Atonement will afford me expiation," or "I shall sin now but I shall repent later." In Chapter 5, Maimonides abruptly interrupts his discussion of the problem of repentance and introduces a new theme—that of free will which is accorded to man. The chapter opens with the well-known passage: "Man is given the option, if he so wishes, of taking the path of goodness and of becoming righteous; or, if he so wishes, of taking the path of evil and of becoming wicked." Maimonides then elaborates (Section 3): "And this is a major principle and it is the foundation of the Torah and of the commandments." He then notes that repentance itself is an outcome of this freedom of choice. In Section 2 he writes: "Because the decision was in our hands, and we deliberately committed transgressions, it is fitting that we repent and abandon our weakness, as the choice now is also up to us; as is stated immediately afterward: 'Let us seek our path, and investigate it, and return unto the Lord.' " Maimonides carries over his discussion of free choice to Chapter 6.

At first glance, this arrangement seems perfectly reasonable: four chapters on repentance followed by two chapters on free choice. It appears that Maimonides concluded his treatment of the subject of repentance and has moved on to take up the problem of free choice. This is however not the case. In Chapter 7 Maimonides returns to the theme of repentance and opens with a passage which seems to be more appropriate as a preamble to Chapter 1: "Since man has been given free choice, as we have explained, he should endeavor to repent and orally confess his sins and turn his back upon his sins." From here on, the whole of Chapter 7 deals with the subject of repentance; and at this point, Maimonides asserts that repentance does not apply only to evil acts; it is also related to bad character traits. Should this not have been included in his statement in Chapter 1? When he stated that "when a man transgresses any one of these," he should have added there: "be it in deed or in thought." In this chapter Maimonides quotes all the wonderful sayings of the Sages concerning the virtue of repentance—for instance, "to the heights attained by penitents, even the completely righteous cannot reach," "Israel cannot be redeemed except through repentance," or "Great is repentance which draws a man near to the presence of God." Finally, in the concluding sections, Maimonides resorts to poetic language in extolling the glory of repentance: "How excellent is the virtue of repentance! Yestereve, a man may have been remote from the God of Israel. . . . Yestereve, he may have been wicked, hated, alienated and abhorrent—and today he is attractive, beloved and befriended." Here Maimonides draws a noble portrait of repentance; the Almighty as it were pines after the penitent person and rejoices in him.

A number of questions are raised by this sequence of the Laws of Repentance. First, Maimonides should have begun with this basic idea postulating the existence of "free choice": logic compels this sequence. If a man has the capability of making his own decisions, then there is room for repentance. If, then, this lies at the very root of repentance, why does Maimonides discuss the laws of repentance for four full chapters before determining and defining the principle of free choice? Second, if the concept of repentance is independent of free will, why should Maimonides include the principle of free choice in the Laws of Repentance? For if, as Maimonides put it, free choice is a "principle of the Torah and of the commandments," it would have been more appropriate to deal with it in the context of the "Laws of the Principles of the Torah," which precedes the Laws of Repentance in Maimonides' "Book of Knowledge." Third, and this is the major problem, why did Maimonides structure the Laws of Repentance in this manner? The first four chapters, dealing with repentance, are followed by two chapters containing a discussion of free choice, which, in turn, are followed by an additional chapter dealing with the theme of repentance. Yet, in Chapters 5 and 6, Maimonides asserted that repentance is only conceivable because of the existence of the principle of free choice, as indicated in the opening passage of Chapter 7: "*Since* man has been given free choice, as we have explained, he *should endeavor* to repent."

To sum up, we are confronted with three enigmas: (a) Why did Maimonides not commence the Laws of Repentance with an explication of the principle of free choice? (b) Why did he not place the discussion of free choice in his treatment of the "Principles of the Torah," it being "a great principle of the Torah"? (c) Why did Maimonides divide the discussion of the problem of repentance, in the Laws of Repentance, into two parts, one preceding the treatment of free choice and one following it?

## *Two Aspects of Faith*

Let us now deal with another problem raised in the course of Maimonides' treatment of the principles of faith. When speaking of the existence of God, which is the content of the first positive commandment, he declares, in *Sefer Hamitzvot* ("Book of the Commandments," which is in the way of an introduction to the *Mishne Torah*), that we are commanded "*to believe* in the Divine"; on the other hand, in the "Laws of the Principles of Faith" in the *Mishne Torah,* Maimonides does not use the same word "to believe" (*le'ha'amin*) but rather the word "to know" (*lei'da*). He writes thus: "The foundation and mainstay of all wisdom is to know (*lei'da*) that there is a Primary Being who is the Creator." The use of both terms, "to believe" (*le'ha'amin*) and "to know" (*lei'da*), seems to indicate that all the principles of faith involve a dual commandment, for the one regarding the existence of God carries implications which pertain to all the other commandments. This precept is at the root of all the commandments, and the principles of faith have their source in this basic idea—"to know (*lei'da*) that there is a God."

It may be said therefore that all the commandments are permeated by this dual obligation "to believe" and "to know." The meaning of "to believe" is evident to us; however, the significance of "to know" is less easily defined.

I do not agree with those who interpret "to know" as meaning "to understand," indicating that each and every Jew would have to philosophize and investigate for himself all that is relevant to the existence of God. I do not believe that this is what Maimonides meant. We cannot "understand" the Almighty; His quality is hidden and unfathomable, and in this Maimonides concurred with the Kabbalists who asserted: "No intellect can apprehend Him." I am convinced therefore that Maimonides did not mean that every Jew had to become a philosopher or, in modern parlance, a theologian. I would say that "to know" (*lei'da*) means that our conviction of the existence of God should become a constant and continuous awareness of the reality of God, a level of consciousness never marred by inattention; "to believe" (*le'ha'amin*), on the other hand, implies no prohibition against inattentiveness. "I believe"—but it may happen that I become distracted at times from the thing in which I believe. But in the term "to know" (*lei'da*) the reference is to a state of continuous awareness—that the belief in God should cause man to be in a state of perpetual affinity, of constant orientation, God should become a living reality that one cannot forget even for a minute. This keen awareness of the existence of God should constitute the foundation of our thoughts, ideas and emotions in every kind of situation and under all conditions. Everything else inevitably depends upon this supreme article of faith.

This "interpretation" actually mirrors an explicit verse of the Bible: "In all thy ways know Him" (Proverbs 3:6). "In all thy ways"—meaning in all situations, in everything you do; whatever path you take, under all conditions—"know Him." Be conscious of God's existence at all times.

A man wakes at dawn and sees the sun rising or goes out at sunset and sees the fiery clouds which drape the horizon in the twilight of a weekday at dusk, and though he may be a physicist or another kind of scientist who is capable of interpreting the phenomena of sunset and sunrise in quantitative mathematical-scientific terms, still he must see in the splendor of sunrise and sunset, in this wondrous cosmic regularity, a reflection of the glory of God, Whose primeval will was central to the dynamics of Creation and still animates all organic matter. I did not conjure this up from my imagination: it actually constitutes the foundation of a substantial number of commandments, namely, the requirement to recite a benediction before partaking of food and upon seeing pleasant sights. It is written in the Midrash: "God help the wicked for they are like the dead, when they wake at dawn and see the sun rising and fail to recite the blessing—'He Who is Creator of light and the Producer of darkness, He Who maketh peace and createth all.' " "To know" (*lei'da*) means to see the sun rising and to immediately say the blessing "Creator of light and Producer of darkness," or to see the sun setting and say the blessing "Creator of sunsets," or to see trees blossom and recite a blessing over this, or to look at the sea and to respond by acknowledging "He Who fashioned Creation."

In nature as a whole—and especially in its systematic regularity and in the technical character of its processes, in the scientific drama occurring within it, in the exact mathematical relationships between the natural phenomena and especially in the permanent laws of physics—the primeval will of the Master of the Universe is reflected. A man goes outdoors on a fair summer's day and sees the whole world blossoming; that man comes "to know" that there exists a Primary Being Who is the originator of all that is; in every budding flower, in every rose opening its petals, in each ray of light and in every drop of rain—"to know that there is a Primary Being and that He is the Originator of all that is."

Yet the "knowing" does not refer to nature alone. It is sufficient that a man reflect on past or present events, enough that he read the morning news in the paper—and he discerns the hand of Providence and hears the shofar calls of the Almighty. Man is under the obligation of fulfilling the positive commandment of "knowing" that there exists a Primary Being responsible not only for nature but for all of history as well.

It is a positive commandment to see God's presence in everything. Thus, in one's own existence, too. When a person feels satisfied, his wife and children are in good health, his affairs are prospering, and he is able to live comfortably, then he feels gratitude toward the Creator of the Universe; he "knows" that there is a Primary Being. He must, as it were, clasp the Almighty to his bosom, for he must sense the reality of His presence in his very house. This is easily proven: were the Almighty totally absent from his house, then it could not be truly blessed. "Thou hidest Thy face, they are dismayed" (Psalm 104:29).

And, God forbid, it may happen that a Jew's lot is misfortune and that he feels lonely and abandoned. He paces back and forth and goes from room to room endlessly in the dim hope of finding "someone," and all the rooms are vast and empty, echoing with silence. Everything is veiled in shadows, the shutters are drawn, and the whole house is shrouded in mourning. Such is a moment in which a man stands confronting abysmal despair and dark desperation; then, too, must he feel the presence of the Almighty: "to know" that everything has its source in a Primary Being, to sense that one is never alone, whether in celebrations or in misfortune and grief. Stealthily the Almighty reveals His presence and from the gray mist of depression the Creator breaks through in all His glory and places His hand on the solitary man's shoulder. He whispers softly to him: "Be consoled, son of man, you are not alone. For have you forgotten that Maimonides stated that 'it is a positive commandment to know that there is a Primary Being Who originated all that is'? You are not alone; I am ever with you."

Here, for example, I am sitting and explaining the Day of Atonement to my students. We are studying the *mahzor* (the prayer book) with its liturgical hymns, the laws and the customs pertaining to the Days of Awe. If need be, I offer philosophical interpretations. From an intellectual standpoint there is much I can transmit to my pupils from what I absorbed from my forefathers and from my mentors about the significance of the day, about the sanctity of the Days of Awe. What I cannot pass on are the experiences that I myself underwent on those days. I cannot give rise in them to that gamut of feelings that a Jew must experience when he says the *Zikhronot* prayer, when he declares "and the Lord God shall blow the Shofar, and shall go with the whirlwinds of the south" (Zechariah 9:14). I cannot possibly transmit the emotion I felt when I heard my grandfather, Rabbi Haim, tremulously breathe the words which describe the service in the Temple on the Day of Atonement: "All this, while the Temple was standing and the Holy of Holies was on its foundations and the High Priest stood and ministered—Blessed is the eye that saw all these!" One could well-nigh see that at that moment Rabbi Haim dwelt in another world, as if he were floating and journeying from Brisk to the Jerusalem of two thousand years ago.

If one wishes to know what the significance of *lei'da* was for Jews in the past, then study the words of the folk song—*"Du"* (Thou)—which is attributed to Rabbi Levi Isaac from Berditchev. "Lord of the Universe," sang Rabbi Levi Isaac, "let me sing you a song of Thou." "Thou—art East; Thou—art West; Thou—art North; Thou—art South." The sun rises—and one sees the Almighty in the illumination of sunrise; the sun sets in an afterglow of haze—and there too one discerns His presence. This is a feeling that a Jew must personally experience; it does not lend itself to transmission via theological tractates and essays, homilies and sermons. It is a feeling—and it must be experienced! I have no idea how this feeling could be instilled in my students. I may not be such a bad schoolteacher, and I can give instruction on various subjects—but not on this.

## *The Unseeing Spectator*

In this context the following selection from Tractate Hagigah (16a) is interesting: "He who is not aware of the glory of his Creator—it would have been better had he not come into this world. And who is such a man? Rabbi Abba said: He who regards the rainbow, as it is written: 'As the appearance of the rainbow on a rainy day, so was the appearance of the brightness round about. This was the appearance of the likeness of the glory of the Lord (Ezekiel 1:28).' " This text is bewildering. Is it possible to believe that the Talmud indeed thought that there was some resemblance between the rainbow and the Almighty? Can He Who is incorporeal and unperceivable to terrestrially-perceptive senses be portrayed as a rainbow? In fact, what the Talmud meant was this: He who looks at a rainbow—one of the most sublime of all cosmic phenomena, possessing the perfection of beauty composed of a symphony of astonishing color which appears in that glorious hour in which the light's radiance is fragmented into a multitude of enchanting colors: a seemingly rational phenomenon, perhaps, adequately explicable according to physical laws of causation—yet he who looks at this ravishing sight and fails to see it as a reflection of the sublime nobility of the Almighty, and as evidence of heavenly beauty but observes a rainbow and nothing more—such a person is blind to the glory of his Creator and his faith is considered defective!

Following this text, Reish La'Kish added: "He who looks at three things—at the rainbow, at the sage and at the *kohanim* (priests)—his eyes become dim." What did Reish La'Kish mean? "At the rainbow" we can understand: He who looks at the glory and splendor of all natural phenomena—the more beautiful and enchanting they are, the greater is their power to bring man near to the Creator. However, Reish La'Kish knew that the nobility of the Divine was to be seen not only in natural phenomena such as the rainbow; a person can discern the Almighty in spiritual, intellectual phenomena which are moving as well.

For example, a Jew sets eyes upon the Nasi, meaning the head of the High Court who, according to Maimonides (Chapter 1 of the Laws of the Sanhedrin), is the wisest of all people, the greatest scholar and Sage of Israel "whose stature is second only to that of Moses our teacher." When one sees the

Nasi and he is a genius in Torah, possessing great intellectual force, a creative mind, deeply penetrating intuition as though attuned to divine knowledge, an encounter with such a person is a marvelous experience. A man sits and listens to a lecture by the distinguished Sage; how illuminating are his insights, how penetrating his grasp, how encyclopaedic his knowledge! It is as though a fountain of knowledge had gushed forth before him, flowing with past learning and intellectual innovation. The beholder is uplifted and carried along by refreshing and enlightening waves, and watches as the Nasi, in the words of the Talmud, goes about "uprooting hills and grinding them together"—uprooting mountains of theory, of logic, of sharpness and of erudition, and grinding them together finely and "resetting" them. And though the Jew who saw the Nasi may himself be a distinguished psychologist or a positivist scientist who is well versed in classifying human thought in physical-technical categories and endeavors to present wisdom in scientific terms, when he confronts "a really great mind," encounters a wondrous example of a great and powerful mind, he inevitably realizes with his entire being, above and beyond all the scientific-positivist explanations, that human thought is dependent upon the Almighty Himself, upon the supreme knowledge of the Infinite One, the Holy One, blessed be He. If a man is a genius, it is because he has grazed the unlimited and eternal process of thought which permeates the universe from one end to the other. When one encounters greatness, one immediately recognizes the presence of the Almighty and feels the ceaseless gushing-forth of knowledge and wisdom from the Primal Intelligence—this, like a flood, saturating every creature blessed with intelligence it comes across in its path. When a Jew encounters such genius or ingenuity, what blessing should he pronounce? He blesses God, "Who apportions something of His wisdom to those who stand in awe of Him." He does not make a blessing on the wise man; rather, he recites a blessing over the fact that the wise man has been given a share of the Supreme Wisdom.

And it is thus that we should understand the above-quoted dictum of the Talmud: "He who sets eyes upon the Nasi"—and fails to discern the Lord of the Universe projecting upon him intelligence and wisdom—"his eyes become dim" as it is written, "and you shall share of your glory with him"—the rays of God's glory which, as it were, were radiated upon Moses and were passed on to Joshua. Whoever beheld the splendor of Joshua's intellectual and spiritual greatness saw that it was a gift of the Almighty, a "portion" of His wisdom. Through his greatness, Joshua, as it were, represented the Almighty's presence in the world, as the rainbow does through its unique beauty.

And this is how a Jew should realize the presence of the Almighty: *lei'da*—"to know"—that there is a Primary Being, to sense an emotional certainty as to His presence. He should also sense this when he sees a *kohen* (priest) blessing Israel, because the *Shekhinah* (Divine presence) rests between the *kohen's* fingers. There are many indications that the blessing by the *kohanim* (priests) is not a commandment which is fulfilled merely by the priests' recitation of the three verses of *Yevarekhekha* (Numbers 22:24–26); rather, it is a special commandment that is fulfilled only when the blessings are said both aloud and in the heart. This commandment is unique not because it requires heartfelt intention for its fulfillment, which is true of other commandments as well, but because it also requires "love." This is the wording of the blessing recited by the *kohanim:* "Blessed be [He] . . . Who sanctified us with the sancitity of Aaron and commanded us to bless His people Israel with love." Another outstanding peculiarity of the priestly blessing lies in the *yehi ratson* (the preliminary invocation) which precedes it in all rites, and not *only* by the Hassidim, who employ the *yehi ratson* formula in other instances as well:

"May it be Thy will . . . that this blessing which Thou hast commanded us to bless Thy people Israel be a perfect blessing, and that it should not involve any transgression or obstacle, from here to eternity." But what transgression and obstacle lurks for the priest while saying this blessing more than during the performance of any other commandment which need not be preceded by such an invocation? To be sure, if he lacks the sincerity of intention, then his blessing will be considered imperfect. But why is there a discussion here of transgression or of obstacles? The danger in regard to the priestly blessing is not that sincerity of intention will be lacking, for this danger exists also in the case of other commandments, but that he will not be capable of the "love" necessary for delivering the blessing—and this would indeed be an obstacle and a transgression. The priest therefore petitions God: "May it be Thy will that the blessing be perfect," that he not fail by acting hypocritically and be indifferent—as a stranger might be—and bless Israel without affinity or love. For no blessing can dwell where love is absent. Love is in fact a stated pre-condition for the fulfillment of this commandment.

It is the custom outside the Land of Israel that the priests do not bless the congregation on weekdays, or even on Sabbath-days. They only do so on festivals. Moreover, the Halakhah rules that a mourner does not recite the priestly blessing—be it, according to the author of the Shulḥan Arukh, during the initial seven days of mourning or, as stipulated by Rabbi Moses Isserles, a full year. This seems very odd. As we know, a mourner is obliged to abide by all the other commandments even during the days of the *shiv'a* (the initial seven days of mourning) while in this case, according to Rabbi Moses Isserles, he is not supposed to recite the priestly blessing for a period of twelve months. The explanation for this can be found in the following verse: "He that hath a bountiful eye shall be blessed (shall bless)" (Proverbs 22:9). If a man is feeling depressed, he is not able to deliver a blessing. One might well ask: Can he not utter the necessary three verses of *Yevarekhekha?* Does he not recite the *Shema* which requires sincerity of intention, and does he not say his prayers? To be sure he can read—but he will be unable to fulfill the obligation "with love" from all his heart. When a person is down and depressed, he is not capable of feeling love. It is a psychological truth that a person who is in distress cannot regard the good fortune and joy of others with love. In other words, the blessing requires that the love of the priest for the whole of Israel should flow from his heart in a spontaneous fashion and be given form by the prescribed words of *Yevarekhekha*—"May God bless and preserve you."

It stems from this that whoever witnesses such an outpouring of love—and it is truly said of Israel that though they may not be prophets themselves, they are at least the children of prophets—as the *kohanim* ascend the pulpit radiating infinite, all-encompassing love, and whoever is fortunate enough to see the High Priest and his fellow *kohanim* bless Israel, and feels how the egotistical partitions between themselves and the people they bless are submerged in the fire of their love, causing them to unite with each other—and sees how there emerges from their midst the blessing resembling the tenderness and love of a father for his only son on the eve of the Day of Atonement before the *Kol Nidrey* prayer: He who observes all this will ask—from whence does this plenitude of human love come? And how can a man achieve such a level of self-effacement so as to be totally geared toward blessing others? It stems from the fact that this is but a reflection of the Divine love that the Almighty has for His own creatures. This is the cause of the great abundance, this is the source of the tenderness and the devotion which characterize great love.

The eternal love of the Creator of the World emanates through the personality of the *kohen:* "the *Shekhinah* dwells between his fingertips." Why does the Talmud specify fingertips? Why not from his forehead, his head, his face? In the case of Moses our teacher, the *Shekhinah* emanated its rays of glory from his face. Why, then, in the case of the *kohanim* does it vibrate from between their fingertips? Perhaps because the fingertips represent man's self-seeking, his tendency to take things and hold on to them. The hand is aggressive; if it grabs hold of something, it does not release it. "Close not your fist to your impoverished brother," we have been commanded. The fingers represent man's possessiveness, his attempt to hold on to assets, occasionally also on to those which are not his. During the priestly blessing, these fingers of the hand are spread apart, extended, as though to proclaim that the moment a *kohen* ascends the pulpit, the usual way of the world in which we too often witness violation of the commandment, "Harden not your heart and close not your fist against your impoverished brother," is transformed and recedes. Its place is taken by love, by care for a friend, by open fingers eager to serve as a channel for the transmission of the grace of the Almighty to all His creatures from here to eternity. As it is written: "And they shall set My Name upon the children of Israel, and I will bless them" (Numbers 6:27). Anyone who encounters such love of humanity, such goodness of heart, such devotion to others, and fails to see in this the reflection of the glory of God, then his soul is dull, like that of the person who sees a beautiful rainbow yet fails to recognize in it the splendor of the *Shekhinah:* "His eyes become dim."

Of special interest in this context is a comment by Maimonides concerning the priestly blessing. At the moment when the *kohanim* ascend the pulpit to raise their hands in blessing, "They stand there," stresses Maimonides (and this is not something emphasized by the Talmud), "their faces to the Holy Ark and their backs to the congregation, and their fingers are curved inward, into their palms, until the prayer leader completes the Benediction of Thanksgiving." Only then do the *kohanim* "turn their faces back to the congregation and extend their fingers and raise their hands to the level of their shoulders and begin the *Yevarekhekha.*" Though this law that the fingers of the *kohanim* must be open is clearly from the Torah, Maimonides specifically indicates that before the *kohanim* open their fingers, they must keep them bent, forming a fist. What is the significance of what they do with their fingers before raising their hands? The closing of the hand in the form of a fist symbolizes the "fist of wickedness" which afterward opens up with the fingers extended, demonstrating the wonderful transformation that occurs within the *kohen* with the fulfillment of the commandment. When he ascended the pulpit, he was an ordinary mortal whose hands are generally close-fisted; but at the moment when the prayer leader announced "*kohanim*" something marvelous transpired, a metamorphosis occurred: his hands opened and at the same time his heart opened, and a hidden font of love was revealed; from here the blessings poured out and the *Shekhinah* shone forth.

That is what Maimonides meant when he wrote: "It is a positive commandment to know that there is a Primary Being." The author of *Hovot Ha'Levavot* wrote that when a Jew walks in the street and passes a mother holding a baby and observes the love flowing from the mother to her infant, he should see reflected in this the grace of the Lord of the Universe. Wherever there is love in this world, *there* dwells the glory of God!

To be sure, the obligation "to know" (*lei'da*) applies to all the principles of faith and not only to the existence of God, for that first principle contains all the rest of the Thirteen Principles. For example, it is not enough to believe simply that the Torah is a gift from Heaven; this belief must become a basic conviction, a burning passion, an experience of the order of "to know." I do not like to talk about myself, but since I cannot tell you what others have experienced, what I relate here must necessarily be my own personal experiences.

Sometimes I study the Torah deep into the night. Of course, these are the best hours for Torah study—things appear clearer, sharper. It happens, in the course of my study, that I sense someone standing near me, bending over my shoulder and peering at my page of *Gemara*, looking precisely at the same subject on which I am focusing, and nodding his head at a new idea whose accuracy I am still considering. My ability to get over what befell me during these past few years[2] is due to the fact that I relate to this principle of "Torah from Heaven" not merely in the sense of "to believe" but also in the sense of "to know."

If a man studies Torah in order to know, to feel, to live—then for him Torah study is not simply an intellectual accomplishment, but a many-faceted undertaking, rich in spiritual and psychological meanings; if then he does not feel lonely and forsaken he regards the Torah as a close friend and he can full-heartedly declare: "Unless Thy Torah had been my delight, I should then have perished in mine affliction" (Psalm 119:92).

The same element of "to know" (*lei'da*) applies to the problem of free choice, also. The assumption that man is free, that he has been endowed with the spiritual courage to make choices and with the power to determine the fate of his religious and moral life—this assumption cannot rely on the idea of belief by itself; it also depends on *knowledge*, on a feeling of being wholly charged by the tension present in this God-given factor of free-choice. Free will should implant in man a sense of responsibility, as Hillel said: "If I am here, everything is here." It was Hillel, significantly, that most humble of men,

---

2. Since the death of Rabbi Soloveitchik's wife, Dr. Tonia Soloveitchik, of blessed memory, on the thirteenth of II Adar 5727.

who emphasized the self, for without the awareness of self the element of "free will" will not be activated in man; without an awareness of self, man can neither create, determine nor decide. "If I am not here, who is?" Hillel knew that the awareness of free choice gives a man a sense of self-importance—not pride, God forbid, but the commitment of each individual to act as if the fate of the whole world was his responsibility, that through one deed he could influence the destiny of mankind for good or for ill. In the words of the Talmud (Kiddushin 40b): "A man should always regard himself as half guilty and half innocent, and the whole world as if it were half guilty and half innocent. If he fulfills one commandment, he deserves to be blessed—in that he tilted the scales in his favor and in that of the world; if he committed a transgression, heaven help him—in that he tilted the scales against himself and against the entire world." Such is free choice! That is the meaning of Maimonides' "to know": a continuous awareness of maximal responsibility by man without even a moment's inattentiveness!

Free choice requires a commitment from man, and it demands courage, forthrightness and intrepidity which one may express as a paraphrase of Maimonides: It is a positive commandment to be conscious of the existence of free choice which makes man responsible for his actions.

When Maimonides, in Chapter 5, Section 5 of the Laws of Repentance, deals with free choice and proves its existence through Scriptural quotations, he puts special stress on the following idea: "And not simply because we adhere to the Faith do we know this thing, but through the clear proofs afforded by wisdom." Why did he emphasize this so much? Because a man should rejoice in exercising the principle of free choice. Anything imposed upon a person or made compulsory by outside factors tends to be forgotten by him; but as everyone knows his own heart best, if a theory or law is discovered by man from within himself, he will remember it always. This was Maimonides' meaning: One is forbidden to take one's mind off the principle of free choice, for it was not given to man only from without or by tradition; it is also something in the nature of self-discovery and must always remain part of the self—the knowledge that man can create worlds and destroy them.

### *Coercion and Free Choice*

Maimonides, as we have seen, divided the Laws of Repentance into two parts, which appear respectively before and after his discussion of the principle of free choice. Why this structure? Because, in fact, he deals with two different types of repentance. That to which Maimonides devotes the first two chapters is apparently not founded on the element of free choice. That is, it sometimes happens that a man comes to repent through external factors and coercion, or through physical circumstances preventing him from continuing his way of sin. The cause underlying this type of repentance is not the sinner's independently arrived at decision to desist from sin; it has come as a result of the pressure of external factors or of an inner feeling of unease in his soul. In other words, free will makes its appearance here, if at all, in its palest form. A man who reaches a decision to repent, in this context, does not exercise the power and freedom to determine the course of his life.

"What is perfect repentance?" asks Maimonides in Chapter 2, Section 1. "That in which the former transgressor is afforded an opportunity of repeating his sin but stays his hand and refrains from doing so because he has repented, and not out of fear or due to incapacity. For example, a man sinfully had a woman. After a time he was [again] alone with her, his passion for her persisting, his physical powers unabated and he continued to live in the same place as before, but he restrained himself and did not transgress again—he is a sincere (perfect) penitent." As Solomon said: "Remember now thy Creator in the days of thy youth," etc. (Ecclesiastes 12:1). If he did not repent before reaching old age, that is, after reaching an age when he was no longer able to do what he had done previously, though it be only imperfect repentance, yet it is efficacious and he may be termed a penitent. Even if a man sins his whole life long and on the day of his death he repents, then all his past transgressions are forgiven, for it is written: "While the sun, or the light, or the moon, or the stars be not darkened, nor the clouds return after the rain" (Ecclesiastes 12:2)—a reference to the day of death meaning that if he remembered his Maker and repented before he died, he is forgiven.

If we examine "the repentance which is not perfect," we reach the conclusion that the factor of "free choice" fills no role here, because the cause of the repentance is not a deliberate decision stemming from free choice; had it been up to the sinner, he would have probably continued to sin. In terms of the exercise of free will, no change has occurred here; only the physical conditions have changed and he no longer has the opportunity to repeat his transgression. Such repentance, though imperfect, is nevertheless efficacious and affords expiation. We may ask, if repentance consists of remorse over the past and resolution for the future, how can this passive type of repentance be accepted? The sinner has sinned his whole life long, he was lustful and pursued pleasures until he fell ill, lost his strength or grew old and lost the physical capacity to sin—what value has his repentance according to the accepted terms of repentance? Is remorse displayed here? It may possibly become more apparent afterward, but for now there is no sign of remorse, only a physical incapacity to sin any longer. To be sure, there is no need to worry, in this case, about resolution for the future. Whether or not he resolves to stop sinning his remorse is one of "sour grapes," as in the fable of the fox. Since he cannot eat them, he deems them to be unripe. If it were up to me, I would throw such an old lecher out of the study hall—but the Almighty is compassionate and gracious, and abounding in kindness and truth: "Thou awaitest him until the day of his death." God is willing to accept his repentance, even in this case, even under these conditions. This is considered legitimate repentance—even though it is clearly not a result of free choice. The sinner can no longer sin; he has already reached "the day of his death," and what else can he do? But even under these circumstances the Almighty is willing to accept him, perhaps because of a flicker of remorse or of a tearful eye. Here is no perfect repentance—but acquittal is granted for transgressions even in this case.

## *The Illness of Sin and the Cure of Repentance*

Indeed, even perfect repentance is not always a result of exercising the principle of free choice, or at least upon the conscious awareness of responsibility in the sense of *lei'da* ("to know"). Even if his decision was not totally due to free choice, he can, nonetheless, achieve what is known as perfect repentance in certain situations. The only difference between this and imperfect repentance would then lie in the nature of the obstacle preventing him from repeating his sin. In the case of imperfect repentance, the former sinner cannot repeat his sin due to physical circumstances—he has aged, he is ill or weak, he is intimidated or inhibited by fear of other men. In a case of perfect repentance, though he is physically able to go on committing transgressions, the former sinner is restrained by a certain feeling; he is held back by a certain state of mind. In the latter case, the factor of free choice may have been activated—but this is not always so. What we are witness to here is a struggle between two inner drives, between two motivations, between lust and love on the one hand and a strong sensation of bitterness and nausea on the other. Sometimes the desire to sin is triumphant; sometimes the revulsion to sin is victorious. In most cases, a victory of this kind does not depend on free choice. It was not the former sinner's free determination that prevented him from sinning again while still in the situation which Maimonides described: "he is still in love with her, his physical prowess is unabated and the circumstances are unchanged."

The prophets and the Torah as well recognized a strong connection between sin and illness on the one hand and between repentance and healing on the other. King David wrote: "Bless the Lord, O my soul . . . Who forgives all your iniquity; Who heals all your diseases; Who redeems your life from the Pit; Who crowns you with loving-kindness and tender mercies" (Psalm 103:2–4). We find a similar concept in the Book of Isaiah (57:19): "Peace, peace to him that is far off, and to him that is near, saith the Lord; and I will heal him"; and again (Isaiah 6:10): "and understand with his heart, and repent, and he will be healed." From this equation Judaism extracted a simple conclusion: If sin were comparable to an organic disease, then its cure must come about accordingly. Sooner or later, an awareness of every organic illness is transmitted through the nervous system to the mind. There comes the point when man begins to realize that something in his organism is out of joint; something in his system notifies him that one of his organs is diseased. The news usually arrives in the same way: through bodily pain. Aristotle long ago noted that pain is perhaps the Creator's most important gift to His creatures, serving as an alarm-bell to alert man of approaching danger. In the words of the Sages: "Whosoever hath a pain, let him go to a doctor." But we all know, God help us, how tragic it can be when the alarm is rung when it is too late. It is a medical fact that in the most serious illnesses, as is often the case with malignant growths, there are no early signs in the form of very sharp pains that cause the victim to gasp with pain—at the early stage of the illness when it would still have been possible to overcome it, as happens in the case of a cut finger. In serious illnesses, a person is attacked by a general feeling of discomfort, of tiredness, of incapacity, apathy and melancholy. Such is the way serious illnesses first affect one. And if the Prophets equated sin with illness and repentance with healing—then, as occurs in illness, there must be warning signs of pain and suffering alarming the consciousness of the oncoming disaster. And, indeed, every sin is accompanied by an inner sense of sin. I am not referring to "knowledge" of sin, or to "understanding" of sin, or to "consciousness" of sin—these are higher stages. I am speaking of the "sense" of sin only, of that feeling of inner disquiet, of that bothersome ache which attacks the sinner, any sinner.

Indeed the first sinner, Adam, felt the ache of sin even before understanding the nature of the sin, in fact even before he knew that he had sinned. When God accused him of sin, Adam had a list of excuses ready to justify his action: he had no awareness of sin. "And Adam hid himself"; if he knew that he had sinned or had awareness of sin, he would not have hidden himself, but would have turned to Him who excels in forgiving and asked to be forgiven. But, he had no awareness of sin, only an unidentified sense of sin, a sort of inexplicable, organic, primitive feeling. What did Adam really feel at that moment? What did Eve feel? Not a sharp, acute pain but an ache of bewilderment: "And the eyes of them both were opened, and they knew that they were naked" (Genesis 3:7). Here was the tree which enchanted and tempted, which fired and inflamed the imagination (Genesis 3:6): ". . . that the tree was good for food . . . and a tree to be desired to make one wise." And all the fantasies and thoughts involving the tree reminded them of their nakedness; the tree itself became abominable and repulsive in their eyes. As is related about Amnon, after he sinned against his sister Tamar, having been driven to do so by a raging, lustful desire, "Amnon hated her with a great hate." So, too, did it happen with Adam and Eve. They now began to loathe the tree. They felt themselves deceived by it, disillusioned and frustrated.

Similarly, concerning the sin of the Golden Calf, it is written: "And it came to pass on the morrow" (Exodus 32:30)—not on the same day but "on the morrow"—"that Moses said unto the people, 'Ye have sinned a great sin' . . . and when the people heard these evil tidings, they mourned: and no one put on his ornaments" (Exodus 33:4). A state of mourning descended upon the people. Only the day before had they celebrated and sung around the Calf, they had danced and encircled, with joy and happiness, drunk with lust and with vulgar pleasure, "and rose up to play" (Exodus 32:6). But: "and it came to pass on the morrow—and they mourned." The sense of sin accompanies the sinner without any possibility of evasion. Intoxication and the blunting of the senses do not allow him to escape from his reaction to sin. "On the morrow," when soberness sets in, the sinner begins to feel the pain caused by sin—not an acute, penetrating pain, but rather a nagging feeling of bereavement, a mood of depression and melancholy.

The same thing occurs in the episode of the spies: "And Moses spoke these words unto all the children of Israel: and the people mourned greatly. And they rose up early in the morning, and went up to the top of the mountain" (Numbers 14:39–40). In the morning, on the morrow, they began to feel the pangs of sin, and these drove them to ascend the mountain.

And if we seek further illustrations, there is also the story of that vulgar creature, Nabal the Carmelite: "And Abigail came to Nabal" to tell him of his impending fate, "and, behold, he held a feast in his house, like the feast of a king; and Nabal's heart was merry within him, for he was very drunken; wherefore she told him nothing, less or more, until the morning light. And it came to pass in the morning, when the wine was gone out of Nabal, and his wife had told him these things, that his heart died within him" (1 Samuel 25:36–37). While Nabal, that primitive creature, was drunk and reveling at the feast, he was incapable of spiritual stock-taking: all his feelings were dulled, his senses dimmed. But for every drunkard, every sinner, every Nabal, every lecher and every coveter, for every brute comes the "morning, when the wine was gone out," when the drunkenness ceases, when wakefulness returns. With the break of dawn, which slowly and gradually scatters the mists of a bacchanalian, lust-filled, insane night, Abigail appears. For every Nabal, for every drunkard, for every sinner an Abigail sits in wait; she may not always appear in the form of the sinner's wife, for she has many guises. And Abigail begins to relate the tale of the tragedy in sin. Abigail's voice finds an echo even in the heart of a primitive and insensitive creature like Nabal. Abigail brings upon Nabal so much fear, remorse and bitterness "that his heart died within him, and he became as stone" (1 Samuel 25:37).

Such is the sense of sin which plagues the sinner. It awakens in him nausea and repulsion—and the repentance which stems from this does not come about because of free choice.

## *In the Morning, When the Wine Has Gone Out*

At this point, let me say something about modern Western society and about the crisis it is undergoing. When I arrived in

America a number of years ago it was a wonderful country; but it was intoxicated with itself and with material prosperity, drunk from success—which made it difficult to speak to the average American. This was also the case with the Englishmen and the Frenchmen; Western society as a whole had become, technologically speaking, immensely powerful; it had reached a high point in scientific achievement and in industrial prowess. It had grown drunk and it was utterly impossible to talk to it. Then a surprising change occurred in Western, especially in American society: "and it came to pass in the morning, when the wine was gone out. . . ." The drunkenness disappeared and people became sober, although this drunkenness had not in itself been evil; in fact, it was an intoxication which made the American a good-natured citizen and an easygoing person. But it was drunkenness. For had America not been so drunk, and had it seen clearly and perceptively, it would have realized sooner many things which it failed to comprehend at the time. Perhaps it would have been able to prevent Hitler's rise to power and the enormous destruction which came in its wake. But America did not perceive the imminent danger; it was concerned with its economy, and accepted the Monroe Doctrine as gospel until it belatedly awakened and confronted the catastrophe which had befallen mankind.

Now we are going through the stage of "and it came to pass in the morning, when the wine was gone out." Abigail is now talking to the people of America. A religious man hearkens and understands what Abigail is saying to him. But she is not talking to religious people only. A capacity for a sense of sin, like a sensation of pain in physical illness, is implanted by God in all of His creatures. Religious and non-religious, believer, atheist and agnostic—Abigail speaks to all equally. When Abigail's words reach him, the irreligious person does not know what to do: he becomes sad and dispirited; he is in a state of upheaval and allies himself with the destructive forces.

He is ready to ruin everything so long as he is not compelled to listen to Abigail and her message.

Those who repent because of the sense of bereavement which overtakes them, or because of the feeling of the impending "morrow," or because of Abigail's minatory message, may be divided into two kinds of people: those whom the sense of sin affects only vaguely, causing in them a kind of primitive disquiet, somewhat like a biological disturbance, and those in whom this feeling leads to a knowledge of sin, thence to an understanding of sin, and thence to a conscious awareness of sin, which is the gateway to true repentance.

Many, such as Nabal, never achieve this understanding and awareness of sin. They never get beyond the stage of the sense of sin, of mourning and of depression, and these feelings prompt them toward that type of repentance deemed by Maimonides "imperfect." Such persons do not seek out the reasons and motives which drove them to sin; they do not really understand the background from which sin sprang. They fail to understand a basic principle—that because sin is exactly the same as any illness, it is never an isolated phenomenon. Any pathologist or biologist will affirm this: there exists no human illness that does not spread and affect the whole body. Even when it is restricted to begin with, it eventually spreads throughout the organism. The fact that an illness makes its appearance in one part of the body does not mean that it is curable there; it must be cured in the weak spot of the whole organism. The treatment of the damaged organ is insufficient in itself; the whole body must be treated. And just as there is a spreading of disease, so there is a spreading out of sin. But the imperfect type of sinner does not grasp this. Abigail intimidates him, and he is troubled only by the specific transgression which engendered the sense of sin, and which is accompanied by pain, depression and mourning. If the sinner is primitive and limited in understanding, he infers that this sin is not "worthwhile," and resolves not to repeat it.

There is no legitimacy here in speaking of free choice; here there is no personal determination by the sinner, who is simply afflicted by two forces, each of which drives him in an opposite direction; he is torn between two magnets, each of which pulls him toward itself with immense force. On the one hand, he is driven by the lust of sin and, on the other, by the fear of awakening—"and it came to pass on the morrow"—and this deters him from sin. He is frightened by Abigail's words, which he knows will reverberate in his ears "in the morning, when the wine was gone out." And even when the sense of dread gains the upper hand, and he withstands temptation, and desists from *sin,* even though "his passion for her persists and his physical powers are unabated"—even then his refraining from sin results not from the exercise of free will but from the pressure of the imminent pangs of "the morrow." Likewise, when someone decides to have a complicated operation in order to be rid of disturbing pains, he is naturally caught between two forces. On the one hand, he is thoroughly afraid of the pains which the operation will give rise to; on the other hand, he is fearful of the fatal consequences of the illness if he does not submit to the operation. In a conflict like this between two compelling possibilities, sometimes one will win and sometimes the other—all depending upon the power of the individual will. But this collision of desire, and the resolution between the two forces, does not depend on the exercise of free choice.

External pressures determine events in this case, not an inner choice which is free of outside influence and stems from a strong sense of personal responsibility.

## *On the Danger of the Repetition of Sin*

This theme finds expression in the confession said on the Day of Atonement. There are a number of beautifully expressive confessionals in the Yom Kippur prayerbook. But the major confession said on the Day of Atonement—and in fact the only one said during *Ne'ila* (the concluding prayer of the Day)—contains the following passage: "We are not so insolent and obstinate as to say before Thee, God our Lord and Lord of our forefathers, 'righteous are we and we have not sinned'; indeed [*aval*], we and our forefathers have sinned." What is the meaning of this confession?

Only if we correctly interpret the word *aval* shall we find in this confession a cogent expression of that repentance which comes in the wake of the sense of sin, when the sinner can no longer bear the great fear and dread. "*Aval* we and our forefathers have sinned"—the *aval* here is not used in the sense of "but" or "however" as, say, it is sometimes used in the Scriptures, such as in 2 Chronicles 33:17: "*Aval* (meaning 'however') the people did sacrifice still in the high places." The *aval* used in the confession we are dealing with signifies "indeed," or "in truth," as if to say "we can no longer evade it, we no longer have a choice: we must repent, we must make confession." And *aval* is used in this way in the Book of Genesis (17:19): "Sarah thy wife shall bear thee a son *indeed.*" Here, too, the meaning of "*aval*" is not "but" or "however"; rather—"this is what will be," "in truth," "this is the emergent fact." You, Abraham, rejoice over Ishmael; you do not take into account the existence of Isaac. But this should not be so. "Sarah thy wife shall bear thee a son indeed." and that son is Isaac, who exists in reality. A similar usage of *aval* appears elsewhere in the Book of Genesis, and it was probably from here that it was taken for the confession: "*Aval* (verily) we are guilty concerning our brother, in that we saw the anguish of his soul, when he besought us, and we would not hear" (Genesis 42:21). Until now we have not admitted to or confessed our sins; until now, the voice of our pleading brother shrilled in our ears and troubled our conscience; until now, we did our very best to repress and ignore the feeling of guilt which gnawed away inside us; we did not want to admit our guilt, we did not dare to give voice to these thoughts. Now we see that the sin surfaces and confronts us; we see that Providence avenges itself upon us, that Simeon is in jail, that Pharaoh conspires against us though we be completely innocent, and accuses us of the preposterous crime of espionage. Is it not perfectly clear to us that we are here called upon to answer for the blood of our brother, whose pleas still reverberate and assail our ears? This must be a punishment from heaven! Our denial of sin will no longer avail. The sin confronts us in all its dread. There is no escaping it. Come, brothers, and let us confess: "Indeed (*aval*) we are guilty. . . ."

And like the admission of guilt by the sons of Jacob, the heads of the Tribes of Israel, so is our confession: "We are not so insolent and obstinate as to say before Thee, God our Lord and Lord of our forefathers, 'righteous are we and we have not sinned.' " Since we are dealing with confession, why, then, do we suddenly begin extolling ourselves, saying that "we are not insolent and stubborn"? What is this self-praise doing here in the midst of our confession? Actually, the passage contains not self-praise, but rather an emphasis on our guilt: "Our Lord and Lord of our forefathers, let our prayer come before Thee, and turn not Your back upon our supplications" though "we are not so insolent and stubborn as to come before Thee and say 'we are righteous and have not sinned.' " Thou knowest why we are not insolent and stubborn in saying "we have not sinned." It is not because we have completely repented in Thy sight. It is really because we can no longer deny our guilt! *Aval* (indeed)—everyone sees it, and it cannot be concealed—"we and our forefathers have sinned."

When a person attains this level of repentance, which stems from a contrite heart and the acknowledgment of sin at the time, how certain can he be that he will not again repeat his sin? And even if such a man in one instance overcame his evil instincts, who will assure us that he will possess the necessary resolution to withstand temptation when the sin beckons once again? What if lust overcomes the dread of "the morrow" and he repeats his sin? Maimonides, concerning such a penitent, stressed: "and his passion for her persists; his physical powers are unabated and he continues to live in the same place." He still covets her and the same circumstances and conditions are unchanged. Who, then, can provide the assurance that he will not repeat his sin?

This matter was raised by Rabbi Yehuda in the Talmud (Yoma 86b): "Who is a penitent? Rabbi Yehuda said: 'One who had the opportunity to commit the same transgression again and again and refrained.' Rabbi Yehuda stressed: with the same woman, at the same time, in the same place." The real penitent must demonstrate on two occasions that though he had the opportunity "and conditions appeared exactly as when he had succumbed, and his desire is at once aroused and tells him: 'Look at that woman, at the same place and in the same situation; go and do what you have done before' " (Rashi, *ad loc.*) and he, nonetheless, refrains from sin for the third time, then from here on his reliability is established—though to my mind there is room for some doubt with regard to one who has sinned from lustfulness. Though he has twice resisted temptation, who knows what can happen in the future? Moreover, Maimonides did not have before him the version of the Talmud which specified "a first and a second time" (nor did Rabbi Isaac Alfasi) and thus asserts that one test of will is enough: "He who is given the opportunity of transgressing as he has done before, and he is capable of doing it," both physically and emotionally, "but refrains from doing so because he had repented"—such a man is considered a "perfect penitent," even if he only proves this once.

## *The Testimony of the Almighty*

The first one to raise the question of how far the penitent could be trusted not to return to his previous defection was Rabbi Sa'adia Ga'on. He believed that all that the Almighty expected of the penitent was that *at the time* of repentance his decision that he would never repeat the sin be honest and forthright even if one could never know if, in fact, he would prove able to live up to his resolution. Therefore, if his intention at the time was earnest and truly meant, then even if he reverted to his sin, his first acquittal due to repentance remains valid. To be sure, the sinner is responsible for the second occasion he sinned as on the first; but the earlier repentance is not thereby revoked. For thus wrote Rabbi Sa'adia Ga'on (from the Hebrew translation of Ibn Tibon): "And let me further clarify: that if a man resolves in the course of his repentance that he will not repeat the sin, his repentance is accepted. And if he be later persuaded by lust to repeat his transgression, his repentance is not (thereby) retroactively effaced; but only the sins which preceded that repentance will be forgiven, and whatever (sins) follow it will be recorded against him. And this applies repeatedly, if he repents, and sins anew: only that which follows each repentance is to be held against him, so long as each repentance is done honestly and sincerely and if, in each case, the penitent firmly resolves not to revert to sin" (*Enunot ve-De'ot* 5:5).

Maimonides' view differs on this point. In contrast to Rabbi Sa'adia Ga'on, he ruled with greater severity concerning the penitent who felt a sense of sin, repented wholeheartedly but was not strong enough to live up to his resolution. Thus he wrote in the Laws of Repentance (Chapter 2, Section 2): "What is repentance? That the sinner abandon his sin and cast it out of his mind and resolve in his heart not to repeat it, as it is written: 'Let the wicked forsake his way, and the man of iniquity his thoughts' (Isaiah 55:7); and that he show remorse over his transgressions, as it is written. 'After my repentance I will be contrite' (Jeremiah 31:19) *and He Who knows all secrets will testify that he will never repeat this sin.*" This last sentence is thoroughly problematic; it seems to impose a condition which the penitent will find very difficult, if not impossible, to meet.

It is possible to interpret this statement of Maimonides in two ways. The first, literally, would mean that the Almighty will testify that the sinner is never going to repeat his sin. After such testimony by Him Who knows all secrets and foresees the future, there is no longer any possibility that the sinner will sin again. Thus interpreted, Maimonides' words clearly diverge from Rabbi Sa'adia Ga'on's definition of repentance as quoted above. It is, however, interesting to note that Chapter 2 of the Laws of Repentance was written completely under the influence of the chapter "On Rights and Duties" which deals with the theme of repentance in Rabbi Sa'adia Ga'on's book. But in the exegesis of the *Leḥem Mishna* upon *Mishne Torah* we find a different interpretation of Maimonides' thinking in this matter. If we accept this interpretation—which appears correct—we will find Maimonides to be in complete agreement with Rabbi Sa'adia Ga'on.

Thus it is written in *Leḥem Mishna:* " 'And He Who knows all secrets will testify' . . . You may well ask: 'How can the Almighty testify thus? Does the choice not remain in the sinner's hands?' And does Scripture not say: 'Even his saintly ones trusteth he not' (Job 15:15)? But it may be interpreted thus—that when he repents he must make God his witness (*'ed*) that he will never repeat the sin, as in the verse (Deuteronomy 31:28), 'and I shall call upon heaven and earth to testify to them,' i.e., that Moses makes heaven and earth his witnesses."

In Hebrew, the word *ya'id* may be used in two ways—first in the sense of to bear witness, to testify, and second in the sense of to mark out or appoint witnesses. If we interpret *ya'id* as used by Maimonides to mean to bear witness, that is, that the Almighty is called upon to testify on the sinner's behalf, then Maimonides differs with Rabbi Sa'adia Ga'on. But in the light of the *Leḥem Mishna*, we may understand him to have used *ya'id* in the sense of "to mark out or appoint as witnesses," as in the passage, "and I shall call upon heaven and earth to testify regarding them." That is to say, when he takes it upon himself not to sin again, the penitent should say: "Lord of the Universe, You are my witness that my intention is sincere and wholehearted." There is something here of the phraseology of a vow and of a resolve for the future. In this interpretation, there is agreement between Maimonides and Rabbi Sa'adia Ga'on, for if, from the start, the repentance was made so "unreservedly and sincerely" that the penitent called upon the Almighty to bear witness to his earnestness, then the repentance is operative, even if he later reverted to sin and failed to stand by his vow.

Thus far we have spoken of what is considered "perfect" repentance. There is however a type of repentance which surpasses even this: namely, "Repentance from Love." All of Maimonides' interpreters identify Maimonides' concept of "perfect" repentance with the Talmudic concept of "Repentance from Love," and Maimonides' "imperfect" repentance with the Talmudic concept "Repentance from Fear." With all due respect, it seems to me that these interpreters err. Actually, "perfect" repentance can also stem from fear (and when

Maimonides wrote that "imperfect" repentance stemmed from "fear and incapacity" he was referring to fear of man and not of God). But there is a level which surpasses even "perfect" repentance and that is "repentance from love." In this situation the sinner's decision to repent does not stem from misgivings and skepticism, and it practically excludes the possibility of ever reverting to his sin.

The term "repentance from love," mentioned in the Talmud, is absent in Maimonides' writings; nor does he use the term "repentance from fear." However, though the terms may not appear, these two types of repentance are, in effect, described by him. Were this not so, we would be justified in being greatly amazed, for anyone who carefully studies the Laws of Repentance knows how comprehensively Maimonides dealt with all the definitions and ideas related to repentance in the writings of the Sages and therefore rejects the possibility that he omitted so basic a distinction as that found in the Talmud between "repentance from love" and "repentance from fear."

### *Repentance of Redemption*

In Chapter 1 of the Laws of Repentance, Maimonides based his thinking on the following statement of Rabbi Matia Ben Harash concerning the four orders of atonement: "If a man commits a transgression against a positive commandment and repents, he is immediately pardoned, as it is written (Jeremiah 3:22): 'Return, ye backsliding children, I will heal your backsliding.' If a man commits an offense against a negative precept and repents, his repentance suspends sentence and the Day of Atonement affords acquittal, as it is written (Leviticus 16:30), 'For the virtue of this very day shall acquit you of sin.' If a man transgresses against commandments punishable by the divine or the judicial death penalty and repents, then repentance and the Day of Atonement suspend sentence and suffering purifies, as it is written (Psalm 89:33), 'And I shall punish their sins with a rod, and their transgressions with afflictions'; but one who desecrates God's Name, his repentance is powerless to suspend sentence, the Day of Atonement affords no acquittal nor does his suffering purify; but all, taken together, afford suspension of sentence and purification only comes with death, as it is written (Isaiah 22:14); 'And it was revealed in mine ears by the Lord of hosts, Surely this iniquity shall not be purged from you till you die' " (T.B., Yoma 86a).

In his penetrating reflections on repentance, Rabbi Kook labored over the interpretation of this difficult passage. What troubled Rabbi Kook was why the penitent should have to remain under "suspended sentence" until the Day of Atonement, and sometimes longer, until he underwent suffering and so on, before acquittal was granted. Rabbi Kook, who, as I picture him, loved all of Israel deeply, could not understand why a penitent, after his repenting, should have to wait further for acquittal. Why should his sins not be atoned for immediately following the act of repentance?

In addition to the problem posed by Rabbi Kook, which I too find perplexing, there exists another difficulty: Why must a penitent wait either for a certain day or for suffering to come upon him; does not repentance possess that instant healing power promised in Scripture (Isaiah 58:19): "and I will heal him"?

In Chapter 7 of the Laws of Repentance, which is written in a noble poetic vein, Maimonides declares: "Repentance brings near those who are alienated. Yestereve (*emesh*) a man was hateful in the sight of the Almighty." Maimonides specifically states "yestereve" rather than yesterday (*etmol*)—which would mean a full twenty-four hours earlier. Maimonides says "yestereve" in the sense of "with the waning of yesterday," at darkness, or perhaps even meaning mere minutes before today's dawn, just recently; just before this, "he was hateful in the sight of the Almighty, despised, forsaken and repulsive—and today he is beloved, desirable, near and befriended." We are confronted by radical transformation in the space of mere minutes. "Yestereve"—five minutes before sunrise: "he was hateful, despised, forsaken and repulsive . . . and today"—five minutes after sunrise—"he is beloved, desirable, near and befriended."

Maimonides continuously emphasizes: "How excellent is the virtue of repentance! *Yestereve* he was cut off from God, Lord of Israel, as it is written (Isaiah 59:2), 'But your iniquities have separated between you and your God': he cries out and is not answered, as it is written (Isaiah 1:15), 'yea, when ye make many prayers, I will not hear'; and he does good deeds and they are thrown back in his face, as it is written (Isaiah 1:12), 'who required this at your hand, to tread my courts?' and *today* he cleaves unto the *Shekhinah.*" Now attachment to the *Shekhinah* is the highest level man can attain: "And cleave unto him" (Deuteronomy 13:5). Naḥmanides, in his interpretation of Deuteronomy (11:22), states in the name of Rabbi Judah Halevi, author of *The Kuzari,* that the meaning is that "they are in themselves a dwelling-place of the *Shekhinah.*" And when the penitent reaches the level of "cleaving unto the Shekhinah," he achieves, according to Maimonides, a state of being "one who performs commandments which are received with satisfaction and joy, as it is written, 'for God now accepteth thy works' (Ecclesiastes 9:7)."

The question must be asked: What kind of sinner is being spoken of here who, before his repentance, is "despised, forsaken and repulsive"? Surely, this must refer to the thoroughly wicked person and not to the Jew who has merely transgressed against some minor commandment. This person is a real scoundrel who has descended to such unspeakable depths that when he cries out in prayer he is not answered, and when he does good deeds they are thrown back in his face. Yet even regarding someone as thoroughly wicked as this, who has undoubtedly transgressed as well against those commandments incurring the divine or the judicial death penalty, Maimonides does not say that this atonement is "suspended" and that he is supposed to wait until the Day of Atonement or for the advent of suffering; he mentions only "yestereve" and then "today." Is this the gradation of expiation and acquittal determined by the Sages? Is the transformation from "hateful, despised and repulsive" to "beloved and desirable" so swift and clear-cut, to the point of "for God now accepteth thy works"? "God accepteth," meaning "is pleased with"—which is something that is even higher than atonement. Yet Maimonides clearly based what he wrote at the beginning of the Laws of Repentance upon the gradations of acquittal enunciated by Rabbi Matia Ben Harash, while here he ignores all of these and describes acquittal as an *immediate and direct* outcome of repentance.

The explanation to this is probably that Rabbi Matia Ben Harash did not deal with *all* the categories of repentance. Apparently, there is one type of repentance which is immediately effective as the transition from "yestereve" to "today" and another type in which time must elapse from the repentance until the atonement is consummated. In the latter case, the repentant has to move along slowly, wait until the Day of Atonement comes, and then he must undergo purgative suffering before attaining acquittal. It all depends upon the internal dynamic of the type of repentance in question. There is one that works like lightning, the sinner being transformed from "repulsive" to "beloved and cherished" with the speed of an eyewink while the other type proceeds slowly and ponderously.

Both kinds of repentance, the speedy as well as the slow, are considered "perfect repentance" as defined by Rabbi Judah. If I may be allowed to distinguish between these two types of repentance and to name them, I would call the first "repentance which acquits and cleanses" ("for the virtue of this very day shall acquit you of sin, to cleanse you");[3] this type of repentance expunges the stains in a slow process of purging and purification. For the second kind, I would turn to Psalm 130 which is in accordance with various Jewish communal traditions, included among the prayers said during the Ten Days of Repentance—this psalm, which begins ". . . from the depths I called you, God," suggests the name for this second type of repentance. It deals with transgressions and asks forgiveness for them; this psalm contains something of the same tremor of anticipation and transition from "yestereve" to "today" as mentioned by Maimonides: "My soul waiteth for the Lord more than they that watch for the morning, I say more than they that watch for the morning"—as if to say, "Now I am full of transgressions and sins, but when dawn comes and the morrow arrives, my soul will be the Lord's." Far more is implied here than mere forgiveness sought by the author in the beginning verses of the psalm. Forgiveness is the result of a gradual process whose various stages have been registered by Rabbi Matia Ben Harash. But the psalmist wants more than gradual expiation. He cries out: "My soul waiteth for the Lord more than they that watch for the morning"; and again he cries out: "Let Israel hope in the Lord; for with the Lord there is mercy." God's loving-kindness is abundant, and He can use it to extricate us from the slow process of forgiveness, to transform it all at once—like the swift transition from the darkness of night to the light of morning. I pray not only for the expia-

3. I once heard Rabbi Haim Heller say, quoting, I believe, the grammarian Rabbi Jonah Ibn Janah's interpretation of Genesis 2:3 (*asher bara elohim la'asot*) as "which God created and made," that it is normal to use in the same sentence both a finite verb and the radical of the verb. This sentence also should be interpreted so: "For the virtue of this very day shall acquit you and cleanse you."

tion of my sins; from God, the possessor of loving-kindness, I seek also "liberation" and redemption from the state of sin. And, in fact, the psalm concludes not by saying that God will forgive Israel, or expiate the sins of Israel, but as follows: "And He shall liberate Israel from all its iniquities." This time he does not mean pardon, purification or the cleansing of stains; he is referring here to complete liberation of the soul.

We find a similar type of repentance described in Isaiah. But the Prophet calls it "repentance of *redemption*" rather than "repentance of *liberation*": "I have blotted out, as a thick cloud, thy transgressions, and, as a cloud, thy sins" (Isaiah 44:22). How long does it take for a thick or even a regular cloud to disperse? Must one wait until the advent of the Day of Atonement? It may sometimes happen instead that "the wind blows and the clouds scatter." The Almighty promises effacement of sin. What, then, of Rabbi Matia Ben Harash's differentiation between four gradations of acquittal and expiation? Isaiah, in God's name, says: "Return unto Me; for I have redeemed thee" (Isaiah 44:22); I redeem thee both from sin and from the pangs of expiation.

References to this repentance of liberation and redemption, which transcends the normal processes of repentance, are to be found not only in the Psalms and in the prophecies of Isaiah but also in the Torah itself. I refer to the portion which is read before Rosh Hashana (Deuteronomy 30:1–3): "And it shall come to pass, when all these things are come upon thee, the blessing and the curse which I have set before thee, and thou shalt call them to mind. . . . And shalt return unto the Lord thy God, and shalt obey His voice . . . then the Lord thy God will turn thy captivity, and have compassion upon thee, and will return and gather thee from all the nations whither the Lord thy God hath scattered thee."

Moses our teacher calls redemption: "and *He* will return"

(*ve'shav*), and this corresponds to repentance: "*Ve'shavta ad adonai Elohekha*" (and *you* shall return unto the Lord thy God). Thus repentance and redemption have the same significance: "and will return and gather thee from all the nations whither the Lord thy God hath scattered thee." For what is redemption from exile? Redemption means returning to one's true origins. The sinner has removed himself from his roots, his origin; repentance serves to restore him to the source of his being. As in spiritual redemption, so it is in bodily redemption—the ingathering of the exiles and repentance, two things which are really one. "And thou shalt return unto the Lord thy God . . . then the Lord thy God will turn thy captivity. . . ."

It is interesting to note that of the two passages of reproof found in the Torah, the first makes reference to a repentance of acquittal and expiation: "And they that are left of you shall pine away in their iniquity in your enemies' lands; and also in the iniquities of their fathers shall they pine away with them. And they shall confess their iniquity, and the iniquity of their fathers . . . then shall their uncircumcised hearts be humbled and then shall they accept the punishment of their iniquity" (Leviticus 26:39–41). This refers to repentance which begins with "pining away in their enemies' lands"—i.e., with suffering—and ends with accepting the "punishment of their iniquity"—i.e., expiation and forgiveness. But the second passage of reproof (Deuteronomy 30:2–3)—which, according to Naḥmanides, is a prophecy referring to our contemporary exile—concludes not with the repentance of expiation but with the repentance of redemption: "And thou shalt return unto the Lord thy God . . . then the Lord thy God will turn thy captivity."

It is this repentance of liberation and redemption that the Talmud calls a "repentance from love," while the repentance of expiation and acquittal it terms a "repentance from fear."

### *The Redemption of Israel*

Whoever delves deeply into Chapter 7 of the Laws of Repentance will immediately understand that Maimonides speaks in it of the repentance of redemption and not of the repentance of expiation, which he had dealt with in the first chapters of the book, before introducing the discussion of free choice. In these first chapters, he had discussed the various issues related to expiation—that repentance affords acquittal from sin, that suffering and the bringing of sacrifices afford acquittal, that one may not remind the sinner of his sin; the modes of repentance—crying out, weeping and supplication, and other matters fundamental to his subject—all this in the framework of that repentance by means of which "premeditated sins are accounted as errors," that is, repentance from fear, which affords acquittal and effaces the sin. In Chapter 7, on the other hand, which is perhaps the finest chapter in the *Mishne Torah*, Maimonides speaks of a penitent who is "beloved and desirable," who "stands before his Creator as if he had never sinned and whose reward, moreover, is great" and for whom "premeditated sins are accounted as merits." In it he speaks in one breath of repentance and redemption: "Israel is redeemed only through repentance and Israel will of a certainty repent and immediately be saved, as it is written, 'And you shall return unto the Lord thy God . . . then the Lord thy God will turn thy captivity.' " In this chapter he speaks of "repentance which draws man near to the *Shekhinah*": he describes the transformation of a nation called *lo ami* (not my people) into a nation of *bnei el hai* (sons of a living God), and of the transformation of a *gever lo yutslah* (an unsuccessful man) into *ḥotam al yad yemini* (the signet of my right hand). In a word, Maimonides fails to mention expiation even once. The repentance described in Chapter 7 is the repentance of redemption. *The sinner who repents in this manner becomes his own redeemer and releases himself from captivity in the pit of sin.* The Messiah's task is not to annihilate evil but to transform evil into goodness, sin into sanctity, hatred into love. "The wolf also shall dwell with the lamb, and the leopard shall lie down with the kid . . . They shall not hurt or destroy in all My holy mountain" (Isaiah 11:6–9). It is in this chapter that we are introduced to the similes of "yestereve" and "today." In the repentance of redemption there is no need to go through the routine of expiation. It comes about with an all-conquering immediacy.

Thus appears the redemption of the individual; let us move on to apply this to the community of Israel.

When the time of Israel's redemption blessedly comes, the messianic ruler will appear all of a sudden with no warning and all will be astonished. In a matter of moments the people of Israel will experience their redemption. "And he rode upon a cherub, and did fly; yea, he did fly upon the wings of the wind" (Psalm 18:10). As the Talmudic Sages say: "If Israel is found worthy of it, then the Messiah will come 'on heavenly clouds' " (cf. Daniel 7:13).

From my father, of blessed memory, I heard that Rabbi Haim Volozhyn was once asked: "How will the Messiah come?" He responded: "Let me describe to you the coming of the Messiah. I come home from the *yeshiva* (academy) on a normal weekday morning, just after the prayer of *shaharit.* My *rebetzin* asks me, 'Haim, would you like your breakfast now?' and I reply, 'Rilka (that was her name), my day's lecture is not yet prepared; I won't eat until I examine the text I am to teach today at the *yeshiva.*' 'All right, Haim,' says she to me, 'as you wish. Until you finish preparing your lesson, I'll go to the market to do some shopping; meanwhile I'll leave the sauce cooking on the stove. Please pay attention, Haim, that it doesn't get burnt. Make sure, please, for I know you well; you tend to forget everything else when you're studying a text.' My wife leaves for the market and I open a book and begin to learn the text at hand. Suddenly I feel the sun shining much more powerfully than it had before. What a brightness! Then I suddenly hear the birds in the garden chirping a new tune, a stirring, enchanting melody. And then I hear a noise coming from the street below. I put my head out of the window and I see Eli the cobbler running in great excitement. 'What is it, Eli? What has happened to the sun's rays? How come the birds are singing so marvelously? How come the trees are suddenly blooming with new leaves? What is happening?' 'What, Rabbi, don't you know?' says Eli, staring at me. 'The Messiah has come.' I immediately race to the wardrobe to get my Sabbath clothing so as to dress up and go out and greet the King—the Messiah. I take out my best suit and, alas, a button is missing. On Saturday night the button fell off and when I asked my wife to mend it she said to me, 'What's the rush? You won't be needing it again until next Sabbath eve.' So now I have to go out and greet the Messiah, and my suit has only two buttons instead of three. While I am standing and deliberating with myself whether to put on my best, but defective, suit or wear something else, or if in fact one may go out and meet the Messiah in one's weekday garb, my wife comes running home and breathlessly says: 'For heaven's sake, Haim, where were you? The sauce on the stove has burnt.' 'Silly woman,' I say to her, 'what do you care about the burnt sauce? Hurry and dress up in your Sabbath best and come to greet the King, the Messiah with me.' "

In this tale, which I heard from the mouth of my father, is encapsulated the whole story of the redemption. A Jew waits endlessly for redemption and then it comes unexpectedly and a button is missing on the suit which he has to wear to go to greet the Messiah. In a similar fashion one may describe the coming of the personal redeemer to every sinner who has been privileged to experience repentance of redemption. "Yestereve," just a short while ago, he was still engaged in wicked and riotous doings, like Nabal and his companions, "and he was very drunk indeed," and he was totally under the spell of his degrading lusts; he was despised, wicked, repulsive. But suddenly, at dawn, he sees the sun shining and the birds breaking out in joyous melody. And coming toward him is the Messiah, the harbinger of redemption. Such is the repentance of redemption, swift, all-conquering, unique—"yestereve" and then "today."

Thus far we have spoken of the characteristics of these two types of repentance. However, we must still learn to distinguish between the repentance of acquittal and expiation, subject to all the rules and gradations of expiation, and the repentance of redemption, which operates outside the framework of these rules. We have already said that the hallmark of the repentance of redemption is that it stems from love, and that the hallmark of the repentance of expiation is that it is motivated by fear. How are the differences between these two types of repentance manifested?

### *Free Choice and the Formation of the Personality*

In order to deal with this problem we must turn for a moment to Rabbi Abraham Ben David's gloss to Section 5, Chapter 5 of the Laws of Repentance. This scholar focused upon a problem which engaged medieval Jewish philosophers: namely, the apparent contradiction between divine foreknowledge and mortal free choice. Rabbi Abraham Ben David argued as follows: "This author [Maimonides] has not acted as the wise customarily do, for a man should not begin something he does not know how to complete. He started by raising problems, but left them unresolved and directed [the reader to rely on] faith. It had been better had he not raised the problems at all and not awakened insoluble doubts in men of simple, wholesome faith who may perhaps ponder over them one day [and stray]. And even though the problem has no definite solution, it is better to rely upon a partial answer than to have none at all. Meaning: if man's righteousness or wickedness were determined by decree of God, we would say that His foreknowledge amounted to predetermination, and this would present us with an almost insoluble problem. But as God has waived this power and has given it over to man, it is not correct to say that His foreknowledge amounts to predestination; rather, it is more like the astrologers who know from another source what roads man will take [but do not determine them]. It has been established that everything a man does, great or small, God has caused to be influenced by the stars, but that God also gave man the wisdom to elude their hold; and this is man's ability to choose good or evil. God knows the power of Fortune and its times—and whether a man's intelligence will enable him to extricate himself from its grip or not. Such foreknowledge is distinct from predetermination."

Rabbi Abraham Ben David wishes to bring out here that when we say that man has free choice, we do not mean that life is without stability or that there is no fixed course for man to follow. Free choice does not mean a state of chaotic anarchy, with sudden and frequent changes of mind that have no rational explanation. If a man switches too often from one mood to another, he is considered insane; if a man constantly changes his mind for no reason, then he is light-headed and fickle; if his actions frequently contradict each other, he will be regarded either as hypocritical or as being downright crazy. In other words, we usually expect a certain display of consistency in a man's thought and actions; we expect him to embody a certain way of life with its own consistency of character. The law of cause and effect, action and consequence, does prevail in a man's life. He reacts to various phenomena in a set manner and not according to haphazard caprice. Many principles in Jewish law are based on the fact that man acts systematically and with a certain degree of consistency. Take, for instance, the Halakha that states "a woman checks, then marries," which is based on the assumption that a woman will prefer not to marry again without finding out whether her former husband is still alive. Or, for example, "people do not lie about things which are likely to become known"; "one may rely upon an agent to fulfill his mission"; "a woman will not openly defy her husband"; "a man does not act impertinently toward his creditor"; "no man pays his debts before they are due"—and all the other presumptions of law which are founded upon human psychology, on a definitive pattern of human behavior. The Halakha did not regard man as an intemperate, irrational creature who walks with his head down and his legs up, whose activities follow no rules and lives by no principles. According to the Talmud, man operates within the law of cause and effect. All of man's actions correspond to a certain pattern of rules of human behavior (just as, in fact, patterns of behavior exist for all of God's creatures). The question now is: If man's behavior and responses are, so to speak, set and predictable, where does "free choice" come in?

There are two answers to this. In the first place, sometimes a man's will power is capable of overcoming the law of causation by which he normally functions; though this entails difficulty, it does lie within his power to act in opposition to his natural inclinations and in divergence from the routine to which he is tied. Secondly, and principally, it lies within man's power to determine the framework of cause and effect within which he lives and acts; this is more important than his occasional departures from the systematic and set framework and his divergencies from the law of causation. Man can be the architect of his own personality; he has the ability to fashion his own character and map out the path he will follow. Indeed, man is capable of determining in advance what his reactions will be to given phenomena and events in the course of his life. When Rabbi Abraham Ben David states, "And it is well known that all of man's deeds, great or small, were given by God to the power of the Fortunes," his meaning is that though life is stamped with causative regularity, "God also gave man the intelligence to elude the hand of Fortune; and this is the power given man for good or evil." Where this law of causation will lead him to swerve to the left or to the right, to do good or to do evil, is up to man. "Free choice" need not play a part each time a man faces a decision of some sort; there is no need for Abigail to come each time and whisper in his ear that after the night of drunkenness indeed "the morrow will come to pass." Free choice, when applied appropriately, can shape in advance the way a man will react whenever an occasion arises where he finds himself confronting any test or trial. By virtue of free choice man can formulate in advance the spiritual dynamic activating him; his reactions become natural, a part of his psychological make-up, and as a result, he need not struggle with powerful drives.

There are a few stories told about great Jews whose lives were plagued by a continuous struggle between conflicting drives, particularly the sexual drive. It appears that the evil inclination was of little concern to them, that they managed to mold and fashion their personalities in line with their wills, and that the "causation principle" operative in their lives was determined by solid, self-established rules. Their natural reactions guided them as to what they could regard with desire and what they should ignore, and as a result it was not necessary for them to engage in a continuous struggle of conflicting drives.

In the light of this, one can understand the connection between free choice and repentance. If the penitent utilizes the power of free choice to form a new way of life for himself and establish a new set of rules which will affect all his natural reactions if he succeeds in shaping a radically new personality for himself, then he is not in danger of backsliding to his former sinfulness. And, indeed, why should he revert to the way of sin? After all, the desires and inclinations which nurtured his sinfulness no longer pertain to him; they no longer play a role in the fabric of his newly-fashioned personality, which is animated by a different set of laws of cause and effect. The passions which previously dominated him and brought about his subjection to corporal-external beauty are no longer alive in him; they have been redeemed and transformed, and in his new personality appear as powers of attraction to supernal-spiritual beauty. Delilah can no longer ensnare the penitent heart of our protagonist; the glory and splendor of the *Shekhinah,* rather, are reflected and mirrored in his redeemed personality, newly reborn.

Even now, he is pulled by enchanting coils and strong passions; he is still "love-sick." But those things which once ignited in him the fires of lust, when he had his other personality, have now totally vanished and consequently there is no longer any danger of his reverting to sinfulness. His desires now lead him to another place entirely.

This repentance which brings about a radical transformation of a whole way of life leading to a rebirth of the personality is *repentance of redemption;* another type of repentance, unlike this kind, is directed against a specific sin—it is *repentance of expiation.* The first type, with which Maimonides deals in Chapter 7 of the Laws of Repentance, is higher than all the gradations of acquittal and expiation, for in it the sinner vanishes and is replaced by a new man who essentially has never sinned and is in no need of expiation, of cleansing, of purification. He is in a wholly liberated and redeemed state.

A further question we have to deal with: What must the repentant sinner *do* in order to be found worthy of repentance of redemption rather than merely attaining repentance of expiation? He must, of course, undergo a complete transformation, a fundamental change in the quality of his life. Yet the question remains: How can this be accomplished? How can a person effect a fundamental change in his entire being? On what should he concentrate in order to realize the fulfillment of a spiritual redemption? It is my feeling that the answer to this can be found in the laws dealing with prayer.

### *Communal Prayer and Individual Prayer*

According to the Halakha, prayer is motivated by *distress* or *need.* If a man is untroubled (and what man, unless he be an utter fool, has no troubles?), if a man feels satisfied that he has no need of anything, then, according to the Halakha, his prayer is worthless. King Solomon stressed this in his prayer (1 Kings 8:38): "What prayer and supplication soever be made by any man, or by all Thy people Israel, for every man knows the affliction of his own heart, he shall spread forth his hand toward this house (the Temple)." Without the pressure exerted on man by "the affliction of his own heart," he has no cause to "spread forth his hands" in prayer and supplication. And in Chapter 1 of the Laws of Prayer (Section 2), Maimonides wrote: "This commandment obliges a man to supplicate and pray every day, praise the Almighty, and afterward plead and supplicate concerning those things which he himself *needs.*" If a man has requests, he should pray; if he has none, he should not pray. And again, in Chapter 2 (Section 1), Maimonides wrote about the section concerning heretics: "And because he saw that this was the most pressing *need*, he and his court instituted this blessing." And, again, in Chapter 1 (Section 4), he wrote: "The 'intermediate ones,' meaning the middle blessings in the prayer of the 'Eighteen Benedictions,' contain petitions for all things, for they are like *paradigms* of every human aspiration and of the *needs* of the community as a whole."

The question arises: If these middle blessings include every possible need which may arise, then why did the Sages have to institute the "supplications" (*Taḥanunim*) which follow these prayers? For according to the Halakha, these supplications represent a sort of extension of the prayers. What, then, is their nature and purpose?

For Maimonides, the difficulty posed is more serious. He considered the added "supplications" as *part* of the prayer of Eighteen Benedictions, even to the extent that the eight considerations of which the worshiper must take particular note when reciting this cardinal prayer apply with equal force to the "supplications" (see Chapter 5 of the Laws of Prayer, Section 13). What is the purpose of the "supplications" as part of the prayers after the worshiper has already prayed *about everything*?

The Sages said: "As their faces do not resemble one another, so neither are their thoughts the same" (T.B., Berakhot 58a). Each man is not only one person in number but is also unique. He is different from others, being characterized by some original quality that no one else possesses. This singularity, this quality unique to him alone, which sets him apart from everyone else, reflects the Divine spark in him. The concept of mourning in Judaism is based upon this assumption. What do we mourn over? We mourn over those who "are gone and not to be found," in the sense of an irretrievable loss.

This goes without saying in the case of the death of a

great leader, a wondrous genius, or a rare philanthropist. Indeed, it is difficult to replace such people. But the tradition of mourning pertains to all men, not only to the noteworthy; it applies to the leader and to the led, to the learned and to the uneducated, to the charitable and to the one who was tight-fisted toward his impoverished brethren. It is written: "He who stands beside the dead, when the soul departs, must rend his clothes; what does this resemble? It resembles a burnt Torah" (T.B., Shabbat 105b). It may be inferred from this that it is impossible to fill the place of anyone who has departed from this world. We do not say, "A cobbler has died, another will fill his place; a tailor has died, another will come in his stead; another clerk will fill the place of the one who has just departed, another shop-assistant shall come in place of the one who is dead." We do not say such things, because every man is indispensable; he is not just "one" who can be replaced by another "one"; he is an individual distinguished by something unique to him and to no one else. Sometimes a person develops his own inner potential, and sometimes it remains locked within him like an untapped treasure that never comes to light. In either case, this unique quality is lost with a man's death.

This is what the Mishnah meant when stating: "Whoever saves a single life, Scripture accords him credit for having saved a complete universe" (Sanhedrin 4:5). Why is a man equivalent to a complete universe? Because he is irreplaceable; with his decease will disappear that uniqueness which he embodies. This is the reason for the custom of rending clothes over the deceased during mourning; the rending tears the cloth irreparably, as if to say: that which has died with the passing of any man is irreparably and irretrievably lost.

Maimonides' stance in the halakhic controversy concerning *ketav elyon* (superimposed script)—whether it is or not, legally speaking, accepted as "handwriting"—is interesting in this connection. The question refers to the case of a person who wrote something, and another came and wrote on top of his writing with *dyo* (black ink). Is the superimposed addition considered "handwriting" or not? Maimonides argued, in reference to the prohibition of writing on the Sabbath, that if the original script was in *sikra* (red) and the superimposed script in *dio* (black ink), then the second person is liable both for writing (the superimposed script) and effacing (the original script). The handwriting of the superimposed script is *not* to be regarded as authentic. If someone writes the names of witnesses who are unable to sign, and then they turn up and fill in the original writing with ink, then their superimposed writing is not considered writing and their signatures are legally invalid. The Ba'alei haTosafot, commenting on this difference between the laws of the Sabbath and the laws of testimony (T.B., Gittin 9, *s.v. mekarke'in*), state that, regarding the Sabbath, the prohibition is against the act of *writing*, because superimposing in black ink over the red is a transgression against the prohibition of writing on the Sabbath. However, concerning the laws of testimony, it is not the act of writing which matters but the *handwriting* itself. The witness must with his own hand affix his signature, which is indicative of his own character and his qualities particular to him and him alone; the witness must write in a script called by the Jerusalem Talmud "writing which can properly be verified"; it must be a script that whoever sees it will immediately recognize it as the writing of such and such, since it may be argued that a man's handwriting constitutes graphological testimony as to the whole nature of his personality. Concerning the Sabbath, it is the act of writing which determines the ruling; concerning testimony, it is the *handwriting*. Thus, in the latter case, the superimposed script does not count; it is that of him who first puts pen to paper—it is the original writing that is decisive.

In relation to the writing of a Torah scroll, Maimonides

also ruled that superimposed inscription is not valid. If, for example, someone transcribes a Torah not "for its own sake" but for some ulterior reason, and someone else comes along and goes over the original in ink but does so *"lishma"*—for its own sake—then this scroll is invalid because superimposed script is not writing. As in the law regarding testimony, it appears that in transcribing Torah scrolls it is not the act of writing (as on the Sabbath) which determines, but the author's handwriting—that characteristic, singular, original, individual handwriting, stamped with the scribe's character—is what gives the Torah scroll its sanctity and validity. If the original script is someone else's, who transcribed it *shelo lishma*—not for its own sake—then another cannot, by going over it and filling it in, sanctify it *lishma.* The content and wording of this scroll is identical with every other Torah scroll; not even one letter is questionable. But the factor that sanctifies the scroll, making it valid, is the original script of the scribe who executed it. In the writing of a Torah scroll, therefore, as in the signature of witnesses, "superimposed script is not handwriting."

This brings us back to the comparison quoted above from the Talmud: "He who stands over the dead, as his soul departs, must rend his clothes. What does this resemble? It resembles a burnt Torah scroll." That Torah scroll, like a man, is irreplaceable, because the handwriting in which it was transcribed is unique and irretrievable.

According to the Sages, there are two types of prayer. One is universal prayer, the prayer of all men. Man is in need of food and health; he wants pardon for his transgressions; he experiences loneliness and he turns for help to the Master of the Universe—for the same prayer applies to all. As Maimonides phrases it: "That they [the prayers] should be ready for the tongues of all men, and that they should be learned by all, and that the prayer of those that stammer should be as perfect as the prayer of the very articulate." In this type of prayer, man prays as part of the community and requests the fulfillment of those needs which are common to all, as enumerated in the Eighteen Benedictions.

The other is individual prayer, which reflects the singular uniqueness of each man, and that is the supplication *following* the universal prayer. The Sages did not determine a standard, permanent formula for this prayer, for they wished to preserve in it the original and innate quality of each individual worshiper.

These two prayers mirror the remarkable paradox of human existence. On the one hand, each man is similar and equal to others; on the other hand, he is alone, independent, a separate individual. So it is with the Torah scroll: the same text, with no changes—but in a different handwriting.

## *Man's Singularity*

How is man's uniqueness manifested? In his central aspiration, in that single goal toward which all the strings of his soul's yearnings are attuned. Man's singularity is expressed in his life's innermost prayer. It may be what others want too—but each wants it in his own individual way. Every man has a dream of his own, and he strives and yearns for what modern psychology terms self-fulfillment. And this he achieves when he realizes his private dream toward the fulfillment of which all his hopes and desires are directed.

It is a man's otherness, his singularity, his personal isolation even when in the midst of a multitude, that determines his lifestyle, that shapes the quality of his thought and actions. In the familiar phrase of the Sages, "Everything is in accordance with the measure of each person."

On a pleasant summer's night a man goes out and sees above him a velvety dark-blue sky filled with softly-shining stars, signaling from vast distances, from hidden worlds; and he is aware of the tranquility which encompasses nature. At such a moment, what are his thoughts? All depends upon his system of associations, upon the type of person he is. If he is a man whose religiousness permeates his being, one who, in addition to fulfilling all the other commandments, fulfills that specific command *lei'da*—knowing that there is a Primary Being—what will he discover on this wonderful night when tens of thousands of stars whisper to him from remote worlds, if not the existence of the Creator of the Universe who spread forth His Divine presence throughout the enchanting tranquility round about, across the silent treetops which listen tremulously to His Voice coming from beyond the purifying mists spread around them? What will that man discover in a miraculous, mystery-filled night such as this if not the breath of Eternity blowing tenderly on his weary countenance? What will he do at that moment, if not respond spontaneously and without aforethought, by singing "Bless the Lord, O my soul. O Lord my God, Thou art very great; Thou art clothed with glory and majesty." One of the astronauts thus reacted spontaneously, when the majesty and splendor of the universe were revealed to him and he began to recite the passage: "In the beginning God created the heaven and the earth." His natural associative stream led him to quote from Holy Scriptures.

If a man was not privileged to be born into a religious home—or to have developed a religious sensibility through his education—he does not deserve our ire but rather our sympathy and pity. Such a man lacks a dimension which would endow his life with a breadth of scope. What will such a person think of when he goes out into an enchanted summer's night? What will his thoughts be? He will think how empty and futile, how hollow and meaningless the world is that operates according to cold mechanical laws. He will see nothing but the desolation of the howling wilderness conforming to certain physical laws. If scientifically inclined, he will attempt to apply these laws to the natural phenomena confronting him. If he is a hedonistic person, how many dark powerful passions and how many hidden lusts will the silence of this many-splendored night awaken in him? For such a man, the dark night will become a symbol of pleasure-seeking. If he has long arms and is avaricious, it may occur to him that there is nothing like the silence of a summer's night for breaking into a bank in order to empty its vault. Indeed, man's thoughts and his trains of association are determined by the type of person he is; all follow the manner in which he has styled the course of his life, all follow the individual nature of his quest. What he wants more than anything else, what his lips whisper when he bows in supplication before the Lord of the Universe, is something between himself and his Creator, which is not meant for the ear of any stranger.

A man's chain of associations depends upon his aspirations, upon that personal supplication whispered in the hour of silence. Some seek the nearness of the Master of the Universe; some long for power or fame; others want to expand their knowledge; and there are those who seek pleasures or money. Prayer represents man in his totality. It represents everything he is and does.

Judaism has always held that it lies within man's power to renew himself, to be reborn and to redirect the course of his life. In this task, man must rely upon himself; no one can help him. He is his own creator and innovator. He is his own redeemer; he is his own messiah who has come to redeem himself from the darkness of his exile to the light of his personal redemption.

The best example of a man's ability to create himself

anew, to change his life's inner prayer, is demonstrated in the act of conversion, of which repentance is but a reflection. Conversion is not, as many believe, a mere matter of immersion in the ritual bath. It is not a mere ceremony. Certainly, immersion is crucial to it, but it is a mistake to believe that the conversion begins and ends with this ritual. Conversion means a radical, decisive and complete change of the person's identity, and the immersion is but a symbol indicative of this transformation. A man descends into the waters to immerse himself, and when he emerges, he is a new person. If I may paraphrase Scripture, it is written: "when you lose it, you find it"—one personality is lost and a second, different one has been found. "Go forth out of thy country, and from thy kindred, and from thy father's house" (Genesis 12:1)—as Abraham, our forefather, the father of all righteous converts, was told. "Go forth" is not a matter of geographical change from one locality to another, but a deeply human and spiritual event. As the Halakha puts it: "A person, having converted, is like a new-born babe." Being born again means a definitive change in his style and way of life, inwardly and outwardly. Without such a change, true conversion does not take place, not even partially.

Like conversion, repentance is also seen as new birth in the sense of receiving a new identity, a whole new personality, a new life. In Chapter 7 of the Laws of Repentance, therefore, Maimonides—when speaking of the repentance of *redemption*—talks of repenting not only over deeds and transgressions but also over evil character traits, a subject not mentioned in connection with repentance of *expiation* in Chapters 1 and 2. This time, he is dealing with a total transformation of personality and not only in regard to a specific transgression. For this, it is not enough to resolve not to commit the same transgression again; this calls for a remolding of the whole personality, including its character traits. If a man refrains from every possible transgression but retains his accustomed traits of anger, jealousy or hatred, he will be incapable of acquiring the new personality which is imperative for redemptive repentance.

### *The Resurrection of the Dead and the Immortality of the Soul*

Let us conclude by explaining a phrase that appears in the opening passage of the Laws of Repentance: "And the exposition of this precept and of the principles which it entails are discussed in the following chapters." What are the "principles" to which Maimonides refers in this context?

He is undoubtedly speaking here of the principle of "free choice," which is a foundation of repentance. However, in using the plural form ("principles"), I believe he was referring to the theme dealt with in Chapter 9, namely, the issues of the World to Come and of the soul's continued existence after death. From Maimonides' reflections on these issues it appears that had the Master of the Universe not created repentance, the principle of the World to Come could not have been perceived. If we believe in the World to Come as one of the Thirteen Principles, then it is owing to repentance "and the principles which it entails," namely the World to Come and the immortality of the soul.

What is the connection between repentance and the World to Come, which is introduced by Maimonides in Chapter 9 of the Laws of Repentance? We have already said that there exists a repentance of redemption whose essence is the total transformation of the personality from one state to another. In the course of this type of repentance, man assumes the role of creator, insofar as God implanted in him the capacity to create himself anew. But is man able to create *ex nihilo*? If everything he was before had been obliterated, if his whole existence had become contaminated, defiled and bathed in sin, if all his prayers had thus far been repulsive and were thrown back in his face, how could a man, out of all these, fashion a new personality for himself? Can he indeed become, as it were, a creator *ex nihilo*? For the Scriptures loudly protest the contrary (Job 14:4): "Who can bring a clean thing out of an impurity?" Who can transform uncleanliness into purity? "Only the One," meaning the Eternal, and no one else has the power to create from nothing—not man, who at best can only fashion something from something. How is such repentance then possible if it apparently entails creation *ex nihilo*?

Indeed, the penitent does not mold himself *ex nihilo* but from something. Though his "something" before repentance consisted of the "abominable and despised and abhorrent," it is a cornerstone for Judaism, emphasized especially in Hassidism and in the Kabbalah, that however great a man's transgressions may be, they fail to penetrate to the innermost core of his soul. Always, and under all circumstances, there remains something pure, precious and sacred in man's soul. If all were corrupted, if sin were to annihilate *the whole personality* without leaving a trace, then repentance would be an impossibility. The idea that in the mystique of man's soul there is an aspect that remains as a pure core, despite the impurity, is reflected in our daily prayers: "My Lord, the soul You gave unto me is pure." The sinner represents only a pseudo-personality, his external self only. All the desires and ambitions which dragged man down to sin were empty and vain. Man's one true aspiration, superseding all others, is to draw near to the Almighty. Mountains of charred ashes and layers of sand may have covered his soul and concealed the burning ember, but it nonetheless continues silently and secretly to flicker. Even then, all that a sinner need do is shake himself out of his state, wake up and identify with his real "self," and reach the sublime moment of prayer directed toward the Almighty, "Who hears all prayer" and about Whom it is said: "Toward You all flesh shall go." *All* flesh: the gates are open to all those who knock upon them in sincerity.

And from this we learn that "all of Israel has a share in the World to Come," that it is the innermost, untouched core of the soul which is forever pure, that enters the World to Come.

# THOU SHOULDST ENTER THE COVENANT OF THE LORD

Maimonides, in his Code in the first chapter of the Laws of Repentance, Section 1, writes: "How does one confess? By saying, 'I beseech You, O God, I have sinned, I have acted perversely; I have transgressed before you, and have done such and such; I am contrite and ashamed of my deeds and I will never do this again.' " Here, before us, are the three well-known elements of repentance: acknowledgment of the sin (*"I have sinned, acted perversely, transgressed"*); remorse (*"I am contrite and am ashamed of my deeds"*), and resolution for the future (*"I will never do this again"*).

Let us pay attention to the fact that in this formula of repentance Maimonides placed the condition of remorse for the past (*"I have sinned . . . and done such and such and I am contrite and am ashamed of my deeds"*) before that of resolution for the future (*"and I will never do this again"*).

As opposed to this, in the second chapter of the Laws of Repentance, Section 2, Maimonides writes: "What is repentance? It consists of the following: that the sinner abandon his sin, remove it from his thoughts, and resolve in his heart never to repeat it, as it says, 'Let the wicked forsake his way, and the man of iniquity his thoughts' (Isaiah 55:7), and also that he express regret for the past, as it is said, 'For after I returned I was regretful' (Jeremiah 31:18)." Here, also, we have before us the two elements of repentance: remorse for the past and resolution for the future. This time, however, the order is different; while, in Chapter 1, remorse for the past precedes resolution for the future, here, in Chapter 2, Maimonides places resolution for the future (*"that the sinner abandon his sin, remove it from his thoughts and resolve never to repeat it"*) first in order of precedence and only afterward does he refer to remorse for the past, quoting an explicit verse from Jeremiah: "For after I returned I was regretful."

The commentators have pointed out this apparent contradiction between the formulae of repentance presented in Chapters 1 and 2 of the Laws of Repentance and have offered various explanations for it. It seems to me, however, that there really is no conflict, since the two chapters of the Laws of Repentance deal with different types of repentance. One type of repentance by its very nature begins with feeling remorse, whereas the other should begin by making resolve for the future. In order to understand the difference between these two types of repentance, we will have to use an analogy from another halakhic category, the release from vows.

## *Two Principles on Release From Vows*

In principle (and according to the majority of the early commentators), the power of a sage to grant release from vows is based on either of two grounds: on the basis of "remorse," or on the basis of what the Talmud calls an "opening." What is the distinction between an "opening" and "remorse"?

According to the explanation of Nahmanides, release

from vows, on the grounds of an "opening," is based on the notion that the vow was made in *error.* The sage can release someone from a vow, insofar as he is able to establish that it was an erroneous or mistaken vow. There are, of course, erroneous vows which do not require release on the part of a sage, such as the case cited in the Mishna of a certain person who "saw others eating [his] figs" and, thinking that these people were not related to him, issued a prohibition to them; afterward he discovered that they were his father and brothers. Such an erroneous vow, made due to an error in identification, does not require release by a sage. A vow requiring release by a sage involves an error which cannot be nullified by itself, but only by virtue of a sage sizing up the vow, and searching for an "opening" in it; and it is through his release that the vow which was originally made with clear intentions—knowingly and without any error—is transformed into an erroneous vow. But when a sage releases a vow by means of the principle of "remorse," he does not transform it into an erroneous vow, for he has found no "opening" to this effect. He cancels the vow, uprooting it as though it had never existed, despite the fact that in this case of "remorse" he found no "opening" to lead him to declare it an erroneous vow.

Release based on "remorse" is derived from the authority of the sage and not through an error in the vow itself. In both cases, the vow is void *ab initio,* but the legal consequences are not necessarily the same. When a sage releases part of a vow by establishing that it has been made in error, the entire vow is automatically considered void, for according to the rule regarding mistaken vows: "a vow which is declared partially void is void in its entirety"—for the error is said to extend over the vow in its entirety. But in the case of release from vows due to remorse, since the release is derived from the authority of the sage, and not from any undermining of the vow itself, only that part concerning which there was "remorse" and release obtained for it by the sage is considered void, while the rest remains operative.

This line of reasoning is cited in the name of Nahmanides in the commentary of Rabbenu Nissim (T.B., Nedarim 27a).[1] What concerns us here is the general rule which emerges from both positions, and that is that there are two principles that apply in the release of vows by a sage: an error or an "opening," on one hand, "remorse," on the other.

### *The Definition of "Error"*

What is the difference—not from a halakhic but from a psychological point of view—between an "opening" and "remorse" as factors in the release of vows? What does Nahmanides mean when he states that a "vow released by opening is somewhat similar to erroneous vows"? We know what the definition of "error" is in the Torah. In cases such as that of "erroneous sale" or "erroneous betrothal," the reference is to a mistake in correct identification of the person or object concerned. I had someone or something in mind and someone or something else turned out to have been there. In an error of this kind, there is no need to seek the release of a sage (and the cases are set out in detail in the Mishna in Tractate Nedarim). When we speak of an "opening" which the sage finds in a vow, according to which he may establish that the vow had a faulty basis, we are not referring to a case of erroneous factual identification, but rather to an error in judgment; the one who made the vow did not err in identification of the object or person concerned but, rather in his *evaluation* of the situation, in not foreseeing the consequences of his vow. An

1. The Tosafists disagree with Nahmanides, but we will not enter into that dispute.

example to this effect is found in the Mishna: "They release for festivals and Sabbaths" (Nedarim 9:6). Rabbi Obadiah Bertinora explains this as follows: "If he vowed to fast, or not to eat meat for a fixed period of time, they say to him: had you paid attention to the Sabbaths and festivals in this period, would you still have made the vow?" That is to say, there is no actual error here, in that he certainly knew that there was a Sabbath within the time he had fixed for his vow, since a Sabbath naturally follows every six weekdays. Where, then, was his error? He failed to realize or to take into account that the vow would interfere with proper enjoyment of the Sabbath. When he comes to a sage to have his vow released, the sage seizes this "opening" which is available to him: "Had you paid attention . . . would you still have made the vow?" and in accordance with this he establishes that the vow is founded on a completely erroneous basis, and cancels it.

On the other hand, when one asks a sage to release one from a vow based on "remorse" there is no error in the vow itself nor in contemplation of its results. There was nothing which the vower failed to consider or realize: he made no mistakes in judgment or recknoning. On what grounds does he now seek release from his vow? On the grounds that his tastes have changed, his feelings, his outlook and criteria are different now from what they were at the time he made his vow. Those things which originally seemed to him to be of ultimate importance now appear to be trivial and foolish. Take, for instance, a person who has been offended by someone and has sworn to avenge the insult. After some time passes, his anger is assuaged and his desire for revenge diminishes and appears out of place. Here the issue is not one of finding an "opening" through an error which he made in his original assumptions or in the logic of his judgments. What happened is that a radical change occurred in the conscience and will of the person who made the vow.

In other words: in release of vows through an "opening" we are dealing with an error of the intellect which did not grasp the full significance nor anticipate the consequences of the vow. The release of "opening" is based on a rational process, on logic, whereas the release of "remorse" is based on emotional factors. My feelings are not what they were at the time I made the vow and I now regret making it.

We thus have before us two types of release from vows. One is according to emotional factors—no error or change has occurred in the vow, but in me, myself. If, for instance, yesterday it seemed important to me to live in a beautiful home, to transfer to a rich neighborhood, it now seems to me to be pointless and absurd. In contrast, the release by "opening" is based on reason. In this case, a person comes to a sage seeking release because his reason has deepened, it is more mature than it was before, and he now understands more than he did previously.

The two types of repentance with which we are dealing may also be defined in this way: one as "repentance of remorse" and the other as "repentance of opening." The first kind, such as occurs in the release of vows due to "remorse," is emotional repentance, beginning with remorse for the past and ending with resolve for the future. The opposite is the case in the other type of repentance, founded on the principle of finding an "opening" in affecting release from vows, in which the process of repentance begins with resolve for the future and concludes with remorse for the past.

### *The Equation: Sin-Sickness*

The propositions that we are dealing with are explainable in the following manner: What is the meaning of repentance of remorse which we have called emotional repentance? The medieval Jewish philosophers, chiefly Maimonides, brought out and expounded the idea that a parallel exists between sickness of the mind and sickness of the body. Maimonides devotes a large part of his "Eight Chapters" (Commentary on *Avot*) to this comparison. The term "sickness of the mind" as used by Maimonides, Rabbenu Bahye and other medieval Sages, do not refer to mental illness such as insanity, as understood today, but rather point to moral deficiencies—in other words, sins.[2]

The idea that sin is the same as sickness is already found in the Bible. There is the following passage, for example: "Of David. Bless the Lord, O my soul . . . Who forgives all thy iniquities; Who heals all thy diseases; Who redeems thy life from the pit; Who encircles thee with love and compassion" (Psalm 103:1–4). It contains a clear parallel between healing and forgiving, between iniquities and diseases. There are many similar passages in the Prophets, such as "Peace, peace, to him who is far and to him who is near, says the Lord, and I will heal him" (Isaiah 57:19, which is also read as part of the *Haftarah* for the Day of Atonement). "And I will heal him"—from what? From his sins, as it says, "and understand with his heart, and return, and be healed (Isaiah 6:10)."

The idea is clear: sin is an abnormal phenomenon. The healthy person, living a normal life, does not fall into the ways

2. By the way, the Sages of Israel in the Middle Ages and in other periods hardly dealt with mental illness on which so much interest is focused today; they were not interested in neuroses and psychoses, schizophrenia and paranoia (except for exceptional cases such as divorce, when they made extremely subtle distinctions to define when a person fits into the categories of madness, such as in the well-known divorce of Cleve in which the great Jewish scholars acted as psychologists and psychiatrists). But, from a theoretical point of view they hardly dealt with it, at any rate much less than we do, perhaps because they simply did not have as many mentally ill people among them as we have today.

of sin. Sin constitutes a sort of spiritual pathology; just as many diseases of the flesh constitute physical pathology, as when the tissues cease to behave in a normal fashion and cells begin to grow wildly, so sin is a sign of spiritual pathology. The conclusion to be drawn from this supposition is of great significance in understanding repentance. If sin is a sickness, then it also has the characteristics of a sickness. What is characteristic of sickness? Suffering. As far back as Aristotle it was established that it is pain and suffering which inform man that he is ill. If sin is an illness, then it too must be felt, i.e., be expressed in suffering. Every organic illness or abnormality reaches the awareness of a human being through his nervous system. The language of sickness, its a-b-c, is suffering. Every pathological phenomenon is generally connected with pain and suffering. The organism informs the human being by means of suffering that he is ill. Suffering, according to Aristotle, is a great blessing conferred by the Creator on His creatures; it serves as a warning of what to expect. Indeed, we all know how many tragedies are liable to occur because pains are discerned when it is too late.

Sin is also a disease—and it, too, reaches human consciousness through the language of suffering, through deep and piercing pain, through spiritual agony which can be sharper and more unbearable than any bodily suffering.

We have discerned the stage of "acknowledgment of sin" in the process of repentance. Before this stage of *acknowledgement of sin,* however, there is another phase which I call the *sensing of sin.* Sensing of sin is analogous in every respect to feeling sickness. Both of these feelings speak in an identical way through the language of suffering.

We all know, to our great sorrow, what bodily pain is. In what way are spiritual suffering and the suffering of sin expressed? How is man made aware of the sickness of sin?

### *Sin As Anti-Aesthetic Experience*

As in sickness of the body, so, also, in sickness of the soul which is sin, man tries to deny, to minimize and to distance himself from the pain. Often, out of fear, whether covert or overt, when we are attacked by pains, we put off the visit to the doctor and console ourselves by saying that they are a figment of the imagination, that very soon they will pass of their own accord. So do we behave, as well, regarding spiritual suffering which comes to make us aware of sin.

What form does suffering take to effect the "communication" of sin to man? Let us refer to the Book of Books for an answer. The Torah tells us about the sin of the golden calf: "And when the people heard these evil tidings, they mourned: and no man put on his ornaments" (Exodus 33:4). In the wake of sin comes a strong feeling of sorrow. The previous day they had engaged in wild, joyous celebration around the calf, but now they felt the bitter sorrow of mourning. The consciousness of the sin reached them and was expressed in the sorrow of mourning. Nor is this the only time that sin is referred to in terms of mourning. The same phenomenon recurs with the sin of the spies: "And Moses spoke these words to all the children of Israel; and the people mourned greatly" (Numbers 14:39). Here, also, mourning follows sin.

What is the sorrow of mourning? According to the Halakha the laws of mourning apply when a person loses something important and precious. The loss of money and property is not a real loss; a real loss is the loss of a dear and beloved person. Mourning is reaction to a loss and it expresses itself in a strong sensation of nostalgia, of yearning, or of retrospective memories. The power of mourning, its cruelty and its loneliness, has its focal point in the memory of the human being. If man was able to forget, to eradicate events from his memory, then there would be no need for mourning. The feelings of bereavement are dependent on memory, which is the greatest blessing of man *qua* man; memory constitutes the entire awareness of the human "I." In times of mourning, however, this blessing becomes a curse.

Memories float up from the past, and when the past comes to the surface and man is forced to compare yesterday with today, he is engulfed by a feeling of bereavement and mourning. Over the course of many years a man becomes accustomed to returning home from his outside affairs; he climbs the few steps before the front door of his house in the same way he has done for years. He rings the bell out of habit and expects to hear, as always, soft steps from the other side of the door. He waits, but the steps never come. He puts his hand into his pocket, pulls out the key and opens the door. It seems to be the same door and the same furniture. Everything is clean and polished as usual. Nevertheless, something has changed. Everything appears to be in exactly the same state and in the same place in which it was before he left his house. Nothing has been moved, only no one is there waiting for him. All around there is peace and quiet which can sometimes be worse than heart-rending cries. Mourning engulfs his whole being.

The sinner also mourns: "And the people mourned." What does the sinner mourn? He mourns that which he has irretrievably lost. What has he lost? Everything. The sinner has lost his purity, his holiness, his integrity, his spiritual wealth, the joy of life, the spirit of sanctity in man—all that gives meaning to life and content to human existence. The mourner mourns the soul of the beloved one he has lost; the sinner mourns his own soul, which he has lost.

Mourning inevitably contains a masochistic element. The mourner tortures and torments himself; he hates himself. In the bereavement of sin there is also a clear masochistic element. The sinner begins to sense a feeling of contempt and disgust toward himself; he experiences masochistic self-hatred. The sin is seen as an abomination, an object of revulsion, something utterly nauseating. The feeling generated by sin is not a moral sensation; the moral sense in man is not such a powerful force. The feeling of sin which drags a person to repentance is an aesthetic sensation, or, more correctly, a negative aesthetic reaction. The sinner feels disgust at the defilement of sin. The suffering of sin lies in the feeling of nausea toward the defiling, disgusting uncleanliness of the sin.

It is interesting to note how an elderly Jew in the old-fashioned city of Vilna—the author of the book *Haye Adam*—many years ago understood so well the aesthetic opposition a person builds up toward sin. The natural inclination or desire of man is for the beautiful, for the aesthetic; man despises the ugly—it is this which draws him away from the sin into which he has sunk, inasmuch as sin contains ugliness, disgust and abomination which repel man's aesthetic consciousness. Thus, when God seeks to draw man to repentance, He arouses not only his moral awareness, which is usually not sufficiently strong to awaken him from his sin, but, more so his aesthetic consciousness which has a better chance of effecting the repulsion of the despised and loathsome sin.

The sinner begins to ask himself, in the words of the author of the *Haye Adam,* Rabbi Avraham Danzig (in his "*Tefila Zakah*—Pure Prayer," said before *Kol Nidre*): "We are astonished at ourselves—how was this abomination perpetrated?" He does not say, "this evil," or "this sin," or "this iniquity," or "this transgression"—but "this abomination." How? How? . . . The sinner is unable to grasp, when repentance begins to knock at the doors of his heart, how he was able to betray the purity of his soul for the abominable sin which now arouses such aesthetic revulsion in his soul.

The Torah spoke in the same vein of idolatry: "Neither

shall you bring an abomination into your house . . . you shall utterly detest it, and utterly abhor it, for it is a cursed thing" (Deuteronomy 7:26). The Torah does not say here, "Do not worship idols." Had it done so, one could have searched for a dispensation to be exempted from the general prohibition. However, it is not the prohibition of idolatry that the Torah emphasizes, but the abomination, the revulsion and ugliness of it. If you have any aesthetic sensitivity whatsoever, if you have spiritual repulsion for an abomination, how could you possibly be drawn to idolatry?

"We are astonished at ourselves," says the author of *Haye Adam.* We are human beings with a sense of beauty, an aesthetic soul, and we are attracted to fine things; how then could we have let ourselves be so attracted to commit an abomination and do contemptible things? "We are astonished at ourselves!"

In the Bible we find a story describing how sin turns into abomination, and how the sinner is pursued and chastised not by his weak and helpless desire for the good, but by his aesthetic drive which proves itself to be powerful, aggressive and full of cunning. I refer to the account in 2 Samuel, Chapter 13: "And it came to pass after this, that Avshalom the son of David had a fair sister, whose name was Tamar; and Amnon the son of David loved her." If the Scripture testifies that she was fair, we do not doubt that she was, indeed, beautiful, and we can imagine how enchanting Tamar seemed to Amnon the son of David. A moment before he sinned, Amnon surely still thought that Tamar represented beauty of which there was none higher, none more splendrous or glorious. This filled him with such powerful love that because of it he sinned and did "this base deed . . . as one of the base men." This was the case before the sin, but immediately afterward: "And Amnon hated her with a great hatred, for the hatred with which he hated her was greater than the love with which he had loved her" (verse

15). He hated her now with such a great vengeance not because he suffered pangs of conscience but because he suddenly realized not only that was she not beautiful, but how ugly and repulsive she was. His sin was an abomination to him. Because of it he came to hate himself—and subsequently hated her. Sin has a masochistic effect. Amnon hated himself and transferred his hatred to Tamar, humiliated through no fault of her own. The same wondrously beautiful Tamar was transformed in his mind into a symbol of abomination and hate. Amnon certainly did not understand what had happened to him, and he asked himself the same question which the author of the *Haye Adam* asked: "I am astonished at myself; how could this abomination have been committed?"

As she had become so hateful and despicable to him, he was not satisfied with calling out to her "arise, begone," but "He called to his servant boy and said to him: put this woman out of here and bolt the door behind her." Even the name of Tamar, his heart's desire, had become an abomination to him. "This woman"—he is unable to form her name on his lips; the feelings of abhorrence and defilement envelop him and choke him, "and bolt the door behind her"—he felt threatened by her presence. Only a short while ago he had so admired her and loved her—and now he was filled with loathing for her.

The sense of bereavement that comes from sin is expressed in feelings of defilement, loathing and self-hatred. Remorse is accompanied by bitter self-recrimination—"we are astonished at ourselves; how could this abomination have been perpetrated?"

In addition to the sense of bereavement, remorse is related to another emotion: the sense of shame—the sense of shame a person can feel for himself. "We are astonished at ourselves"—meaning, also, that we are ashamed of ourselves. "I was ashamed and confounded": the feeling of disgust mingles with the feeling of shame. The awful monstrosity of the act of sin plagues the sinner and leads him to feel remorse. This remorse comes as a result of emotions, not from reasoning; a person's intellect plays a negligible part in it. What was responsible for the transformation which occurred in Amnon's soul turning into hate, desire into revulsion? Neither the mind nor the intellect. He had no time for reasoning things out. These emotions which came as an instinctive emotional reaction to the sin brought about this transformation. They are the natural reactions of revulsion and shame and not processes of reason, understanding and knowledge. Amnon could not understand why he suddenly hated her to the point that he was unable to tolerate her presence, just as he did not know why her charms had so enchanted him originally. Of course, the unfortunate Tamar could not understand what had happened, and she saw his present behavior as bringing even greater humiliation upon her than the sin he had just committed by assaulting and raping her. "And she said to him, do not add this greater wrong of sending me away to the other that you have done to me." She failed to grasp that this was the instinctive and natural reaction of the sinner to the sin itself and to the object of his sin as well. Amnon now identified Tamar with the sin itself.

### *Repentance Which Requires No Resolve for the Future*

Repentance which comes in the wake of an emotional shock of the sort that came over Amnon is repentance motivated by emotion. It is, of course, understood that wherever there is an emotional reaction to sin, when the sin is rejected not for intellectual reasons, but in an emotional and instinctive manner, through the natural feelings of shame and disgust which overwhelm the sinner causing unbearable torment to his soul, then the sinner is no longer required to make a resolution regarding the future. It becomes superfluous in such a case. The essence of repentance lies in remorse, in the feeling of shame toward himself, in "we are astonished at ourselves, how could such an abomination have been committed," in that feeling of "and Amnon hated her with a great hatred"—and, consequently, how can he repeat the sin? Can we suspect someone of repeating his sin when the love which drove him to sin has turned to unfathomable hatred and disgust? The torment of his soul and the feeling of shame in themselves block the way of the sinner. In this type of repentance there is no need for him to resolve not to repeat the sin in the future. We can rest assured that he knows what sin is with his entire being which is pervaded with the aftertaste of sin, and it is this torment which now fills him with hatred instead of love, disgust instead of desire, scorn instead of admiration. There is no greater preventive measure which can assure us that he will not repeat the sin.

In repentance of this sort, where confession expresses itself in the words "I am contrite and ashamed," as Maimonides phrases it in Chapter 1 of his Laws of Repentance, it is pointless to say "and I will never do this again." He is not going to repeat it, having been burned by the sufferings his soul has endured which have deeply penetrated his being and left indelible impressions on him. Wherever the sinner says "I am ashamed" it implies a reference to emotional repentance which comes out of the spontaneous and natural reaction to sin and not from intellectual reasoning. The instinctive feeling that causes *remorse* is thus the central motif of repentance. The sinner reacts to his sin, just as the sick man reacts to his pains. He will restrain himself from repeating those things which bring him so much suffering. Resolve for the future—for this, there is no apparent need. Remorse and shame—these are what restrain him from sinning again. So when Maimonides says: "and I will never do this again," his intention does not seem to have been that a resolution for the future was to serve as a means of holding back the sinner. Probably, what he meant was that as a result and in consequence of feeling shame (*"I have sinned, I have acted perversely . . . and I am contrite and ashamed")* due to my having sinned and experienced the suffering from sin, I am confident that "I will never do this again."

### *Repentance Which Begins With Resolution for the Future*

There is, however, repentance of another kind, and this is what we have referred to as intellectual repentance, the repentance that comes from an "opening," or error. While in emotional repentance the "castigator" which reproves the person comes out of his own inner emotions, in intellectual repentance the "castigator" is his intellect. This repentance is not based on the reaction to the sin; usually there is no feeling of sin, for not everyone achieves the same level of reaction to sin as Amnon did. Not everyone is capable of feeling the constructive value of suffering which purifies man and refines and sanctifies him; not everyone attains this. Many are those whose path to repentance goes along an entirely different route; they get to it not through an emotional reaction to sin but through mental awareness of sin. In this form of repentance, the element of shame is missing from the outset; from the very beginning the sinner does not feel any soul-pangs; he does not sense the contamination of the sin, nor does he shudder at its repulsiveness. Instead of being shocked emotionally and reacting instinctively as Amnon did, this kind of sinner understands with his mind, with his intellect, the soul-wreckage caused by the sin. These are two essentially different ways. The first penitent *feels and senses* the destruction to his soul. The second, that of the second section of Chapter 2, *understands and is aware* of the damage to his soul. He grasps and realizes to what level he has descended.

The first one is like a mourner. In mourning one does not comprehend; one feels. The second one is an intellectual type; he can estimate and imagine to himself the hazards that await him because of his sin; he grasps the dimensions of the sin, its terrible significance, its consequences. He is aware of what he has lost in the wake of sin and of his need for repentance. All this he knows, understands and apprehends. However, his awareness of sin, as well as his understanding and comprehension of it, is entirely the fruit of mental processes, of his intellect and mind. He knows about everything, but he has no soul pangs. He understands the full nature of sin, its depth and breadth, and knows of its destructive powers, but he feels no contempt and hatred for himself. He does not experience terrible pangs of remorse, paved with suffering and replete with pain. His repentance is similar to the case of release from a vow in which one comes before a sage, with a request based on the fact that one's former enemy is now "a scribe and an important person." He retracts his vow by means of an "opening," because of an error in judgment regarding the sin; he had great expectations from his sin and it became clear to him that he had after all erred in his calculations. Repentance and acquittal based upon an "opening" is intellectual repentance, as it emerges from understanding and not from feeling, through apprehension of an error, rather than from shame at the defilement of sin, from awareness of sin, rather than from a sense of revulsion and hatred. The basic distinction is that here love is not transformed into hatred and the beauty does not turn into corruption; the person with whom he sinned does not appear monstrous or abominable as in Amnon's case, of which it is said: "and he hated her . . . put this woman out now from me." On the contrary, the love remains as before and its attraction still has great force. It is only that the mind, the reason, will not allow him to sin anymore. A mighty battle rages within the sinner between his mind and heart; a titanic conflict takes place between the emotions and the intellect. A strong intellect joined to a powerful will can eventually overcome the mighty force of lust which pulls him to sin. The nature of a repentance such as this lies not in remorse for the past, but in a daring decision that no matter how great the attraction of sin may be and however much he may desire and long to sin, he will not repeat it.

The will and the intellect unite to defeat the passions, to overcome the emotional drive which impels him and puts him under the bewitching spell of sin. The will and the intellect make a joint decision to oppose lust and passion. This is not spontaneous remorse over what has been; on the contrary, yesterday still attracts—but opposing it is the steadfast resolve of the intellect and the will regarding the future. Awareness of sin leads to repentance of the mind which indicates a resolution for the future as well. Remorse comes later. "After I returned I was regretful." Remorse comes as a result of the resolve for the future; it is a conclusion and active consequence of the strong will to change the sinful way of life and mode of thought.

Note carefully the verse from Jeremiah which Maimonides quotes in this context: "For after I returned I was regretful." Before my return I would not have been able to be remorseful. The power, the splendor and glory of the sin charmed me, just as the Tree of Knowledge enticed Eve with its charms: "And the woman saw that the tree was good for food, and that was a delight to the eyes, and a tree to be desired to make one wise. . . ." Only after a mighty struggle envelops a person's reason and his passions, and only after the intellect together with the will emerges victorious from this struggle, only then does the person begin to recognize, little by little, that the life of sin is one of vanity and emptiness and that it is worthwhile to overcome the charms and pleasures of sin for the sake of the life of purity that follows repentance.

"After I returned I was regretful, and after I was instructed I smote my thigh"—here Jeremiah drafts a blueprint for repentance that comes from knowledge, and his words are read in the *Haftarah* for Rosh Hashana. "After I was instructed"—that is the remorse and shame for having sinned which comes only after undergoing the intellectual process of repentance and attaining knowledge of the sin.

"What is perfect repentance? It is when an opportunity presents itself for repeating an offense, and the offender refrains from doing so because he is penitent, not because of fear or inability to act. For instance, if a man had sinful intercourse with a woman, and after time passed he found himself alone with her, with his love for her still persisting, his physical powers unabated while living in the same district where he had sinned before, yet he refrains and does not transgress, he is then a perfect penitent." These are the words of Maimonides at the beginning of Chapter 2 of the Laws of Repentance. We have before us a case which is exactly the opposite of that of Amnon, in which he hated the woman "with a great hatred." Here his "love for her still persists." When he repents of his sin—what type of repentance is it? The repentance of a mind! The repentance of reason!

Reason agrees with passion that sin is attractive and enticing, but at the very same time it argues that sin is defilement and fornication which in the end bring the sinner down to the lowest level and cause his personality and character to disintegrate, taking away the very basis of his existence. The intellect beckons the sinner to repent, while he is still under the magic spell of sin.

This is not spontaneous repentance, but rather a way of many obstacles. "What is repentance?" continues Maimonides in the second section of Chapter 2. "It consists of this: that the sinner abandon his sin, remove it from his thoughts, and resolve in his heart never to repeat it, as it says, 'Let the wicked forsake his way, and the man of iniquity his thoughts' " (Isaiah 55:7). Why does Maimonides go to such great lengths to describe all of these stages? By doing so, he gives expression to the strenuous battle of the will in which the penitent is engaged, struggling until he makes up his mind "never to repeat it." Only after this long, drawn-out process does he arrive at remorse for the past, having made his resolution for the future. "And so he regrets the past, as it says, 'For after I returned I was regretful' (Jeremiah 31:18)." Remorse for the past occurs only after a person succeeds in translating his rational awareness and intellectual outlook, which are expressed in his resolution for the future, into an intense emotional experience—and this is a slow and difficult process.

This kind of repentance of an "opening" has great strength; it is not emotional, spontaneous repentance but has a reasoned, intellectual quality. It is not emotional repentance, but repentance of the intellect. The first kind of repentance begins with the feeling of sin, the second with the knowledge or acknowledgement of sin. Which of them is greater I do not know. Maimonides calls this intellectual repentance "perfect repentance," since the person has passed through the hell of the war of his will and has overcome his mightiest foe, his own self. I think, however, that the first kind of repentance, which comes spontaneously and emotionally, is also "perfect repentance."

### *Two Sanctuaries Within Man*

I believe that both types of repentance which we have mentioned and the ability of man to attain any one of them can be considered divine gifts. We have already emphasized in previous discourses that the very phenomenon of repentance, the fact that a person is able to rise above his lowly state and ascend the mountain of the Lord, is one of the most wondrous favors with which the Creator has endowed His creatures.

The grace of repentance has a dual nature and this is revealed by two factors: first in the fact that the human personality is the true sanctuary of the Holy One, blessed be He. The greatest of all holy temples, even more sacred than the Western Wall, is the human soul, the divine dwelling place. "And let them make me a sanctuary, that I may dwell among them"—if the Holy One, blessed be He, did not dwell within man, repentance would not be possible. The Divine Presence within man—this is the first act of grace. The second one, which is a divine favor throughout eternity, is the fact that the Holy One, blessed be He, who chose the human soul as His dwelling place, does not remove Himself from man even after he sins. "The eternal God is a dwelling place" (Exodus 25:8)—what is God's dwelling place? "Behold, the heaven and heaven of heavens cannot contain Thee; how much less this house which I have built?" Where does the Holy One, blessed be He, live? Where is the dwelling place of the eternal God? The home of the Holy One, blessed be He, is in man, in his heart, in his soul; and He does not depart from there even when man has sinned and defiled the holy sanctuary within him. The Holy One, blessed be He, continues to dwell within the depths of the soul of the sinner: "He who dwells with them amidst their defilement."

The Holy One, blessed be He, has two dwelling places within man. He is to be found in two homes, in two sanctuaries. One is the sanctuary of feeling, in the Holy of Holies of human sentiments, such as love, wonder, mercy, goodness of heart, awe of the exalted, joy, sorrow, amazement. In all of these it is possible to find a manifestation of the Divine Presence. The second is the sanctuary of thought. When a person thinks, when he studies Torah, when he purifies and sanctifies his intellect, the instrument of his knowledge and reason—there the Holy One, blessed be He, can be found. One dwelling place of the Eternal God is within the human heart. The second dwelling place of the Eternal God is inside the human brain. When a man sins and the Holy One, blessed be He, continues to dwell within him, both emotion and cognition cry out in revolt and battle with him until he is brought to either of the two kinds of repentance, whether it be repentance of the emotions or that of the mind. When a person becomes a penitent it is because the Holy One, blessed be He, Who is present within him has aroused and altered him to do so.

## *The Oath Formula in Confession*

We now have to find the answer to another question which was raised previously. In the formula of confession of emotional repentance described in Chapter 1, Section 1 of the Laws of Repentance, Maimonides writes that the guilty person must say, after he has expressed remorse for the past: "and I will never do this again." We then asked: Why is there a need for resolution for the future in emotional repentance, which is rooted in total revulsion, according to the paradigm of "and Amnon hated her with a great hatred." It should be clear to all that the sinner has no intention of ever repeating the sin. We tried to explain this as being the conclusion reached from repentance itself and not a resolve for the future. But, nonetheless, Maimonides does include this phrase in the verbalized formula of confession. For what purpose does he do so?

In order to elucidate this matter, let us turn back to the second chapter of the Laws of Repentance, Section 2. There Maimonides, in speaking of perfect repentance, establishes that aside from expressing remorse for the past and making a resolution for the future there is something else that is required of the repentant sinner: "And he calls on the One who knows all secrets to be his witness that he will never again repeat this sin." What does he mean by this?

The author of the commentary *Lehem Mishneh* puzzled over Maimonides' inclusion of this phrase and asked: "How can the Holy One, blessed be He, testify for him? Surely the choice is not in His hands?" He explained this in the following manner: "It means that when man repents he has to take God, may He be blessed, to be his witness that he will never repeat the sin, in the same way as 'I call on heaven and earth to be my witness,' where heaven and earth are called upon to act as witnesses." This, then, is the meaning of Maimonides' statement that aside from remorse for the past and resolve for the future "he calls to witness"—that is to say, the sinner summons God, or heaven and earth as it were, to testify to the truth of his intentions. The source for this is in *Psikta d'Rav Kahanah:* "Israel declared before the Holy One, blessed be He: Master of the Universe! If we repent, who will testify for us? He told them: I will testify for you . . . as it is written, 'Return Israel unto (*'ad*) the Lord your God'—that is, the Lord your God is witness (*'ed*)."

Where is this idea "and he calls to witness Him who knows all secrets" to be found in the formula of confession, either in the one Maimonides brings (Chapter 1, Section 1) or in the one which appears in the accepted order of prayers? All the versions of confession and prayers of forgiveness in the holiday prayer book contain the required elements of confession—acknowledgment of sin, remorse, resolve, etc.—yet the summoning of a witness or witnesses to testify to the veracity of the repentance is an element which seems to be missing.

If we look closely, however, we find that this element does indeed appear both in Maimonides' version as well as in all of the other versions we have. In Chapter 1, Section 1, Maimonides writes: "With regard to all the precepts of the Torah . . . when a person repents of his sin, he is under the obligation to confess before God, blessed be He." What is the meaning of those last few words? If he has to confess, of course it is before God that he confesses! In Chapter 2, Section 5, Maimonides also writes: "This only applies to transgressions which take place between man and his fellow man. But sins committed against God do not have to be made public . . . he is, rather, supposed to repent before God, blessed be He, declaring his sins in detail before Him and confessing." Certainly we know that he need not confess before people, but only before the Holy One, blessed be He. It seems to me that Maimonides stressed the fact that the confession is "before God, blessed be He" and that enumerating one's sins is done "before Him," in order to emphasize the idea of summoning the Holy One, blessed be He, to witness his confession, according to Maimonides' assertion that "he calls to witness Him who knows all secrets." Confession is said before God—the only witness invited to attend the occasion.

How is this idea expressed in the formula of confession which we say in prayer? In the words "I beseech Thee, O Lord!" with which the confession formula opens, and particularly in the second "I beseech Thee" in the High Priest's confession: "I beseech Thee in Thine Ineffable Name." The Talmud asks: "From whence do we know that the confession must begin with 'I beseech Thee'?" and replies: "Acquittal is mentioned here and subsequently at Horeb; just as there it has

'I beseech Thee,' here too it has 'I beseech Thee.' And from whence that it is with the Ineffable Name? Acquittal is mentioned here and subsequently in connection with the beheaded heifer; just as there the Ineffable Name is used, here it is also used" (T.B., Yoma 37a.). Rashi comments (*ad loc.*) that the formula "I beseech Thee, O Lord" is an indispensable part of the confession. Why should it be of such great significance? Why can the High Priest not begin with "Thy people Israel have sinned, transgressed and committed iniquities before thee," and continue: "Please grant acquittal to their iniquities, etc., as it is written in the Torah of Moses thy servant, etc."? Why is there here a "scriptural decree" to add the words "I-beseech-Thee" and "Lord" (= the Ineffable Name)? We should attempt to understand a "scriptural decree" as well!

It has already been pointed out by the *Tosefot Yeshanim* that the phrase, "I beseech Thee," seems to be out of place here, for the first section of the confession consists of an acknowledgment of sin and contains no petition in which the phrase "I beseech Thee" fits. What then does the penitent request when he says "I beseech Thee, O Lord"? It seems that what he requests with these words is that he be allowed to approach God. Confession is a private conversation between the Holy One, blessed be He, and the sinner; the sinner begins by requesting permission from God to start the conversation. Sin places man at a distance, alienates him from the Holy One, blessed be He, as Maimonides puts it: "Last night he was alienated from the Lord God of Israel . . . as it is said, 'Your iniquities have alienated you from your God' " (Laws of Repentance, Chapter 7, Section 7). An iron curtain separates the sinner from God. The sinner has no right to stand before God; how, then, can he confess? For confession requires him to summon the Holy One, blessed be He, and appoint Him as witness to the saying of his confession; and it is impossible to appoint witnesses in their absence. Therefore, the petition comes at the beginning of the confession with the supplication, "I beseech Thee, O Lord!"—please, allow me to remove the barrier in order to come before You so that I may repent and say confession. Immediately after this he says, "I have sinned."

In the second type of confession, as stated in the Jerusalem Talmud and as it appears in all the versions in the standard holiday prayer books, the formula changes from "I beseech Thee, O Lord (*HaShem*)" to "I beseech Thee in the Name of the Lord (*baShem*)." I have already explained in the past that the word *"baShem"* is not connected with the word *"ana"* (I-beseech-Thee) which precedes it, but with what follows, so that it says: "In Thy Name please acquit," i.e., with the power of Your great Name please grant acquittal for our sins and iniquities. Thus, I have directed the leader of prayers in the synagogue in which I pray to say *"ana,"* to pause and only afterward to continue: *"baShem kaper na!"* (although he was angry with me for "ruining" the melody . . .). Now I have a different way of explaining the matter.

The expression "in the Name" seems to inform us that we are really voicing an oath. The phrase "in the Name" reminds us of the command "do not swear falsely *in* My Name" or of one who swears *in* the Name of the Holy One, blessed be He. "I beseech Thee in Thy Name" will mean, then, "I beseech Thee," I promise and swear "in Thy Name." "I beseech Thee," accept my repentance, for I promise and take an oath on my resolution for the future (which does not appear in the confession of the High Priest) "in Thy Name," that I will never repeat the sin. Because of this I beseech You: "Please acquit us of our sins, iniquities and transgressions," etc. These few words contain Maimonides' entire system of confession. The first "I beseech Thee, O Lord" consists of a prayer-petition to be found worthy of standing before God, while the second "I beseech Thee in Thy Name" is for calling upon God to bear witness to the intent and truth of the confessor-penitent's sworn resolution for the future, as by "he calls as witness Him Who knows all secrets that he will never repeat this sin."

All the early authorities are of the opinion that if a person promises to fulfill something and mentions the Name of God in saying so, then it is considered to be an oath. The very mention of the Divine Name turns the promise into an oath. So we say, for example, "May it be Thy will, O Lord, that I will never sin again" (from the prayer of Rav Hamnuna, "O God, before I was formed"). What is the meaning of this prayer? It seems to clash with the principle of choice. Rather, this is the explanation: "May it be Thy will" that You believe me, "O Lord!"—that I take it upon myself in the presence of witnesses (more correctly: may You please act as my witness) "that I will never sin again."

Every resolution for the future in repentance contains for all practical purposes not merely an expression of good intentions, but a promise under oath. This is what Maimonides meant when he said: "He calls to witness Him Who knows all secrets that he will never repeat this sin." Every oath which contains the Name of God means that it sets up God as a witness. This is a feature of all kinds of confessions, from that of the High Priest ("I beseech Thee in Thy Name!") to all the confessions included in the standard order of prayers.

"We beseech Thee, may our prayers reach Thee; do not ignore our plea. For we are neither insolent nor obstinate to say before Thee, Lord our God and God of our fathers, 'We are just and have not sinned.' Indeed we and our fathers have sinned." Here we have confession that comes with repentance. We have sinned—that is, we are ready to repent. The emphasis is: "before Thee, Lord our God and God of our fathers"; why is it not enough to say "before Thee"? Because confession that does not mention the Name of God is not considered valid! For without the Name of the Holy One, blessed be He, it is not an oath, and without an oath confession is not valid.

### *Toward the Formation of a Renewed Covenant*

Why an oath? It is possible to understand the need for an oath in a case of intellectual repentance, for a person is engaged in a mighty battle of the passions, and an oath is liable to strengthen his resolve not to repeat the sin. "From whence do we know that one may take an oath to fulfill the commandments? As it is said: 'I have sworn and may I fulfill the statutes of Thy righteousness.' " But in the case of emotional repentance, when the sinner himself no longer wishes, and is perhaps not even capable of repeating his sin, there is obviously no need for guarantees regarding his future behavior; why then obligate him to take an oath?

In order to answer this question, we should first go into another matter, that of the sanctity of Israel, a principle which has been established both in the Halakhah and in the Aggadah. The sources for this kind of sanctity are twofold. First, there is the sanctity of the *Patriarchs,* which is our heritage passed on from generation to generation, beginning with our forefather Abraham down to this very day. Like the Torah itself, sanctity too is a tradition handed down from generation to generation. Second, there is the sanctity of the *self,* which every Jew has by right. In addition to the sanctity that an Israelite inherits from his forefathers, he has another kind of sanctity given to him by the Holy One, blessed be He, Who endows each and every member of Israel in every generation with this special sanctity. Here, there is no distinction between a scholar and an uneducated man, between a person of high character and a simple man, between a Jew who reveres God and a mean one—all share equally in the sanctity that belongs to Israel. Rashi, in his commentary on the Torah, enunciated this principle in a clear fashion. On the verse "For thou art a holy people to the Lord thy God, and the Lord has chosen thee to be a special possession to Himself, out of all the nations that are upon the earth" (Deuteronomy 14:2), Rashi says: " 'For thou art a holy people'—your sanctity [comes] from your forefathers but in addition, 'the Lord has chosen thee,' " that is to say, you have two kinds of sanctity, that which comes to you by inheritance, and, in addition, each Jew is given sanctity in his own right.

These two degrees of sanctity are rooted in separate covenants enacted between the Lord and Israel His people. There were actually three covenants but two of them are counted as one, namely, the covenant made at Horeb, with those who received the Torah, and the covenant made in the plains of Moab with the people entering the land. Israel was sanctified through these covenants and this sanctity was passed on by inheritance from generation to generation. Together, they comprise the sanctity of the Patriarchs, or what Rashi calls "the sanctity [you have] from your forefathers." Besides these two covenants there is a third one described in the portion *Nitzavim* (Deuteronomy 29). This one applied not only to that generation, but to every member of Israel throughout the generations for all time, as it is written: "Neither with you only do I make this covenant and this oath, but with him that stands here with us this day before the Lord our God, and also with him that is not here with us this day" (Deuteronomy 29:13–14). From this is derived the original, independent sanctity of every individual in each generation in every era. We thus have a dual connection with the Master of the Universe, both as individuals and as the descendants of our forefathers.

What is the difference between the sanctity which derives from the covenants on Mount Sinai and Mount Moab and that whose source is in the later covenant? The Talmud stipulates that an oath made to nullify the Divine commandments is invalid since one is "[considered to be] forever forsworn from Mount Sinai." Where do we find it written that Israel took an oath at Mount Sinai? "We will do and we will hear" is a declaration, a promise, but not an oath. We find an oath—as Nahmanides points out in his commentary on the Torah—in the covenant mentioned in the portion *Nitzavim* where it is written "this covenant and this curse"—a curse always denotes swearing. The expression "forever forsworn from Mount Sinai" therefore refers to this oath, as it applies to every person in Israel in each and every generation until the end of all time.

Study the matter: every sin profanes and blemishes the sanctity of Israel. "A Jew who has sinned is nonetheless a Jew." Nevertheless, from the standpoint of sanctity, there is a tremendous gap between a sinner and a just person.

The source of the sanctity comes from the enactment of the covenant, that is, in the contract that Israel and God have mutually agreed upon. Sin indicates that one party to the agreement has not fulfilled its terms, and it follows that even if the sin was committed inadvertently or under duress, the agreement is void and the sanctity, which was his by right if he held to it, is abrogated.

As to the sanctity of the Patriarchs, it is passed on by inheritance from Abraham and from Moses, and no sinner has it in his power to break its operativeness; the covenant has been given to the community of Israel by right from the Patriarchs and no power is capable of nullifying it. But the personal sanctity he has in his own right by power of the covenant which also applies to "him that is not here with us this day," even though it was enacted with the entire congregation of Israel ("for thou art a holy people to the Lord thy God"), applies separately to each and every individual. So, when the individual sins, he blemishes the element of sanctity which is dependent on his responsibility to keep to the conditions of the covenant. He cannot touch the "communal" sanctity of Israel, and since "a Jew who has sinned is nonetheless a Jew," he retains his share in the sanctity of the nation, of the congregation, as a whole, theirs by virtue of the sanctity of the Patriarchs—even though as an individual he has severed his connection to it through sin, and his share in the sanctity of Israel has been blemished. From this, it follows that a penitent is apparently a flawed and blemished personality. Yet, the Talmud says: "Where penitents stand, even the perfectly righteous cannot stand" (Berakhot 34b). How can we reconcile these different statements?

The solution to this problem lies in the correct definition of repentance. Repentance not only cleanses the sinner of the pollution of sin, it implies a sort of re-enactment of the covenant between an individual person and the Holy One, blessed be He. It follows that repentance is not only purification of character, it also sanctifies the "persona," qualifying him once more to be a partner in the covenant. To attain such status, it is necessary, first of all, that a person actually stand before the Lord in a "face to face" confrontation. One cannot appoint any agent to make a covenant, and since repentance brings a renewed state of personal sanctity, then there is no escape from this direct, face-to-face confrontation. Not only that, but re-enactment of the covenant with an individual requires a definitive commitment by oath, meant by: "this curse." Attention should be paid to the fact that in making a covenant with the community, with the entire nation, such as at Mount Sinai or in the plains of Moab, an oath was not necessary, while for re-enactment of the covenant with any one individual in any generation, an oath is required. "You stand this day all of you before the Lord your God . . . that thou shouldst enter into the covenant of the Lord thy God and into his curse which the Lord thy God makes with thee this day."

Therefore, without taking into consideration whether this is repentance of the emotions or of the mind, every act of repentance requires official acceptance and a sworn commitment by the "persona" which is tantamount to re-enactment of a covenant between the Holy One, blessed be He, and the sinner. This is why the Talmud says: "Ezra established for Israel that they should read the curses . . . in Deuteronomy before Rosh Hashana" (T.B., Megilla 31b). Regarding this, Rabbenu Nissim Gaon asks, if so, then should we not read the portion of *Ki Tavo* (in Deuteronomy) before Rosh Hashana? The answer to this is in the negative because the enactment of the covenant mentioned in *Ki Tavo* has no connection to the act of repentance. The sinner can never be excluded from this covenant, since regarding the sanctity it bestows on the community of Israel, it is said "though he has sinned he is nonetheless a Jew"; but, as to the other kind of sanctity, connected with the enactment of the covenant which says "You stand this day all of you before the Lord your God," it is toward its renewal that a person works when he repents of his ways during the ten days between Rosh Hashana and Yom Kippur, which have been set aside for that purpose.

The preparation for repentance which one makes during these ten days is not merely for relinquishing sin and for character purification; it is supposed to pave the way for the reenactment of that marvelous covenant which allows man to, once again, stand before God.

In this respect, repentance is similar to conversion. A convert is considered to be a Jew in every way. He, too, must receive both kinds of sanctity: that of the Patriarchs and the sanctity of the self. How can a convert assume the sanctity of the Patriarchs? From the precept based on the verse, "Thou shalt be the father of a multitude of nations" (Genesis 17:5), it has been ruled that a convert should pray to God with the standard formula: "God and God of our forefathers." Upon converting, the proselyte assumes fully the heritage of sanctity which belongs to all Israel, as an integral part of the nation, concerning whom it is written, "Thou art a holy people unto the Lord thy God." How does a convert assume sanctity of the self, that is, how is he included in "the Lord thy God has chosen thee to be His own treasure"? By accepting upon himself the yoke of the commandments! This portion of the conversion ceremony is not a meaningless ritual, but is rather a re-enactment of "You are standing this day before the Lord your God," an assemblage which explicitly included "the stranger that is in the midst of thy camp." How were these strangers-converts accepted into the camp of Israel? Nahmanides, in his commentary on the Torah, suggests that the reference alludes to strangers who at that time had actually thrown in their lot with the people of Israel, or possibly to all the converts who would ever tie their fate in with them. Thus, even the convert was included in the covenant made with every individual who is part of the congregation of Israel. Were it otherwise, the convert would lack one of the two kinds of sanctities which distinguish the Jew, and we all know that a convert is judged by the same laws as every other Israelite.

The convert's acceptance of the yoke of the commandments during ritual immersion is what serves as the enactment of the covenant between him and the Holy One, blessed be He. The historical event of "You are standing this day before the Lord" is re-enacted each and every time a proselyte converts and seeks shelter under the "wings of the Shekhinah." The acceptance of the yoke of the commandments by a convert thus has two aspects. The first is the literal aspect of the proselyte's assuming the obligation to observe all the commandments, and this obligation goes into effect as soon as circumcision takes place, assuming it has been done for purposes of conversion and for performing the commandments. The second aspect is that acceptance of the yoke of the commandments which goes into effect upon ritual immersion is tantamount to entering into a covenant with God. In the opinion of the Ba'alei HaTosafot, immersion must be performed in the presence of a legally constituted court—not for witnessing the immersion itself but for the formal acceptance of the yoke of the commandments which is an act that requires the presence of a court. And why must it be a court of three? That is inferred from the verse, "God standeth in the congregation of God; in the midst of judges He judgeth." That means that the Shekhinah is present amidst a court of three. Why is formal acceptance of the yoke of the commandments necessary in the presence of a court, when the proselyte has already assumed them upon himself? And why is it necessary to have a court of three present at this formal ceremony? This is because of the fact that what actually takes place is the enactment of a covenant, with the court representing, as it were, the Shekhinah Itself—the "before God" the proselyte faces for the enactment of the covenant.

## *The Bondage That Releases All Bonds*

We must now try to understand the full significance of the homily of *Psikta d'Rav Kahanah* which was mentioned earlier. "Israel said before the Holy One, blessed be He: Master of the universe! If we repent, who testifies for us? He said to them: I will testify for you, as it says, 'Return, Israel, unto *('ad)* the Lord your God'—the Lord your God is witness *('ed)*." The Talmud brings a different homily based upon the same verse: "Great is repentance, for it reaches unto the throne of glory, as it is written, 'Return, Israel, unto the Lord your God' " (T.B., Yoma 86a). Where is the source of this idea? It is based upon the fact that the verse does not say "Return to *('el)* the

Lord your God," but rather "Return unto *('ad)* the Lord your God." The word *'el* ("to") means that I am going in a specific direction and have not yet reached my goal, while the word *'ad* means that I have already reached that goal, that my hands can reach out and, so to say, even touch the Throne of Glory itself. When Maimonides speaks of the repentant sinner, he describes him as "cleaving unto the Shekhinah" (Laws of Repentance, Chapter 7, Section 7), that is, one who has repented cleaves and is united with the presence of God. But a connection with the Shekhinah is brought about in one way only: through the enactment of a covenant. Without enacting a covenant it is impossible to achieve the unique state that characterizes the relationship between God and man, epitomized in the verse, "You are standing this day before the Lord your God."

The Holy One, blessed be He, is King of the entire universe, and He has a close relationship with the world and all inhabitants thereof, "even with the horns of rams and the eggs of lice"—most of all with mankind that was created in the Image of God. But amongst all these, His relationship with Israel is unique. The difference between God's relationship with all other creatures and the one He has with Israel is like the difference between "to (*'el*) the Lord" and "unto (*'ad*) the Lord."

This is the significance of the homily from *Psikta d'Rav Kahanah:* "Israel said before the Holy One, blessed be He: Who testifies for us? He said to them: I will testify for you, as it says, 'Return, Israel, unto (*'ad*) the Lord your God.' " How may a Jew achieve this status of "unto the Lord your God"? Is it possible for any human being to really cleave unto the Shekhinah? A union of this sort can only be achieved by renewal of the covenant with the Holy One, blessed be He, and this can be accomplished through the act of perfect repentance, which brings man not only "to" God but "unto" God Himself.

To go back: the relationship of an oath in the name of the

Lord had a dual nature. First, an oath necessitates reference to the name of God. Maimonides actually enumerates this requirement amongst the 613 precepts "to swear by His name, may He be exalted, as it is written, 'And you shall swear by His name' (Deuteronomy 10:29)" (Positive Precept No. 7). An oath of this type is sworn "by" the Name of God, but there is another kind of oath, sworn "to" the Name of God. This is demonstrated aptly by the verse in Isaiah: "That unto Me every knee shall bow, every tongue shall swear" (45:23), a verse which has been incorporated in slightly modified form in the *"Malkhuyot"* prayers for Rosh Hashana. Some have explained this to mean that every knee shall bow unto Thee and every tongue shall swear "by" Thee, that is, by Your Name. That does not seem to be what the verse intended to say, for the word "unto me" (= *li*) extends to both the bowing and the swearing. Thus, the reference is to swearing "to the Name" and not "by the Name"—what significance does such an oath have? What is meant by taking an oath "to You"? It means that every oath and obligation to which a man commits himself must be for God alone, and for nothing else. Just as it is forbidden to bow one's knee to any other created being—only to the Creator Himself—so, too, is it forbidden to swear any oath, to subjugate oneself or make a total commitment to anyone or anything except to God Himself.

Not only must one swear by God's name (it is a transgression to swear by God's name in conjunction with anything else, such as "by the Holy One, blessed be He and by the Heavens"), but the oath, any kind of oath, must be addressed to God only. The same sort of prohibition seems to exist against taking an oath in conjunction with a created being even when the oath is meant for the Holy One, blessed be He.

An oath whose aim is the fulfillment of selfish impulses, such as revenge, the attainment of wealth or the pursuit of fame is unlawful—it also borders on violating the prohibition against taking an oath by God's name—in conjunction with any other. Indeed, taking an oath to God Himself is the central motif of the *Malkhuyot* prayers recited on the High Holy Days, which proclaim that a Jew is not allowed to subjugate himself to any power or cause other than to the Holy One, blessed be He, the ruler of the entire universe.

Man's bondage to the Holy One, blessed be He, must be absolute and unconditional. It means that man can never be subjugated in any way by his fellow man. Bondage to God is all-encompassing and by definition releases man from all other ties and bonds.

A very eminent psychiatrist once said to me: Had I the authority to do so, I would eliminate the prayer recited on the High Holy Day that begins with the words, "Cast Thy fear," as fear is the major cause of the mental illnesses that beset mankind. In order to preserve one's mental health one should be free of fears, and so there is certainly no reason why one should ever pray for fear.

Though I am not a psychiatrist, what he said helped me to understand the true nature of that prayer which was ordained by the Sages of Israel. And that is what I told that psychiatrist: Everyone seems to be beset with fears of all kinds. Some are afraid that they will not be able to succeed in their careers, others fear losing their wealth or status or that they will fail to attain sufficient prominence. Many people are afraid of sickness and bodily weakness. In generations past, fear of leprosy engulfed the world; today people live in fear of cancerous growth. Many people do not go to see a doctor even when they have pains lest he diagnose "the disease." Man is plagued constantly by all sorts of lesser fears. I am not a psychiatrist, but I do know that one major source of fear can wipe out all of these lesser fears. What fear can overtake man, thereby uprooting all other fears, such as that of failure, of poverty, of old age, of rejection or of disease? Only the fear of the Lord! That is the reason behind the expression in the High Holy Day prayer, "Cast Thy fear, O Lord our God, upon all Thy handiwork and Thine awe upon all that Thou hast created." We pray that this great fear will free us from those other ones which lurk everywhere, upsetting our lives.

The same thing applies to human bondage. Only when man has one king, to whom he owes allegiance and absolute loyalty, can he be considered a liberated and free person. Subjugation to anyone else borders on idolatry.

People subjugate themselves in many ways. What can be better or more desirable than binding oneself to one's family and children? The Torah teaches us to love and cherish our children and brings as an example, "as a father takes pity over his children." At the very same time, the story of the Binding of Isaac is perhaps there to teach us that parental love must not be transformed into absolute bondage, which has idolatrous connotations.

Bondage to the state can also become idolatry. Were all the great men of the world to ask me to sign a declaration pledging my unreserved loyalty to the state which fulfills the highest ideals of Jews today, I would by no means be willing to do so. Subjugation of this kind is tantamount to idolatry!

Only one kind of bondage is permissible and that is to the Holy One, blessed be He, to the Torah He has given to us to guard our ways and to the set of spiritual values with which He presented us. If the state assists us in accepting this bondage, then we would be justified in professing devotion to it; but if the state interferes with these loyalities, there could be no room in my heart for any love for it.

This ideal of Judaism is epitomized in the *Malkhuyot* prayer. Family, friends, the state—none of them are absolutely binding. The only oath that can utterly bind us is allegiance to the Holy One, blessed be He, "for unto Thee every knee shall bow [and unto Thee, to Thee alone] every tongue shall swear."

The only pledge we must keep is the one made for the enactment of the Covenant—"that thou shouldst enter into the covenant of the Lord thy God and into His oath." This oath releases man from all other pledges and bonds. If man is subjugated in other ways and bound by other oaths, he cannot assume allegiance to the oath of the covenant. "Said Moses to Israel: Is it with your knowledge that I pledge you to this oath?" Did you think that was the same as any of your other obligations? Of course not! "I cause you to take this oath, by my leave and by leave of the Holy One, blessed be He!" All other obligations and pledges are cancelled when a free and liberated person stands before God in order to enter into His covenant and His oath.

### *On This Sanctified Day*

On the eve of the Day of Atonement, at sunset, as individuals and as a community we come to the synagogue to stand before God and renew, by means of absolute repentance, the covenant of "You are standing this day, all of you, before the Lord your God"—that covenant which was defiled and violated by us through our sins. Then, the prayer leader goes over to the lectern together with two other distinguished members of the community, constituting a court of three, and they make two proclamations before the congregation.

The first proclamation declares that everyone who is present, without exception, is qualified to stand before God and petition Him for acquittal and renewal of the covenant as well: "At the assembled gathering above and at the assembled gathering below, with God's permission and with the permission of the community, we hereby declare it permissible to pray together with the sinners." Everyone is capable of repenting and entering the renewed covenant. Moses, too, declared: "You are standing this day, all of you, before the Lord your God, your heads, your tribes . . . even all the men of Israel."

The second proclamation which the prayer leader, who on the Day of Atonement takes the place of the High Priest, says together with the two distinguished members of the community is to declare null and void all the oaths and asseverations and obligations and bondages which are liable to prevent the assembled congregation from "entering into the covenant of the Lord and into His oath." As long as man is enslaved by his impulses, passions and whims, so long as man is not free from cravings for wealth and honor, luxuries and comforts, of the lust for power and the desire for revenge, he cannot enter into the great oath which we all strive for on Yom Ha-Kippurim, the Day of Atonement.

Man, by his nature, is drawn to idolatry. He allows himself to become enslaved to impulses and drives which master him and, in the end, bring about his own self-destruction; they demand a price which he cannot pay, stifle the spark of life in him and darken the light of his soul. These masters appear in various shapes and forms—in the image of a fake culture, in the form of an absolutist state, in the shape of public opinion or as the ideal of beauty, the desire for orgiastic pleasures or the urge for permissiveness. These forms of idolatry impose oaths and asseverations upon man and keep him in their snare. Yet, as the Day of Atonement begins, we must liberate ourselves from their hold, and that is why we say the *Kol Nidre* prayer, to declare all these oaths and asseverations to be "null and void, ineffective and non-existing."

We enter into the sanctity of the Day of Atonement by declaring our total freedom. We proclaim that we are free men, independent, not tied by burdensome bonds to such trivial things as the love for money, for honor and fame or lust for power. We proclaim that we are free to enter ourselves completely into the wondrous oath and stand before the Lord our God: "That thou shouldst enter into the covenant of the Lord thy God and into His oath which the Lord thy God maketh with thee this day; that He may establish thee this day unto Himself for a people and that He may be unto thee a God, as He spoke unto thee and as He swore to thy fathers, to Abraham, to Isaac and to Jacob."

In this state of freedom from all types of bondage, on this sacred day, we renew our state of holiness in two ways: through the sanctity of the Patriarchs and through the sanctity of our selves.

# BLOTTING OUT SIN OR ELEVATING SIN

In Chapter 1, Section 1 of the Laws of Repentance,* Maimonides wrote:

> With regard to all the precepts of the Torah, both affirmative and negative, if a person transgresses any one of them, either willfully or in error, when he repents and turns away from his sin, he is under a duty to confess before God, blessed be He, as it is said, "When a man or woman shall commit any sin that men commit . . . they shall confess their sin which they have done" (Numbers 5:6–7)—this means confess in words; and this confession is an affirmative precept.

And Maimonides continues:

> How does one confess? By saying, "I beseech Thee, O Lord, I have sinned, I have acted perversely, I have transgressed before Thee, and have done thus and thus, and lo, I am contrite and ashamed of my deeds and will never do this again." This constitutes the essence of confession.

"This constitutes the essence of confession"—these are the core components and basic framework of confession. Of course, various additions may be made, but they must always center around the three fundamental components, which are: (1) acknowledgment of sin ("*I have sinned, I have acted perversely, I have transgressed*"); (2) remorse ("*I am contrite and ashamed of my deeds*"); (3) resolution for the future ("*I will never do this again*"). These three stages constitute "the essence of confession." And Maimonides adds: "The more one confesses and elaborates on this matter the more praiseworthy he is. And, also, those under an obligation to bring sin-offerings and trespass-offerings, who bring their sacrifices for sins committed either in error or willfully, are not acquitted [of their sins] by means of these offerings until they repent and confess in words. . . ." In other words, sacrifice alone cannot bring acquittal—confession is a *sine qua non* and without it repentance cannot take place. Even if one has decided to abandon sin and to radically alter one's way of life, it does not amount to a complete act of repentance; without confession acquittal is denied. Confession is mandatory not only for those who, having sinned, are obligated to bring sacrifices, but also for "those who have incurred the judicial penalty of death or punishment of stripes"—"they do not attain acquittal through death or [by the punishment of] stripes, until they repent and confess. Similarly, one who inflicts a wound on another person or causes him monetary damage is not acquitted even after he has paid [the injured party] what he owes him, until he confesses and penitently resolves never to commit the same offense again. . . ."

Note carefully that only the first half of the formula of confession which Maimonides sets forth as obligatory is identical with the formula employed by the High Priest in the Temple on the Day of Atonement ("I beseech Thee, O Lord! I have sinned . . ."; cf. Mishnah Yoma 3:8). In place of the second half ("I am contrite and ashamed . . . I will never do this again"), the High Priest used to offer a prayer and say: "I beseech Thee, O Lord, acquit me of the iniquities and the transgressions and the sins which I have committed before Thee!" Maimonides deleted the *prayer* portion from the formula of confession of the High Priest and replaced it with two other elements which do not appear there at all. They are: remorse ("I am contrite and ashamed . . .") and resolution for the future ("I will never do this again").

Elsewhere in the *Mishneh Torah* (Laws of Sacrificial Procedure, Chapter 3, Section 14), Maimonides ruled that every sacrifice must be accompanied by confession. "Whoever brings a burnt-offering, confesses; a sin-offering, confesses; a trespass-offering, confesses. . . ." What is the formula of confession to be used by one who sins in error and is obligated to bring a sin-offering? The answer to this question seems, at first, to belong to the Laws of Repentance, in which is found the formula for confession quoted above. However, in the Laws of Sacrificial Procedure, Maimonides sets forth another formula of confession (Chapter 3, Section 15).

> How does one confess? One says, "I have sinned, I have acted perversely, I have transgressed, and have done thus and thus and I have come back in repentance before Thee and this is my acquittal."

If we compare the two formulae of confession, the following significant differences can be discerned between them. The first one, in the Laws of Repentance, has the phrase "before Thee" appear immediately after "I have sinned, I have acted perversely, I have transgressed," while in the second formula, in the Laws of Sacrificial Procedure, it appears later, in the phrase "I have come back in repentance before Thee." At the same time, in the second formula, the element of resolution for the future ("I will never do this again") has been dropped; instead, there appears the phrase "and this is my acquittal," whose meaning is far from clear.

In light of this, it may be said that the concept of confession has more than one dimension. It is not an act that has an independent existence, nor is it something that stands on its own. It is, rather, the finale, the conclusion of another act—that of "repentance."

As we have already explained on several occasions, repentance is not a sudden occurrence. It does not begin at nightfall of the eve of the Day of Atonement, just moments before the recitation of confession. Repentance sprouts forth and grows in the course of a long and drawn-out process typified by doubt and speculation, soul-searching and spiritual reckoning. First comes the inner stirring which generates actual repentance. A great gap often intercedes between the idea and the act, for crystallized thinking is the end-product of intuitive, undefined thoughts. They take hold of one in the darkness of the night, they emerge from the innermost recesses of the secret self, and man tries to fend off some of them and hide them from himself, not to mention from others. The road that leads from these first stirrings to the actual contemplation of repentance is long indeed, and even then, after the rational idea is clearly formed in thought, it must be reborn and translated into action.

To do this necessarily entails expressing the thought of repentance in words and working it out in logical terms. Pure thought on its own, no matter how exact and penetrating, is simply not grasped until it is formed into words. We know many truths about ourselves that we do not dare express in public, and even avoid saying them to ourselves. It is not easy to give expression to our thoughts—all the more so when these thoughts are unflattering—but without doing so no act of confession can take place. Indeed, confession is no simple matter.

Were it an easy thing to confess, the Torah would not have demanded it of us, for what need is there for a commandment to do something that requires no effort? And if Maimonides made a point of stressing the requirement of doing confession, that alone is a sign that it is only achieved with difficulty.

Confession is not something that comes about suddenly, and it is certainly not the mechanical recitation of a set formula—it is, rather, part and parcel of repentance, the climactic finale of a drawn-out, exhausting process. And just as repentance cannot be considered complete until it has brought man to confess, so, too, confession is not valid unless it bursts forth from within the fiery depths of the furnace of repentance.

A basic principle of the laws of property is that "matters [that are only] within the heart are of no significance" (literally: "are not matters") (see T.B., Kiddushin 49b). If your intention is serious, if you really plan something, say it. As long as man has not confessed, his "repentance" is not considered complete. He may think in his heart: "From now on I shall observe the Sabbath, I'll close my store at the start of the Sabbath, I shall be straight and honest in all my dealings and cheat no one, I'll study Torah at regular and set times." All these are commendable thoughts, but as long as they are not expressed verbally, they do not comprise an act of repentance. Confession is the climax of the process of repentance; only after confession has been made can repentance be effective. Is this not what Maimonides wrote in Chapter 3, Section 2 of the Laws of Repentance? "And what is repentance? That the sinner abandon and strip himself of his sin and resolve in his heart never to do it again . . . and also that he be contrite over [what he has done in] the past . . . and he must confess in words, with his lips, and declare verbally all that which he has resolved in his heart."

Thus, according to Maimonides, confession is the concretization of repentance. Speech, the verbalizing of confession, endows the thought of repentance with reality. It is the climax and final chord of the long and tortuous internal process of repentance.

## *Confession—*
## *A Separate Category*

There is yet another dimension to confession.

Were confession only the ultimate act in the process of repentance, the following ruling of Maimonides would be unintelligible: "Transgressions which one has confessed on the Day of Atonement, one confesses again on the following Day of Atonement even though one has remained steadfast in repentance" (Laws of Repentance, Chapter 2, Section 8, based upon a discussion in the Babylonian Talmud, Yoma 87b). If confession is the ultimate act in the process of repentance, what place is there for "confessing again" if one "remains steadfast in his repentance"? We may thus infer that confession has another aspect—that there is a duty to confess *per se*, even if it be long after repentance has taken place.

Additional evidence of the fact that confession has an independent existence, apart from completing the process of repentance, is furnished by considering the confession of the High Priest on the Day of Atonement. Were it solely a constituent component of the act of repentance, how could the High Priest "do repentance" two and three times on the very same day—corresponding to the number of times he says the confession? Moreover, how does the High Priest come to confess for the entire community of Israel? If confession is part of the act of repentance, each and every person should be required to come to the Temple court to confess in person, for how can the High Priest *repent* on behalf of all of Israel? Can one repent on behalf of another, be it even his brother, father or son?

We see then that in addition to the law which views confession as intrinsically linked to repentance as the verbalization of penitential thoughts which have found expression, there is another law regarding confession. It consists of the act of confessing before God sins for which repentance is not necessary—either because they are not one's own sins or because one has already repented of them. When is confession of this sort mandatory? Whenever one encounters a "force of acquittal." The Day of Atonement by its very nature is an "acquitter" of this sort, and thus there is an obligation to confess on that day that is not connected to any act of repentance.

We have discerned two categories of confession: (1) confession which is an integral component of the repentance process, and (2) confession which comes as a form of propitiation. When a sinner is *able* or *desirous* of obtaining an acquittal, he has an obligation to confess.

The sacrifice of sin-offerings involves both of these aspects of confession. On the one hand, the bringing of a sacrifice requires confession which is an integral part of repentance, to the extent that without confession it is said that "the sacrifice of the wicked is an abomination" (cf. T.B., Shavuot 12b). If a sacrifice must be accompanied by repentance and if repentance without confession is not valid, then assuredly sacrifice requires confession. But another confession is made when bringing a sacrifice—that which is said *on* the sacrificial animal itself, by the one who brings the sacrifice and places his hands on top of the animal, prior to its slaughter. This confession comes *after* the act of repentance. If a person sets aside an animal for a sin-offering after he has repented and confessed—i.e., after his act of repentance is complete—even though he has already attained the status of a perfectly righteous man, he still must place his hands on the animal and confess. Why are two confessions necessary?

They are necessary because, as we have already stated,

there are two kinds of confession. The first is confession of repentance and acquittal, and the second one is for propitiation and appeasement. True, man may be cleansed and acquitted of all his sins after having completed repentance; nevertheless, when he seeks to come before the Holy One, blessed be He, he cannot come with only words of praise; he must first propitiate God, and this is done by means of confession.

This distinction between the two types of confession is the explanation for the varying formulae of confession which are included within the *Mishneh Torah.* In the Laws of Repentance (Chapter 1, Section 1), Maimonides deals with the first type of confession: "With regard to all the precepts of the Torah . . . if a man transgresses any one of them . . . when he repents and turns away from his sin, he is under a duty to confess. . . ." And there too: "And also those who are under an obligation to bring sin-offerings and trespass-offerings . . . are not acquitted [of their sins] by means of these offerings unless they repent and confess in words." It is not the absence of "laying on of the hands" (*smikhah*) which bars the acquittal that comes with sacrifice, but the absence of the first type of confession of repentance, which makes it a "sacrifice of the wicked," is an abomination. In the Laws of Sacrificial Procedure (Chapter 3, Sections 14–15), in contrast, Maimonides deals with the second type of confession—that of propitiation which accompanies the "laying on of the hands between the two horns [of the animal]." This explains the difference in the wording of the two formulae as they are set forth by Maimonides.

In the first: "And he must confess with his lips (in words) and declare those things which he has resolved in his heart" (Laws of Repentance, Chapter 2, Section 2); "The more one confesses and the more detailed a confession one makes, the more praiseworthy is he"(*ibid.,* Chapter 1, Section 1). In confession of repentance, man must call forth that which is hidden in the inner recesses of his heart—everything that has caused him sleepless nights, the doubts and hesitations, and the pangs of remorse he has experienced, the tribulations that have come upon him in the course of acknowledging his sins. All that has pushed and impelled him onto the path of repentance man is obligated to recall and declare in the course of his confession: "The more one confesses and the more detailed a confession one makes, the more praiseworthy is he." But in the context of the second type of confession, that which appears in the Laws of Sacrificial Procedure and the Laws of the [Temple] Service on the Day of Atonement, there is no suggestion that improvisation, additions or details in the making of confession are required. It contains a definite and set formula, and allows for no additions or subtractions of any kind.

Furthermore, if we examine them more closely, we find that where the phrase "before Thee" appears in each formula reveals the fundamental difference between the two types of confession. In the first type of confession, the phrase "before Thee" is part of the section that entails "acknowledgment of sin": "I have sinned, I have acted perversely, I have transgressed before Thee." Here man incorporates within his confession the whole gamut of his thoughts and feelings. He pours out his sorrows and his heartbreaks, his aspirations and his disappointments, his trials and tribulations, the torments of his spirit and his painful inner struggles; they are all brought out in detail, and the more one elaborates in this vein, the more praiseworthy is one's confession, all of it being, as it were, accounted for "before Thee"—before God. In "acknowledgment of sin" man acknowledges that he has placed a distance between himself and God. When man acts sinfully, he contaminates his own soul as well as his surroundings, and excludes, as it were, the Holy One from his presence. "I have sinned, I have acted perversely, I have transgressed—before Thee!" I have sinned, and as a consequence I have removed You from myself and have cast myself far from You.

This outpouring of feeling, which is an inherent part of the repentance process, is identified with the first type of confession. In contrast, in the second type of confession, the formula is predetermined; man is not obligated to dredge the depths of his soul and relive everything which led him to that point. In this case, the confession consists purely of a formula of conciliation, following the act of repentance. It is for this reason that the phrase "before Thee" does not appear within the introductory part describing the sin, but later on, in describing the "after-the-fact" situation: "I have come back in repentance before Thee"—I am again "before Thee." I feel Your nearness. Closeness makes words unneccessary. Here it is not: "The more one confesses the more praiseworthy is he."

## *Despair and Faith Together*

The second type of confession, that which appears in the Laws of Sacrificial Procedure, also has three parts: (1) acknowledgment of sin ("I have sinned, I have acted perversely, I have transgressed"), (2) repentant return ("I have come back in repentance before Thee"), and (3) acquittal ("and this is my acquittal"). In fact, this confession of propitiation mirrors the inner dialectic and inherent contradiction within the whole concept of repentance. For repentance is actually built upon two conflicting principles, upon two rules that are seemingly incompatible with one another.

The first of these basic principles is embodied in the concept "acknowledgment of sin." Basically, acknowledgment of sin emerges out of a feeling of despair and resignation. Man surveys his deeds and says: "I have sinned, I have acted perversely, I am guilty, that is, I admit my guilt; I recognize and acknowledge the fact that I am a sinner; I accept the judgment; I offer no defense, excuse or justification for my behavior. There are no mitigating circumstances; I am not worthy of loving-kindness and mercy—justice has been done. Wherever I turn there are none who are willing to pardon me, and they are right, for why should anyone show me favor?" Even Prophecy and Wisdom are justified in carrying out their sentence, as the Sages have so majestically stated: "They inquired of Wisdom, 'What is the punishment of a sinner?' Wisdom said, 'Evil pursues the wicked' (Proverbs 13:21). They asked Prophecy, 'What is the punishment of a sinner?' Prophecy said to them, 'The sinful soul shall die' (Ezekiel 18:20)" (T.J., Makkot 2:6). The sinful soul shall die, evil pursues the wicked—the awesomeness of sin itself tears man to pieces and there is no escaping it. "The sinful soul shall die," cries Prophecy—all the roads are closed before the person who is sunk in sin. "Evil pursues the wicked," echoes back Wisdom. Sin takes man in its clutches and refuses to release him from its grasp. This is acknowledgement of sin in the fullest sense. How does this lead to the path of repentance? Only the Master of the Universe Himself knows the answer to that: "They inquired of the Holy One. 'What is the punishment of a sinner?' He said to them: 'Let him repent and he shall be forgiven,' as it is written, 'He instructs sinners in the way' (Psalm 25:8). He instructs sinners in the way to repent" (*ibid.*). Only God can extricate man from the awful and terrible state resulting from his acknowledgment of sin and can transform him to one who is, in Maimonides' words, "beloved and desired before the Creator, as if he had never sinned at all" (Laws of Repentance, Chapter 7, Section 14). And elsewhere Maimonides describes the transformation in these terms: "One day a person may be despised of the Lord, abhorred and loathed and cast far away—and the next day be loved and desired; a close friend" (*ibid.,* Section 6).

The feeling of acknowledging sin is one of self-degradation and abnegation, of who am I and what makes me worthy of coming before God and seeking His nearness. Acknowledgment of sin gives expression to everything that is tragic in man's predicament as he realizes that his life has reached a dead end, and that his very existence is meaningless and empty. On all sides he is engulfed by Ecclesiastes' plaintive cry, "Vanity of vanities, all is vanity," and in the midst of this nothingness man feels that he is loathsome, an outcast, an abomination. The horror of this condition brings utter despair, an overbearing sense of guilt, and a feeling of worthlessness.

This is one of the basic components of the repentance process—but there is another one which is antithetical to the first, yet is an integral part of the very same process, and whoever fails to achieve it cannot become a full penitent. This element is faith in the Creator of the Universe and in man's spiritual potential. This belief says that despite the fact that man may become an abomination and a loathsome being, he still has the capacity to uplift himself and escape from the cage of his despair. Maimonides emphasizes this point time and again—the option is open to man; it is up to him to choose; what great powers have been granted man!

It is this sense of power that tells man that even when all the roads are barred to him, there still exists somewhere a secret path that twists and turns between hills and valleys, that climbs to dizzying heights and drops to bewildering depths, that goes forward and retraces its steps backward, and he knows that if he follows this path no one can stand in his way. Should he insist upon joining others on the main thoroughfare, he will find himself confronting a barrier. Who goes there? What right have you to be here? The highway is closed to the sinner. Even the angels of mercy will not permit him to pass, for no one may approach the King's gate wearing the sackcloth of sin and transgression. Nevertheless, though the highway be blocked, it is still possible to travel the hidden byways that wind their way through the jungle. Though the main gate be sealed, there is always a tiny window through which man may seek entry. The public thoroughfare does not lead man to the goal—only the solitary road. And every man must travel his own individual path.

Just as man senses that there is at least one path that remains open to him, so must he have faith that there remains at least one burning coal in the pile of smoldering embers deep in his heart, one flickering spark from which he can kindle a new flame.

"Repentance brings near those who are afar," wrote Maimonides in Chapter 7 of the Laws of Repentance: "How lofty is the quality of repentance! One day man may be alienated from the Lord, God of Israel . . . and the next he cleaves unto the *Shekhinah*" (Sections 6–7). Everything depends upon man's will: "Permission is granted unto every man [to choose]."

The prophet Ezekiel lived in a time of destruction and general despair. The Jews of his generation bemoaned that they were "pining away in their iniquity." There are times when a whole generation may feel that it "is alienated from the Lord, God of Israel," that it is "despised and cast far away."

An acknowledgment of sin which leads one to a state of helplessness and utter exhaustion is the first part of the process of repentance and confession: "I have sinned, I have acted perversely, I have transgressed, that is to say, I am polluted by sin, I am alienated from the God of Israel, I am a despicable outcast."

However, this awful feeling does not necessarily lead to

unmitigated despair. Man is capable of a complete change of mood: "I have come back [to stand] before Thee." This is the dialectic of the process of repentance, the inherent polarity of the conflicting forces within the soul of man which come to the fore when man stands "before Thee." One day he is loathsome and the next he can be appealing and beloved. Only an instant separates one day from the next—one quantum jump.

What is meant by the concluding phrase, "and this is my acquittal"? This is prayer, and it is as if man were to say, "May it be Thy will that my prayer serve as my acquittal, that Thou accept it mercifully and in propitiation."

If we study it closely, the formula which Maimonides stipulates for us in individual confession contains the same elements found in the confession of the High Priest on the Day of Atonement. First, acknowledgment of sin: "I have sinned, I have acted perversely, I have transgressed." Then an element that is the diametric opposite of the despair resulting from acknowledgment of sin: the possibility to free oneself from sin and overcome it. In the confession of the High Priest, this is expressed by citing a biblical verse, "As it is written in the Torah of Moses, 'For the virtue of this very day shall acquit you of sin to cleanse you of all your sins; before God, you shall be cleansed,' " whereas in the confession of the individual, this idea is contained in a single word (in the Hebrew): "before Thee"—if I can come before Thee, then I believe and am convinced that acquittal and catharsis are given options just as it is written in the Torah of Moses.

After that came the element of prayer. The High Priest prayed: "I beseech Thee, O Lord, acquit the sinners and the transgressors. . . ." What is the prayer of the individual? It consists of the two words (in Hebrew): "and this is my acquittal," that is to say "may this be my acquittal." Why is the prayer of the High Priest so detailed and elaborate in contrast to the prayer of the individual which is brief and enigmatic? We must assume that Maimonides had a source on which he relied. For our purposes, what is important to note is the correspondence in structure and content between the two confessions, that of the High Priest and that of the individual. Both are made up of the same components: (1) acknowledgment of sin, which means utter resignation, self-effacement and self-renunciation, (2) return in repentance, that is, raising oneself from the fathomless pit of despair and achieving the lofty pinnacle of standing "before Thee," and (3) prayer, saying, "Oh, grant acquittal," "may it be Thy will to accept my repentance."

Every act of repentance is built upon this structural model. Thus, after Nathan the prophet reproved David for his sins, we read: "And David said unto Nathan, 'I have sinned against the Lord,' and Nathan said unto David, 'The Lord hath put away thy sin; thou shalt not die' " (2 Samuel 12:12–13). What sort of confession and repentance have we here? All David said was one word: "I have sinned," and for this he deserved pardon and forgiveness! Rabbi Elijah, the Gaon of Vilna, noted that in the Masoretic text of the Bible, after the phrase, "I have sinned against the Lord," there is a gap, a blank space. David actually wanted to say much more, to make a detailed confession, but he became choked up with tears and could not utter another word. At that moment, David achieved complete self-negation, a sense of sheer worthlessness. He was so profoundly shaken that he could say no more. But Nathan the prophet sensed the drama that was taking place in David's soul, after he managed only with the utmost of difficulty to utter the words "I have sinned." He saw that, at that very moment, David was wholly immersed in repentance, how he was undergoing the entire process of repentance, from acknowledgment of sin to self-elevation and prayer. That was how Nathan could say to him, "The Lord hath put away thy sin."

## *"When Any Man of You Bring an Offering"*

Let us return to Maimonides' text: "And also those who are under an obligation bring sin-offerings and trespass-offerings, when they bring their sacrifices for sins committed in error or willfully, are not acquitted [of their sins] by means of these offerings unless they repent and make a verbal confession as it is written, 'He shall confess that wherein he has sinned' (Leviticus 5:5). And, also, those who have incurred the judicial penalty of death or punishment of stripes do not attain acquittal by [suffering] death or [the punishment of] stripes unless they repent and confess" (Laws of Repentance, Chapter 1, Section 1). Note carefully that in relation to those obligated to bring a sacrifice, Maimonides rules that they must "confess verbally," while in relation to those who have incurred judicial penalties, he rules that they must "confess," and omits the phrase "verbally." Also, in relation to the latter, he does not cite a verse in order to substantiate his ruling, as he does in relation to the former, and in the subsequent section as well: "Similarly, one who inflicts a wound on another person or causes him monetary damage ... does not attain acquittal unless he confesses and penitently resolves never to do so again, as it is written, '[when a man or woman shall commit] *any* sin that men commit ... [they shall confess]' (Numbers 5:6)." Another difficulty arises concerning the wording of this section in the latter verse, "any sin that men commit." This incorporates within it all possible types of confessions; why then did Maimonides find it necessary to cite a specific verse in relation to the confession over sacrifices, "he shall confess that wherein he has sinned" (which in the Torah refers only to sins requiring varying offerings)?

In Chapter 6 of the tractate Sanhedrin, the following Mishnah appears: "When he is about ten cubits away from the place of stoning, they say to him, 'Confess' . . . and if he does not know what to confess, they instruct him, 'Say, may my death bring acquittal for all of my sins.' " The implication is that saying "may my death . . ." is equivalent to making a formal confession, and that it is not necessary to recite a pre-determined formula. Yet, on the basis of what Maimonides writes in the Laws of Sacrificial Procedure (Chapter 3, Section 15), which we cited earlier, it would appear that confession does require a set text: "How does one confess? One says . . ." Why, then, do those who have incurred the judicial death penalty say any words they wish, some version of "may it be Thy will . . ." while those who bring sacrifices are supposed to recite a lengthy and pre-determined confession formula?

We will understand this by learning about the structure and content of confession. Those who have incurred judicial sentences do not need "acknowledgment of sin," for the court has already condemned them for their sins. All that remains for the sinner to do is to make petition that the death penalty or punishment of stripes bring acquittal. It was for this reason that Maimonides felt compelled to cite a special verse in connection with the requirement to confess when bringing sacrifices so that we would not mistakenly assume that confession here was the same as with those who have incurred judicial penalties. The confession over sacrifices, Maimonides emphasizes, is a "verbal confession," meaning that it consists of an explicit formula somewhat similar to the specific texts of the blessings which the Sages ordained. This is not the case in relation to the confession of those who have incurred judicial penalties, for they do not need to confess in order to attain a broken spirit and recognize their sinful state. The court has already established that by announcing its verdict and there is no longer any need to use a prescribed formula.

The specific terminology of the confession which is said together with the bringing of sacrifices may also be understood from a different perspective. If we probe deeply into the philosophical origins of sacrifices, we will discover that the whole idea of the ritual for the Day of Atonement, at the center of which is the burning of sacrifices upon the altar, is based upon one central idea, and that is—to use Nahmanides' term—that man is the "property" of the Creator of the Universe. Man's whole essence and being, his flesh and his thoughts and his deeds and his achievements and his possessions, his wife and his children and his home, are not really his, but belong to God who created man. On the Day of Atonement, every act of confession is preceded by the recitation of "the soul is Thine and the body is Thine." Without establishing this premise, man cannot place himself before God in prayer.

The Torah forbade all human sacrifice. The example it uses to describe the abomination of idol-worship is, "for even their sons and their daughters they consume with fire on behalf of their gods" (Deuteronomy 12:31). Yet, although the Torah forbade human offerings, it did not invalidate the *idea* behind it that man should sacrifice his own self—"that it is proper that [man] spill his blood and burn his flesh" (cf. Nahmanides, Leviticus 1:9)—rather than just bring a bull or two pigeons or turtle-doves. God does not seek offerings from man, he seeks man himself.

This is the foundation of sacrificial practice, and it is on this idea that the story of the binding of Isaac is based. On unconditional self-sacrifice of body and of soul the Jewish faith is founded. Judaism does not reject the idea behind human sacrifice. If man is the property of the Holy One, blessed be He, when he hears the voice of God calling to him, "Take now thy son, thine only son . . . and offer him . . . for a burnt-offering upon one of the mountains which I will tell thee of," he has no other choice than did Abraham: "And Abraham rose early in the morning and saddled his ass . . . and went unto the place of which God had told him." The Torah renounced human sacrifice, and even forbade it—out of the quality of mercy. "Had it not been for the mercy of the Creator who took [other] consideration from us" (cf. Nahmanides, *ibid.*), strict justice and absolute truth would have dictated "When any man *of you* bring an offering" and stopped there: "of you"—literally so! It was mercy which came and added: "ye shall bring your offering of the cattle, even of the herd or of the flock."

Others have already pointed out the fact that the name of God that appears throughout the story of the binding of Isaac is "*Elohim*": "God (*Elohim*) did prove Abraham . . . God (*Elohim*) will provide Himself the lamb for a burnt-offering, my son . . ." etc. Only after the angel stays Abraham's hand and calls out to him, "Lay not thy hand upon the lad," does the Ineffable Name of God appear for the first time: "And the angel of the *Lord* called unto him out of heaven. . . ." Up until then, the quality of strict justice had prevailed, according to which Abraham had no "right" to his son Isaac or to derive pleasure from his offspring. His son did not "belong" to him, and on this there was no dispute or room for discussion or evasion. "And God (*Elohim*) said unto him": the quality of strict-justice called out to him. This was an order which had to be fulfilled without any reservations. Abraham heard the command, and he followed and obeyed it.

In a world of strict justice, the only acceptable way is for man to sacrifice himself. When man sins, it is as if he summons the quality of strict justice to judge him. By sinning, he loses his most elementary right, the right to his own self. "For in the day that thou eatest thereof thou shalt surely die." Sin means death. The quality of strict justice is never willing to concede. "If Thou exactest strict judgment, who can stand before Thee?"

When man brings a sacrifice after having sinned, he must imagine that it is he himself who is being offered upon the altar. When the blood of the animal is sprinkled, he must imagine that it is his own blood that is being sprinkled—that his own hot blood, which in its passion drew him to sin, is being sprinkled upon the altar of his sin; that the fats which are consumed upon the altar are not the animal's, but his own fats, which congealed in his heart and gave him over into the hands of sin. Only by virtue of God's august mercy is man redeemed from having to sacrifice himself, for it is God who arranged for a ram to take the place of Isaac. It is for this reason that it is always (with two exceptions) the Ineffable Name of God that appears in the context of sacrifices, for the quality of Divine mercy is revealed in the sacrificial rites.

When an Israelite brings a sacrifice to attain acquittal for having sinned, what is it that actually achieves the acquittal? Is it through a sin-offering worth two *shekalim*? Certainly not! Acquittal comes only with confession and acknowledgment of sin, which means self-nullification and negation, absolute submission and subservience, utter sacrifice of the self and his whole being and all that he owns, as if he has laid himself upon the altar.

"I have come back in repentance before Thee and this is my acquittal." Repentance itself—that is the acquittal, the expiation. Repentance takes the place of the sacrifice of myself which I had a duty to offer upon the altar. It stands in my place and it is as if I myself were stretched out upon the altar. "And [Abraham] offered [the ram] for a burnt-offering in the place of his son." In the prayers for the Day of Atonement we petition God to remember "the ashes of *Isaac*," not the ashes of the ram, for in essence it was not the ram that was sacrificed, but Isaac himself.

This, then, is the nature of the verbal confession that accompanies the bringing of a sin-offering. The confession itself is the spiritual sacrifice which man offers. "And this is my acquittal"—confession has brought about an annihilation of my whole being, just as the sacrificial animal is utterly consumed by the flames upon the altar.

### *Repentance Motivated by Love Versus Repentance From Fear*

In the *Selihot*, the penitential prayers, we thank God for having "shown us the way of repentance." But, in fact, there is more than one way open to us—there are at least two.

The first way is by: blotting out evil.

The second way is by: *rectifying* evil, and elevating it.

The following passage from the Tractate Yoma (86b) will help to clarify this distinction:

> Resh Lakish said: Great is repentance, for because of it, premeditated sins are accounted as errors, as it is said: "Return, O Israel, unto the Lord, thy God, for thou hast stumbled in thy iniquity" (Hosea 14:2). "Iniquity" is premeditated, and yet he calls it "stumbling!"—But is that really so? For has Resh Lakish not said that repentance is so great that premeditated sins are accounted as though they were merits, as it is said: "And when the wicked turneth from his wickedness and doeth that which is lawful and right, he shall live thereby" (Ezekiel 33:19)? That is no contradiction. One refers to a case [of repentance] motivated by love, the other [to repentance] which comes from fear.

This passage, admittedly, raises difficulties. Why should the wicked be given a "bonus" by having his premeditated sins accounted as though they were merits? What has he done to deserve such treatment? Moreover, what is the meaning of repentance from love as against repentance from fear, and in what way do they differ from each other?

In order to explain this problematic passage and to understand the two ways of repenting, we must first direct our attention to the principal philosophic problem underlying repentance, with which the great Jewish thinkers have grappled, including Rav Saadia Gaon, Rabbi Jonah Girondi, Rabbenu Behaye, Rabbi Hayyim of Volozhin and many others. Philosophers of other nations have also wrestled with this problem, and consequently refuted the value of repentance.

The problem of repentance is intertwined with an apprehension of the concept of time and how it relates to human existence. Rabbi Jedaiah Ha-Pnini was the one who coined the phrase: "The past is nothing, the future is not yet, and the present [passes] like the blink of an eye." According to this conception, man's life is meaningless, he has no hold in time whatsoever. But the truth is that man does exist within two distinct dimensions of time: (1) in memory, and (2) in expectation for the future.

Memory replies to the question: "Who am I?" I am he who remembers these feelings and those experiences, these moments of happiness and those moments of sorrow. In memory, the "I" sustains its continuity. In the liturgy of the Day of Atonement, we say to God: "Thou recalleth (*zokher*) the deeds of old and remembereth (*poked*) those who existed in ancient times." What is the difference between "recall" (*zokher*) and "remember" (*poked*)? Both bear the connotation of "visit," as in the verse, "And the Lord remembered (*pakad*) Sarah" (Genesis 21:1). It was as if God came to visit Sarah; until that moment the heavens had been sealed before Sarah in her barrenness, but then God "remembered" her and visited her. And just as God remembers the beings of ancient times, so does man remember and revisit the past which is preserved in his memory. Whoever dwells constantly on the past loses his mind, for it is man's nature to leave it behind him and move forward. But from time to time man is compelled to remember and revisit the past, to recall the issues and experiences which are not yet dead and buried and are in many ways still very much alive within him.

On the other hand, when man asks himself "Who am I?" he hears the reply, "I am he who foresees and anticipates the future. I am he who, with God's help, plans for tomorrow and the day after, for the coming week and for next year." When a person is young, his memory is short and his expectations are greater, and for an older person memory is long and expectations are lessened. But both young and old float upon the current of time and are carried from a known and familiar past to the unknown future, still wrapped in mystery. The present is the bridge that connects the two.

What does a sinner do when he comes to repent of the wrongdoings he committed in the past (there can be no repentance without "remorse for past deeds"), with all the sins committed in bygone years strung up in his memory? Sometimes a person is immersed in sin for ten or fifteen years. (I know of someone who wanted to repent after seventy years of sin!) What will happen when he looks back and recalls all those years of violating the Sabbath, of exploitation and of thievery? Are not all these years part of his personality, part of this "I"? Will he continue to consider himself part of those years or can they be wiped out as though they never were?

Sometimes one will "erase" certain years of a lifetime. Ex-convicts, for example, tend to completely forget the years they spent behind bars. They simply decide to erase those years from their past. "Yet the chief butler did not remember Joseph, but forgot him" (Genesis 40:23). He did not remember, and actually he wanted to blot out of his memory the whole unpleasant period he spent in jail, probably because he wanted to forget that he had ever been in prison. But when one blots out a part of his past he also severs part of his being; his past shrinks and his personality is dwarfed. An "operation" of this sort is not easily carried out. A man of fifty or sixty years of age can by no means erase in a moment a third, or a half, or even three-quarters of his life. What, then, should he do if he wants to repent at this stage of his life? Can he go on identifying himself with those years of sin? If he does so, it is as if he admits the existence of evil and acknowledges it as one of his permanent personality traits.

Philosophers have dealt with this problem at great length, and it brought Nietzsche and Spinoza to deny the possibility of repentance. Maimonides discloses his view of the matter in Chapter 2, Section 4 of the Laws of Repentance: "It is characteristic of repentance that the penitent cries out continuously before the Lord . . . and keeps far away from that wherein he sinned, and changes his name, as if to say: 'I am a different person and not the same one who committed those deeds.' " In other words, a man of seventy who repents erases with one blow his whole past and is like a newborn babe. . . . I have seen penitents do just that—and the consequence? They became different and estranged from their families and friends, who appeared to them to belong to another eon, a different world, a period when they were entrenched in sin which has now been erased from their consciousness. All feelings and experiences connected with that period were dead to them to such an extent that they even severed all ties with their parents, children, brothers and sisters.

In effect, that was what God demanded of our forefather Abraham: "Get thee out of thy country, and from thy kindred and from thy father's house. . . ." Our forefather Abraham tore himself away from his past and severed all his ties with it. In Maimonides' words: ". . . and changed his name, as if to say: 'I am another person and not the same one who committed these deeds.' " Abraham was then forty-three years old. He renounced and put behind him forty-three years of his life. Indeed, the Torah begins to recount the history of Abraham's life only after he has reached the land of Israel, for it was only then that Abraham the Hebrew was "born."

Maimonides also indicated this in his exact choice of words: "One day *a person* may be despised of the Lord, abhorred and loathed and cast far away, and the next *he* is loved and desired and close at hand, a friend." Before repentance, he was "this person" and afterward he became "him." But they are not the same person; the beloved one of today is not the despised person of yesterday; the friend close at hand is not the same loathsome person who was cast far away.

The question whether repentance implies continuity or severance, whether it sustains the past or utterly nullifies it, depends upon the nature of the repentance. There is repentance which does allow for continuity and which accords recognition to the past, and there is also repentance whose goal is the utter annihilation of the evil in the soul of man. Certain situations leave no choice but for the annihilation of evil and for completely uprooting it. If one takes pity and lets evil remain, one inexorably pays at a later date the awesome price of six million or ten million victims. The biblical imperative of blotting out the remembrance of Amalek is not a matter of racial hatred but rather the uprooting of a nation that embodied such evil that could not be rectified except by a clean break, by sheer annihilation, for fear that this evil will continue to thrive and insinuate itself in good times as well. Repentance of the individual can also be of the kind that requires a clean break, with all of man's sins and evil deeds falling away into an abyss, fulfilling the prophecy, "And Thou wilt cast all their sins into the depths of the sea" (Micah 7:19). Not only are the sins cast into the depths of the sea, but, also, all the years of sin—ten or twenty or even thirty years of the sinner's life. It is impossible to sift out only the sins and leave the years intact.

The years that have fallen aside leave an empty space, and yet the Holy One, blessed be He, gives man "credit" for those years. He "overlooks transgression" as it were, ignoring and uprooting from time all those years which the penitent has cast into the depths of the sea, together with all their entangling webs of relatives and friends.

The Holy One, blessed be He, appears then, in the words of the liturgy of the Day of Atonement, as "He [who] is patient and condones those who go astray." The quality of strict justice cannot fathom this and asks in wonder: How is it possible to obliterate what has occurred? Logic, too, is outraged at the possibility of uprooting part of man's consciousness, excising part of man's memory. Both Nietzsche and Kant claimed that this was impossible, but Judaism says: Yes, it can be done. Abraham was the first to demonstrate that it was indeed possible, that man can make a clean break and start anew!

Repentance of this sort leaves man only a limited sense of feeling of "return." To where shall he return? He returns to his starting point, to where he stood prior to embarking upon the road of sin, and everything that has occurred in the meantime disappears, as if it had never been. The Holy One, blessed be He, then recompenses him for this loss by pardoning his sin and erasing it from the books.

This is the first way of repentance, but there is another way—not by annihilating evil but by rectifying and elevating it. This repentance does not entail making a clean break with the past or obliterating memories. It allows man, at one and the same time, to continue to identify with the past and still to return to God in repentance.

"When thou shalt besiege a city a long time, in making war against it to take it, thou shalt not destroy the trees thereof by wielding an axe against them" (Deuteronomy 20:19). How much more so should one not destroy, frivolously, ten years or tens of years of one's life! What, then, shall the penitent do with all those years of sin? He does not want to identify with them, and yet he cannot blot them out. What shall he do?

When the goal is annihilation of evil, there cannot be any compromises. Evil must be utterly destroyed and cast into the depths of the sea. But there also is another way of dealing with evil, and that is by rectifying it and uplifting it. This way of repentance does not transform the penitent into "another." Here, there is no clean break between "this person" of yesterday and the "he" of today. It is not necessary to blot out and erase the past. The future can be built upon the foundations of the past. How so? By elevating and exalting evil. How does one exalt evil to such an extent that it ceases to be evil? How does the "despised and abhorred" of yesterday become the "beloved and desired" of today, without erasing and annihilating yesterday?

Repentance of this sort does not require man to return to the starting-point where he was originally, but rather infuses him with a burning desire to come as near as he can to the Creator of the universe and attain spiritual heights undreamed of before he sinned. Man then becomes infused with strength and power he did not have previously.

From whence does it come?

## *The Dynamics of Sin*

The intensity of sin and the sense of guilt and shame that overwhelms man in its wake are such strong drives that they impel the penitent upward and outward in the direction of the Creator of the universe. The years of sin are transformed into powerful impulsive forces which propel the sinner toward God.

Sin is not to be forgotten, blotted out or cast into the depths of the sea. On the contrary, sin has to be remembered. It is the memory of sin that releases the power within the inner depths of the soul of the penitent to do greater things than ever before. The energy of sin can be used to bring one to new heights.

The Talmudic sage, Resh Lakish, was renowned as a man who sinned grievously and repented. According to Rabbenu Tam (Tosafot, Baba Metzia 84a), Resh Lakish was an accomplished scholar before he became a thief. After he fell to thievery, Rabbi Johanan succeeded in convincing him to repent of his ways, and thereafter Resh Lakish became "even greater" than he had been before. How did this happen? Certainly, while he was out thieving and robbing, he wasn't engaged in the study of Torah! What, then, made him greater after he sinned than he had been before? Sin itself!

The penitent who does not wipe out the past nor tear the pages of sin from his memory, but rather makes a point to use the memory of his sins to enhance his longings for holiness that are bursting forth from inside of him—such a person achieves the quality of repentance which elevates evil to a state of goodness. With regard to such a penitent, the Holy One, blessed be He, does not "overlook transgression" but "bears sin and transgression." It is as if He lifts up and elevates sin and transgression to unimaginable heights.

"Now these are the last words of David, the saying of David the son of Jesse, and the saying of the man raised on high, the anointed of the God of Jacob, and the sweet singer of Israel" (2 Samuel 23:1). The plain meaning of the phrase "raised on high" is that King David was endowed with greatness by God, but our Sages interpreted the phrase homiletically to mean that "he (King David) raised on high the yoke of repentance" (T.B., Mo'ed Katan 16b). David was the penitent *par excellence* who was raised on high so as to serve as an example to all of Israel. What was it that made David so great that, in Rashi's phrase (*ad loc.*), "Israel sings in the Temple only his songs and his melodies"? The answer is: the fact that he sinned and repented, that he took sin and out of it constructed the yoke of repentance.

In light of this, Resh Lakish's comments which were cited earlier can now be understood: "Great is repentance that causes premeditated sins to be accounted as errors." Resh Lakish was here referring to repentance by means of which sin is annihilated. Such repentance erases sin, but it has no creative power and does not germinate or give life to anything new. Premeditated sins are accounted as errors, as though they never took place at all. They are wiped away. But in his second comment Resh Lakish said that "repentance is so great that premeditated sins are accounted as though they were merits," and here he was referring to repentance by means of which sin is elevated and exalted. This motivates man to fulfill the precepts with a vigor and a zest lacking before he sinned and causes him to study and learn Torah in a different manner. What was it that made Resh Lakish worthy of being the closest friend of Rabbi Johanan, the most esteemed Sage of his day? The fact that he had repented and that, by means of repentance, he had elevated and exalted the evil used for thievery to the goodness that lay in the study of Torah.

Repentance in which evil is elevated is brought about by love, and, because of it, premeditated sins are considered as merits, while repentance in which evil is blotted out is instigated by fear, and, because of it, premeditated sins are accounted as errors. In repentance of love, love rises with the flames of repentance and burns brightly in the fires fanned by sin; the bonds of love pull man up to great and exalted heights. It is concerning repentance of this sort, that the Sages said: "Great is repentance that touches the Throne of Glory" (T.B., Yoma 86a).

You may ask: How is it possible for one who has repented to get nearer and ascend higher than he was before he sinned?

How is it possible for sins to act as a dynamic force leading to holiness? Is it not written: "Who can purify the unclean? No one!" (Job 14:4)? God alone knows the answer to this mystery. The Master of the Universe, the Creator of all, He is the one who made it possible to purify the unclean, and perhaps the idea of uplifting evil belongs in the same category.

The following phenomenon may also explain the dynamics of sin.

There seems to be a tragic flaw inherent in the nature of man from which no one can escape. The people and things that we love and cherish most are not fully appreciated as long as they are alive and present with us. We realize what they meant to us only after they are gone and their image has become faded and unreal. They seem to twinkle from afar as the stars in the night; we admire them but cannot touch them. How many near and dear ones did we have whom we did not succeed in appreciating fully, as long as they were with us: mother, father, teacher, wife or husband?

I am not speaking of those people who failed to properly observe the precept of honoring their father and mother or of those who neglected to show due respect to their teachers or love to their marital partner. I am speaking, specifically, of those who showed the utmost honor to their parents and who esteemed their teachers and were dedicated to their husband or wife. Even these people must suffer the burden of feelings of guilt for not having done what they could while their loved ones were still alive. Whoever fails to be tormented by such remorse does not know the real meaning of grief for a dearly loved one who is gone forever.

The practices relating to *shiva* (the initial seven-day period of mourning) and *shloshim* (the first thirty days after death) and the year of mourning are all practices of mourning which the sages have instituted in accordance with the nature of man. But the essence of mourning consists not only of grief for one who has gone but also in the pain of "would that I could"—if I only could, I would make amends now for what I didn't do when I could have acted differently, but, alas, it is no longer possible to undo the damage.

The following story related in the Talmud illustrates this most poignantly: "When Rav died, his disciples walked after him (in the burial procession). When they returned, they said: Let's go and eat bread alongside the Dank River. After they had eaten they asked themselves whether the requirement of *zimmun*, reciting a joint grace after meals, was applicable only if they had decided to say the blessing over the bread together (before the meal) or whether it was also applicable when they had casually sat down and said, let us eat together. They were at a loss for an answer. Thereupon Rav Ada bar Ahava got up and tore at his garment where it had been rent before and said: 'Rav's soul has left him and we haven't even learned [the laws] of grace after meals!' " (T.B., Berakhot 42b).

Rav Ada bar Ahava rent his garment the first time in grief over the death of Rav, the Master of all of Israel. Everything that Rav Ada knew he had learned from Rav, his great master. No one had meant more to him than his teacher, Rav. Yet he suddenly realized that he had hardly known his master. This happened when he was confronted with a facile question of law and he did not know what had to be done. Only at that moment did he become aware of what he had lost, and it was then that he tore his garment a second time, out of grief at not having really known his master as he should have, for he had been even greater than anyone realized. "Rav's soul has departed from him and we haven't even learned [the basic laws of] grace after meals!" We have not even learned properly something as routine as grace after meals. It was then that Rav Ada and his colleagues realized that their master was gone, whereupon they tore their garments a second time. At that moment, Rav Ada surely would have given his life to be able to spend five more minutes with his illustrious teacher and discuss the problem about grace after meals which he had not managed to study sufficiently before. But it was now too late. He found himself before a stone wall. An unbridgeable chasm separated him from his master and there was no way he could possibly span it.

It was then that he rent his garment for a second time—in grief for his beloved master and for the loss he felt.

The longing for one who has died and is gone forever is worse than death. The soul is overcome and shattered by fierce longing. Just before Rosh Hashana, I imagined that my father, of blessed memory, was standing beside me. He was the one and only *rebbi*, master and teacher, that I ever had. I put my life down before him and said: "My father, my teacher, I have had so many new insights concerning the laws of the Day of Atonement . . . certainly there are amongst them some which would have pleased you, and also some which you would have rejected. . . ." That was how I imagined myself speaking to my father, knowing that I would receive no response. Oh, what would I have given to be able to discuss Torah with him, if only for five minutes! But I knew that my beloved father, who had once been so close to me, was now far away, and my heart burst with the desire to talk to him for even five minutes, which had not seemed so valuable while he was still alive.

The same is true regarding my mother and my wife. Several days ago I once again sat down to prepare my annual discourse on the subject of repentance. I always used to discuss it with my wife, and she would help me to define and crystallize my thoughts. This year, too, I prepared the discourse, while consulting her: "Could you please advise me? Should I expand upon this idea or cut down on that idea? Should I emphasize this point or that one?"

I asked, but heard no reply. Perhaps there was a whispered response to my question, but it was swallowed up by the wind whistling through the trees and did not reach me.

### *The Intensity of Longing*

Every person, during his lifetime, is confronted by the tragedy of longing for one who was near just a short while ago and now is irrevocably gone. These longings are accompanied by severe pangs of guilt which plague one relentlessly and may even drive one mad. How intense is the desire to make contact with a loved one who has gone afar! But how unrealistic it is, how impossible it is to achieve, for these souls which we so long for are far removed from us, shrouded under the comforting wings of the *Shekhinah.*

The penitent one who does *teshuvah* undergoes a similar experience. When a Jew sins, he banishes the Holy One, blessed be He, from his presence. Desecrating the Sabbath, eating forbidden foods, illicit sexual relationships—all set an iron curtain between man and God. At first man may not sense what has happened, he may not realize what has actually occurred, just as one fails to grasp the horrible tragedy of the death of someone dear. Only after the initial excitement, after the *shiva* (seven day period of mourning) or the *shloshim* (first thirty days after death) have passed, does one feel the loss, does one sense that one's home has been destroyed and the most intimately precious part in one's life is no more.

This happens to anyone who has lost someone dear to him. The same thing applies in the spiritual realm when God has departed from man in the wake of his sins. At times the loss may be felt right after the *shiva,* but occasionally thirty or forty years pass before one finally senses the emptiness and the void. Mourning by the sinner over his separation from the Holy One, blessed be He, is like mourning over the death of a beloved mother or father. It may come late, but come it must. Nothing can hold it back when it does.

Then comes the fear and loneliness, the estrangement and alienation. The emptiness of life becomes devastating and a deep sadness clutches at the soul. Only the intimacy with God that man attains while standing in prayer sustains joy in life, gives man a ray of hope. Without it, "the earth is given into the hand of the wicked" (Job 9:23).

No matter how old he is and what stage he has reached in life, a Jew begins to long again for the Master of the universe, in the same way as Rav Ada bar Ahava longed for his master and I long for my wife. But while our longings are a fantasy, since one who has died will never return, longing for the Master of the universe is realistic, and man is drawn to Him and rushes toward Him with all his strength.

He runs faster than he used to before he strayed afar. The intensity of the longing that bursts forth after having been pent up for so long impels him forward. For example, were I actually to see my father, would I not run after him as fast as light itself? So, too, the sinner who has repented runs after the Creator, with all his might and strength, in a storm and in torment; his whole being is sucked in and drawn upward towards the Infinite.

This impulsion of longing raises the individual who has repented to a level above that of the thoroughly righteous man. He has not forgotten his sin—he must not forget it. Sin is the generating force, the springboard which pushes him higher and higher. For such a person, repentance does not mean a clean break with the past, but rather continuity; for him the Holy One, blessed be He, does not "overlook sin" but "bears sin and iniquity."

There is another reason why a repentant sinner is greater than a truly righteous man. The Kabbalists (and the psychologists agree with them) say that two forces repose in the soul of man, constructive forces and destructive forces. Love is a constructive force. Standing opposed to it, jealousy and hatred are destructive forces. The Torah enjoins us to nurture and develop the constructive spiritual forces within us: "Love thy neighbor as thyself"; "Despise not . . . Desire not"; "May the Lord show you mercy"; etc. The positive forces are by and large static and passive in nature, while the negative forces are dynamic and aggressive.

This should be obvious to everybody. Compare, for example, love and hate. A lover is much more passive and much slower to react than one who hates. What won't a person who hates do in order to hurt the object of his passion! Neither rain nor sleet nor snow will deter him from an opportunity to do harm to his enemy, but a friend who is called to a meeting on behalf of someone he loves will often find an excuse to stay at home and will claim that it is either too hot or too cold or that he can't leave his wife alone at home. That is the nature of love which is far less aggressive than hate. Hate is stronger than love, jealousy is more powerful than endearment. Hate is more emotional and more volatile than love. The destructive forces are stronger than the constructive forces.

A thoroughly righteous man is not given to feelings of hatred or jealousy; he is distinguished by natural feelings of love and mercy and kindness. These feelings often lack force and spirit. But a man who has sinned and has repented may be able—if he proves worthy—to utilize the dynamism of the forces of evil which had enveloped him before and elevate them, and to make them operate on behalf of the forces of good.

The very same hunger and zest which drove him to do evil and sin can be utilized to do good and observe the precepts.

The very same eagerness and dedication with which he invested his labors in order to make money illicitly, he can now invest in the labor of charity and in doing deeds of loving-kindness.

By sinning, he discovered new spiritual forces within his soul, a reservoir of energy, of stubbornness and possessiveness whose existence he had not been aware of before he sinned. Now he has the capacity to sanctify these forces and to direct them upward. The aggression which he has discovered in himself will not allow him to be satisfied with the standards by which he used to measure his good deeds before he sinned; it will rather push him nearer and closer to the Throne of Glory.

When one reaches the exalted level of elevating evil, one can no longer say, "and this is my acquittal"; one can no longer say, "I have brought my sacrifice, I have made a break with the past and now I am a different person." No, I am not a different person, I am not starting anew; I am continuing onward, I am sanctifying evil and raising it to new heights.

This, indeed, was the power of the High Priest on the Day of Atonement, and it was this that gave him the strength not only to pray but also to command: "Oh, acquit us!" He did not say, "And this is my acquittal," and begin things anew. Rather, he cited Scripture itself to support his position: "As it is written in the Torah of Moses Thy servant . . . 'Before the Lord, be you cleansed!' " We have the capacity, on this day, to cleanse ourselves and uplift ourselves to great heights, to the Throne of Glory itself. Is there anyone who will dare to bar our way?

"The Day of Atonement is the time of repentance for everyone, for the individual as well as for the multitude; it is the goal of the penitential season, appointed unto Israel for pardon and forgiveness" (Laws of Repentance, Chapter 2, Section 7). The repentance of the Day of Atonement is the repentance of uplifting and exalting sin. "And in His temple everything saith, Glory" (Psalm 29:9), said the Psalmist. "This is the incense of the Day of Atonement" was how our Sages homiletically interpreted this verse. And the verse immediately preceding it states: "The voice of the Lord maketh the hinds to calve and strippeth the forest bare." On the Day of Atonement, the Holy One, blessed be He, demands of man that he strip the forest bare, that he take his life in his hand and enter the jungle of his soul where the animal that is in man hides out. God does not ask man to cut down the trees or to uproot the entire jungle. The world needs jungles just as it needs irrigated fields and beds of flowers. Jungles contain much that is vital and essential; in the depths of the wild a healthy aggressiveness prevails, but woe to the forest through which the voice of the Lord does not penetrate, the voice which makes the hinds calve and strips the forests bare. Our desire is not to destroy the trees, and we do not aim to burn down the jungles but to turn them to the voice of God! And after that has been achieved: "And in His temple everything saith, Glory—This is the incense of the Day of Atonement." What is incense? A mixture of galbanum and odoriferous spices. Why is it necessary to adulterate the odoriferous spices with foul-smelling galbanum? So as to demonstrate that it is possible to take something evil and mix it with good spices and, as a result, not only does the galbanum not detract from the sweet smell of the incense, but this mixture of good and bad actually enhances and augments its fragrance. On the Day of Atonement, incense is burned in the innermost sanctum of the Temple, and on that very day evil ascends to the Holy of Holies—it is not erased by Him who "overlooks sin" but is sanctified and purified by the elevation of sin.

On the Day of Atonement we are not bidden to tear out pages from the Book of Life or from the history of man. Man is not required to cover-up and conceal the bad years, the years of sin; rather he has the capacity to sanctify and purify them. Do we not pray to God: "Pardon our iniquities on this Day of Atonement; blot out and remove our transgressions and sins from Thy sight, as it is said: 'It is I who blot out your transgressions, for My sake; I will remember your sins no more' "? We thus begin with a prayer for annihilating evil, for blotting out iniquities and remembering them no more. But further on, a second idea is expressed in this very same prayer, the idea that repentance in which sin is annihilated is not enough: "And it is said: 'For the virtue of this very day shall acquit you of sin, to cleanse you, before God: be you cleansed' "—that is, uplifting and exalting sin. By means of repentance, one can rise and at the same time raise evil to such heights that it may even, together with the incense, enter into the Holy of Holies.

This, then, was the prayer, the command of the High Priest: "Before God, be you cleansed!" It was as if he had declared: Be not satisfied with "He who overlooks sin." Cast your eyes upward towards "He who bears sin and iniquity." It is true that the goal of the sacrificial ritual is to achieve acquittal, to blot out evil and obliterate it. Nevertheless, the goal of the whole service of the Day of Atonement is purification, which is why the High Priest does not say meekly, "And this is my acquittal" as does the individual in making confession upon his sacrifice. Instead the High Priest demands, loudly and clearly: "Oh, grant us acquittal!"

# EXPIATION, SUFFERING AND REDEMPTION

Let us now deal with two further aspects of repentance and begin by discussing the concept of suffering which is an integral part of the process of repentance.

The Talmud, in Tractate Yoma, tells us: "Rabbi Matiah Ben Harash asked Rabbi Elazar Ben Azariah in Rome: 'Have you heard of Rabbi Ishmael's fourfold distinction between the types of expiation?' He replied: 'There are, in fact, only three, and repentance is required for each one of them.' " This means that it is impossible to achieve expiation unless it is linked to the act of repentance. This applies to all of the different orders of expiation.

Rabbi Ishmael defined the three types of expiation as follows: (A) "If a man transgresses against a positive commandment, and repents, he is immediately pardoned, as it is written (Jeremiah 3:22): 'Return, ye backsliding children.' " In this case, where there has been a transgression against a positive commandment, repentance is efficacious immediately and there is no need for any waiting period. (B) "If a man transgresses against a negative commandment, and repents, his repentance affords him a suspension of sentence and then the Day of Antonement affords him expiation, as it is written (Leviticus 16:30): 'For the virtue of that day shall acquit you of sin to cleanse you.' " In other words, repentance affords a suspension, postpones the imposing of a penalty until the Day of Atonement and the "virtue of that day" affords expiation. (C) "If a man transgresses against commandments punishable by the divine or judicial death penalty, and then repents, this repentance and the Day of Atonement afford him a suspension of punishment and suffering purges him *(memarkin),* as it is written (Psalm 89:32): 'Then will I visit their transgression with the rod, and their iniquity with stripes.' " In the case of such grave transgressions, it is suffering that brings about purgation and completes the process of atonement. Thus we encounter the use of the grammatical root *mrk* meaning "scouring" and "expunging." When one makes a utensil *kosher* after it has been defiled, it undergoes *merika* (the process of scouring). That which was absorbed by the utensil is expunged by scouring it. (In simple Yiddish the process of scouring or *merika* is called *kasheren,* meaning to make *kosher.*) It is suffering that scours and "makes *kosher*"; suffering is what consummates the process of expiation of sin. As it is written: "Then will I visit their transgression with the rod, and their iniquity with stripes"—meaning that for a crime and a transgression one must pay, in some cases, by being whipped or by suffering punishment inflicted by the rod. These are the three types of expiation. To them one must add: "Concerning one who is guilty of desecration of the Divine Name, repentance does not afford suspension, neither does the Day of Atonement afford expiation, nor does suffering cleanse. In this case, all three together afford suspension, and only death can bring purgation."

This distinction in the Talmud between the different types of expiation provides the basis for Section 4, Chapter 1 of the Laws of Repentance: "Though repentance affords expiation for everything and the Day of Atonement expiates as well, transgressions divide into those for which there is immediate expiation and those that require a passage of time for expiation to be granted. How is this so? A man transgressed against a positive commandment, and so on." And here Maimonides elaborates upon the different types of expiation offered in the Talmud in the name of Rabbi Ishmael. But instead of using the term "suffering cleanses *(memarkin),*" Maimonides employs a different phrase. He writes on this point: "And the suffering he undergoes completes *(gomrin)* his expiation." Furthermore, Maimonides adds: "And he cannot receive complete expiation until he is visited with suffering, as it is written: 'Then will I visit their transgression with the rod, and their iniquity with stripes.' "

Maimonides' phrasing raises a number of questions. To begin with, why did he replace the original Talmudic usage of *merika* (scouring, purgation) with *gemira* (completion, consummation) of expiation? Secondly, it is unclear why he repeats: "And he can never obtain complete expiation until suffering comes upon him." Just before this he enumerated the different types of expiation—expiatory repentance, conditional repentance, the act of repentance followed by the Day of Atonement which suspends the sentence and suffering which comes upon him and completes the expiation. And his sins can never be atoned for "until suffering comes upon him." What reservation is he making here, or what is he adding to what has already been said? And why, indeed, does he indicate precisely "until suffering *comes upon him*" rather than "until he undergoes suffering"? Similarly, why does he use different kinds of terminology? It seems to me that Maimonides wished to make another point in this addendum, and we are called upon to make an attempt to discover his meaning.

Let us put aside Maimonides for a moment and return to the Talmudic passage dealing with the distinction between the types of expiation. It states that without suffering expiation is not possible for those grave transgressions which are punishable by the divine or the judicial death penalty. Such transgressions include the violation of the Sabbath, incest, prohibitions regarding food and the eating of animal blood, fasting on the Day of Atonement, and so on. I must confess that whenever I studied this passage in Tractate Yoma I was stricken with fear, for the Almighty does not grant expiation for grave transgressions unless suffering is endured. In the words of Maimonides, "such sins can *never* be expiated." And when, on the Day of Atonement, we confess our sins we recount in the *Al Het* a great number of grave transgressions, punishable by the divine or the judicial death penalty, transgressions inexpiable by the Day of Atonement. Rather, the virtue of the Day affords "suspension" of sentence, but we do not know for how long this suspension will be in force nor what the scope of the suffering we may be destined to endure is *going to be.* It is possible, God help us, that the amount of suffering it may be necessary to undergo to deserve expiation of grave transgressions which are by no means rare occurrences is limitless.

Moreover, if the Day of Atonement does not afford expiation of grave transgressions, which are perhaps the majority of the sins we commit, but suffices only to afford us a "suspension of sentence," what then is the meaning of the following passage: "For the virtue of this very day shall acquit you of your sins to cleanse you"? How is it possible even to speak of acquittal and purification when the sentence for these transgressions has only been "suspended" and expiation has not yet been granted?

True, the Day of Atonement "suspends sentence," and without the Day of Atonement even suffering would not suffice to achieve purgation. But what is the meaning of the phrase "suspends sentence"? What, in fact, does the Day of Atonement accomplish? In what way does this day anticipate the expiation which will be achieved later through suffering?

## *Of Pardon and Forgiveness*

When speaking specifically of expiation afforded by the Day of Atonement, we are referring to two things. First, in relation to punishment, the Day of Atonement affords expiation in the sense of "reducing sentence." The Day of Atonement, therefore, is a day of commuting sentences or of the reduction of the amount of suffering. As the Sages of the Kabbala put it: On the Day of Atonement severe judgment (*din kasheh*) is replaced by mild judgment (*dina rafie*); the measure of grace takes the place of the measure of strict justice. The Sages of the Kabbala interpret the passage (Genesis 22:9) "and (Abraham) bound Isaac his son, and laid him on the altar upon the wood" as meaning that the measure of grace represented by Abraham binds and constrains the measure of strict judgment, symbolized as the "Fear of Isaac" (Genesis 31:42). So far we have touched on one aspect of the expiation afforded by the Day of Atonement, that of pardon (*mehila*), which brings remission or a reduction of sentence.

Pardon (*mehila*) is a concept that does not pertain only to sin and to the Day of Atonement. It is a juridical concept and has application in the area of civil law as well. When a man is in debt to a friend who "excuses" him by waiving repayment of all or part of the debt, then the debtor is released from the bondage or obligation under which he labored until that act of "pardon" (*mehila*). Such is the case regarding the pardon that is conferred by the Day of Atonement. A man transgresses, incurring guilt, and the Day of Atonement affords him a remission of sentence.

However, in addition to conferment of pardon, the Day of Atonement also contains the element of forgiveness and expiation. This is because transgression not only requires a suitable punishment, it also defiles and damages the sinner's soul. It causes a deformation of man's spiritual make-up and severs the sinner from the source of his God-given vitality and spirit, as it is written: "But your iniquities have separated you and your God" (Isaiah 59:2). On the Day of Atonement the Almighty pardons man, releasing him from his obligations and freeing him from the bondage linking sin and punishment. But still this pardon does not clear man's soul of the corruption which has infected the essence of his being. The soul remains in a state of alienation from the Lord of the Universe. It is the function of repentance to purify the personality, to renew it and to restore its *status quo ante*, prior to the sin, to re-establish relations between man and the Almighty. This is not pardon (*mehila*) but forgiveness (*seliha*); it is a process which cleanses and sanctifies the metaphysical dimension of the personality. Not only the act of pardon, but forgiveness as well, is contingent upon the grace of the Day of Atonement, as it is written: "For the virtue of that day shall acquit you of your sins to cleanse you; before the Lord be you cleansed."

Pardon, therefore, means the remission of punishment, in the same way as release is from a debt. The Day of Atonement possesses the unique characteristic of commuting sentences, as the divine quality of loving-kindness overcomes the quality of strict justice, as in the case of "and (Abraham) bound Isaac his son" (Genesis 22:9). This motif is central to the prayers of Rosh Hashana which focus on the trial of Abraham's faith (the binding of Isaac). This is also true of the afternoon prayer on the Day of Atonement in which all the liturgies touch upon this trial of Abraham's faith.

Legally speaking, the Almighty is by no means committed to granting anyone pardon. According to the law, a creditor is not called upon to release his debtors from their obligations of repayment, nor is he in any way required to do so. It is only the intervention of the quality of mercy and its ascendancy, on the Day of Atonement, which renders pardon possible. The Day of Atonement is, therefore, a day of divine grace.

On the Day of Atonement, more than on Rosh Hashana, we discern the mystical significance of the *Akeda* "and (Abraham) bound Isaac his son, and laid him on the altar upon the wood." The Day of Atonement, in addition to being a day of pardon, is also a day for purification.

The word "pardon" (*mehila*) does not appear in the Bible save, perhaps, for one place, where it is written (Deuteronomy 32:18): "and hast forgotten God that formed thee (*meholelekha*)." Our sages (*Sifrei Ha'azinu,* paragraph 319) interpreted this homiletically as meaning "a God Who pardons you for all your transgressions." The Bible used the phrase *kapara* (atonement, acquittal, expiation), instead of *mehila* (pardon). "For the virtue of the day shall acquit you," meaning pardon from punishment and commuting of sentences. Loving-kindness takes precedence over strict justice and the transgression is expiated—that is to say, pardon is granted. But, clearly, the erasure of the transgression does not signify the soul's purification or its return to the *status quo ante.* For this is another function of the Day of Atonement which not only affords pardon and expiation but also purifies and bestows forgiveness. "Lord Who pardons and forgives our sins," it is written. Why the dual usage? This is because of the two elements which characterize the Day of Atonement. "Pardons"—that is, commutes sentences, releases from obligation and bondage; "forgives"—that is, brings absolution and restores the soul to its original state. We do not declaim "Lord Who pardons and forgives and expiates"—for pardon and expiation are used synonymously. "Pardons" and "forgives" are, in the terminology of the Torah, parallel to "acquits" and "purifies."

## *A Trace of Something ("Mashehu")*

How are sentences commuted? What is involved in this process? It remains a mystery. Though we cannot fully comprehend it, we are not exempt from making an effort to understand something about it and, at the same time, to learn more about the quality of the Day of Atonement. It is exaltingly expressed in the Day's liturgies, beginning with those of Rabbi Eliezer Hakalir which, I believe, best capture the mood of the Day's sanctity. The Sephardi prayerbook does not contain Hakalir's liturgies. It has other profound, well-composed and splendid liturgies by Rabbi Yehuda Halevi and Rabbi Abraham ben Ezra, but these lack the passionate feeling for the sanctity of the Day which erupts and flows from those of Rabbi Hakalir and Rabbi Simeon Hagadol (even though their form is relatively imperfect). The closer I study the liturgies of the Day of Atonement the more I become convinced of their well-planned arrangement. Far from being included through chance selection they are integrated into a system geared to conveying and transmitting the fiery sanctity of the Day of Atonement. I turn to these liturgies when attempting to understand the nature of the Day of Atonement and its many dimensions. I shall try to explain their significance in halakhic terms.

I believe that pardon, acquittal, forgiveness and the release from obligations vouchsafed by the quality of mercy of the "King Who gives pardon" (*melekh mohel*) on the Day of Atonement operate through three principles:

(A) The element of a "trace of something," the principle of reduction (*tsimtsum*). The origin of a "trace of something" in the Bible is found in Psalm 147:5: "Great is our Lord, and of great power. His understanding is infinite."

(B) The element of redemption (*pidyon*) or substitution and exchange. Its scriptural origin is in Genesis 22:13: "And

Abraham went and took the ram, and offered him up for a burnt offering in the stead of his son."

(C) The element of the lottery, of chance. Its origin is in Leviticus 16:8: "And Aaron shall cast lots upon the two goats—one lot for the Lord, and the other lot for the scapegoat (*le'Azazel*)."

These are the three principles according to which the Lord of the Universe commutes sentences; through them is fulfilled the phenomenon of Abraham binding his son Isaac "on the altar upon the wood" and the quality of mercy succeeds in constraining the quality of strict judgment.

What is the element of a "trace of something" (*mashehu*)? In Judaism the *mashehu*, the small minor detail, the quantitatively unimportant factor, can be immeasurably significant. Anyone who has studied the *Shulhan Arukh* (Code of Jewish Law) knows that a trace or particle of something forbidden mixed with something a thousand and even a million times greater can sometimes suffice to contaminate the whole. A trace of *hametz*, unleavened bread, which falls into a large cauldron of sauce, on Passover, disqualifies the whole. This rule applies, as well, to the produce from which tithes and priestly dues have not yet been set aside, to idolatry, and in general to those things "which are permitted under other circumstances" when they become mixed with substances of like kind. In relation to these, a trace of leaven, a particle of produce from which the priestly tithes have not been removed, a drop of forbidden wine, suffices to spoil vast quantities to which it is added. Generally, in a mixture which is allowed under other circumstances, a particle of something does not defile the whole except when there is an admixture of like substances (the exception to this is that a trace of leaven on Passover renders forbidden a mixture even of unlike substances). And the question arises: that small forbidden grain which defiles or that tiny drop of idolatrously used wine which got mixed in is not dissimilar in appearance, in size or in taste from a thousand other particles of grain or from a drop of any other wine. Why, then, shouldn't such a particle or drop, submerged or diluted in a far vaster quantity of the substance, lose its separate identity and be neutralized? There is no adequate explanation for this, but the conclusion that must be drawn from this law is that the Torah has never been impressed by large quantities, great numbers, or enormously huge objects. Had the Torah been affected by numbers and size—then the Lord of the Universe would not have selected *Knesset Israel* as His chosen people. "The Lord did not set His love upon you, nor choose you, because you were more in number than any people, for you were the fewest of all people. . . ." That which is small and seemingly insignificant is just as important in the eyes of the Lord of the Universe as the great, and powerful.

Perhaps that is the explanation of the passage (Psalm 147:4–5) which we say each day in our prayers: "He counteth the number of the stars; he calleth them all by their names. Great is our Lord, and of great power: His understanding is infinite." Why does it say "His understanding is infinite (*ein mispar*)" and not "His understanding is endless or limitless"? It appears that the passage should be interpreted as follows: The Almighty sets the number of stars, He arranges the order of the stars in the solar system and He rules over the mighty and innumerable heavenly constellations. He Himself is infinite, great and ominipotent, and yet "His understanding is infinite" (literally, His wisdom hath no number), meaning that in His boundless understanding and for His omniscient and all-encompassing wisdom, numbers have no significance. The Creator of the Universe Who brought forth 310 enormous worlds, millions of stars, giant solar systems which stretch across fantastic spaces measurable in millions of light years—it is possible to believe that He prefers magnitude, vastness and power; for "Great is our Lord, and of great prowess." On the contrary, it is rather, from His viewpoint, that "His wisdom" is immeasurable (i.e., not affected by numbers), meaning that large numbers are of no significance to Him. In His eyes the small grain, the minute particle can possess just as much importance as do enormous astronomical systems. Providence does not defer to quantity. And it is because of this that "one grain of wheat redeems the whole heap (T.B., Hullin 1376). The Torah commands man to set aside a portion of his crop for the *kohanim*—the priests. Seemingly, this would appear to mean that man must offer up a substantial contribution, something proportionate to the size of his heap of grain. But the law is that even if the heap of grain was sufficient to fill a threshing floor, the offering of a single grain was considered sufficient to fulfill one's formal obligation. (In truth, the Sages determined that one part in forty or one part in fifty or one part in sixty should be given.) And it is noteworthy that in the Talmud the reasoning which applies to the ruling that "one grain of wheat redeems the whole heap" is also valid to the problem of "mixing." That single grain of wheat, if it is from the pile from which tithes and priestly dues have not yet been set aside (*tevel*), and it is mixed with the balance of the produce that has been tithed (*holin*), renders the whole heap violate. (From the Talmud it appears that the power of a single grain to spoil does not stem from the rule applying to "substances permissible under the circumstances," but from a separate and specific law, and this is what Maimonides rules as well in the "Laws of Forbidden Foods.") Just as one grain of wheat is sufficient to release a whole heap from the obligation of the heave-offering, thereby annulling the status of the whole heap as one from which tithes have not yet been set aside, so it lies within the power of a single grain to render forbidden a whole heap of wheat. But in truth this law of a "trace of something" is relevant to us now only as an analogy, so that we may expand this concept to encompass the morality of Judaism and man's responsibilities to his Creator.

In Judaism, it is not only the great heroic deed that is considered important—a fate so wondrous in the eyes of all that future generations will be filled with awe ruminating upon how a man could attain such a high level of utter dedication as, say, when Abraham prepared to sacrifice Isaac. Judaism does not stand only upon heroic pinnacles such as the *Akeda*, but just as much is it founded upon simple, day-to-day deeds. Anyone who studies the Talmudic chapter dealing with "the hiring of workmen" in Tractate Baba Metzia (86b) will see how enthusiastically Abraham our forefather greeted the three angels who appeared before him in the guise of wayfarers. Abraham bestirred himself wholeheartedly in order to observe the commandment of offering hospitality toward the three anonymous wayfarers. And in return for this simple commandment which was observed by our forefather Abraham, the people of Israel were amply rewarded—so it is stated in the Talmud—with the Manna, the pillar of cloud, with Miriam's well and so on. This deed of Abraham's was not an heroic act. Rather, it was a straightforward demonstration of humanity expressed through hospitality toward wanderers.

Indeed, sometimes a simple manifestation of human kindness, a display of decency toward people, stands on the same plane as a dramatically courageous act. The homily (in *Midrash Rabba* to the Book of Lamentations) concerning the attempts of our ancestors to plead with the Almighty to spare the Temple from destruction is justly famous. Abraham presented one argument, Isaac advanced another; the Patriarch Jacob, our teacher Moses and the Prophet Jeremiah all offered arguments and pressed their claims with the Almighty. But God did not accede to their pleas until Rachel came forward. She alone succeeded in eliciting a positive response, expressed in the verses which we read on the second day of Rosh Hashana: "Weep no more and wipe the tears from your eyes, for you shall be rewarded for your deeds and your sons will be reinstated in their Land." Why was Rachel, rather than Abraham or Moses or the rest of our illustrious forefathers, thus privileged? Indeed Abraham and Isaac both presented the argument of the "*Akeda* of Isaac"—and what greater act of heroism and supreme dedication could be posited? Our mentor Moses, savior of Israel, loyal servant of God—who could be expected to intercede with the Almighty more effectively than he? And the same applies to the rest of our ancestors. But it was the pleas of Rachel that bore fruit. Why was that so? Because Rachel had aided her elder sister, and had signaled Leah to precede her in marriage to Jacob. This act of compassion toward an unfortunate sister is what carried weight and stood the test of time, more so than all the intrepid acts of valor, such as the "sacrifice of Isaac" and the many other heroic deeds of our ancestors.

This exemplifies Judaism's evaluation of deeds. Sometimes the small, modest, unseen act, the seemingly insignificant deed, unnoticed and hardly discernible, is precisely the one which fills a higher place than great and renowned heroism.

It is possible, I believe, to enlarge upon this halakhic concept of a "trace of something" found in relation to the laws of the ritually permissible and prohibited to encompass problems of the civil law as well. Here, too, a "trace" or "particle of something" has a decisive importance.

Resh Lakish's ruling (Sanhedrin 8a), based upon the verse, "Ye shall hear the small and the great alike" (Deuteronomy 1:17), is well-known: "That indicates that you must be as concerned with a lawsuit concerning one *perutah* as with a suit concerning a hundred *mina*." The Talmud's question there is interesting: "For what practical purpose is this laid down? If it is to urge the need to give equal consideration and investigation, is this not self-evident?" That is, the judge must devote as much thought to a case concerning a penny as to that concerning a hundred, and must adjudicate as truthfully. But this, says the Talmud, is self-evident and would not call for a specific biblical verse. The Talmud then answers: "[The meaning is] that the case must be given due priority, if it should be first in order." The quotation was needed in order to demonstrate that judges must not give precedence to cases involving a sum of one hundred to those cases involving a mere penny; if a case involving a mere penny comes up first it must be dealt with prior to one concerning a sum of millions, and judgment must not be deferred until afterward.

The Hatam Sopher points out that when Jethro proposed to Moses that he lighten the burden of his magistracy, he said (Exodus 18:22): "And it shall be, that every great matter they shall bring unto thee, but every small matter they shall judge." But when Moses accepted Jethro's advice (Exodus 18:26) and, also, when Moses repeated the story in Deuteronomy 1:17), he changed the phraseology of Jethro's proposal and instead of "every *great* matter" he inserted: "The *hard* cases they brought unto Moses." This, says Hatam Sopher, characterizes the difference between Jethro's attitude to law and that of Moses. Jethro believed that when there was a dispute between two people "in a small matter," involving a small sum, there was no need to bother Moses with it. It was sufficient, Jethro felt, that the "leaders of tens" deal with it. Moses should sit in judgment only when great sums were involved. This is the attitude of a gentile who says: "Every great matter they shall bring unto thee." And to this day, in fact, gentiles have claims courts for dealing with cases involving minor sums. But in Moses' view it was not the sum under contention which determined the importance of a case but rather the problem of law which was at issue. If the law was direct and clear, even if the case involved the sum of a million dollars, then lower courts should adjudicate in the matter, he believed. But if it was "a hard case," and complex, then it should be "brought before me," even if it involved a single penny. The amount of money at stake played no part in determining the importance of the case. One can discern in this halakhic principle additional far-reaching implications. It is well known that in the Halakha there is the concept of "money purchase" (*kinyan keseph*). Concerning movable goods there is a controversy between Rabbi Yohanan, who says that according to Torah law purchase occurs with the transfer of money, and Resh Lakish, who says that "pulling"—gaining possession—is what constitutes the transfer of ownership according to the Torah. However, regarding real estate all agree that ownership changes with the transfer of money. How much money must the buyer give the seller in order to gain right to a piece of land? The whole price? Most of it? Half of it? The law is that a single coin changing hands is sufficient to establish the purchase. If a man buys a multi-storied skyscraper worth fifty million dollars and hands over a single penny to the seller, then he has gained rights of possession to it. Though there is a controversy between the authors of the *Turei Zahav* and *Sefer Meirat Einayim* (commentaries on the *Shulhan Arukh*) as to whether the penny is from the price itself and thus when the remainder is paid the buyer can deduct it from the fifty million dollars and pay the price minus one penny, or whether the penny was paid only to gain possession and the price must afterward be paid in full. Either way, the penny is what establishes the purchase.

It is quite certain that this ruling concerns only transactions that take place between two Jews. In regard to the purchase of real estate from gentiles, the purchase is not finalized until the whole price is paid; the transfer of a penny does not conclude the sale. The Tosafot in Tractate Kiddushin (14b; cf.

Ho'il) state that according to Rabbenu Tam, "a pagan cannot purchase real property by [the transfer of] a deed. This is because in the chapter, '*Hezkat Habatim*' (in Tractate Baba Batra 54b), it is stated that the moment a pagan receives the monies, he removes himself." Rabbenu Tam's ruling is based upon the fact that the Talmud uses the term "monies" (*zuzei*) rather than "money" (*kesef*), and from this he inferred that what was meant was the sale price in full.

Support for this position may be found in another passage in Tractate Kiddushin (16a): "Whence do we know that property is acquired by money? Hezekiah said: Scripture says (Jeremiah 32:4–4): 'Man shall buy fields with money.' " In this connection, the Tosafot (cf. *amar*) ask why Hezekiah did not cite the verse about Ephron (Genesis 23:16): "And Abraham weighed to Ephron the silver." And the Tosafot responded: Because in discussing Abraham's transaction with Ephron we are speaking about a Jew purchasing something from a gentile, while the passage "men shall buy fields for money" in Jeremiah refers to a Jew buying from another Jew, i.e., Jeremiah purchasing from his uncle, Hanam'el. In Abraham's negotiations with Ephron a money purchase does take place when the buyer hands over the entire sum of money: "And Abraham weighed to Ephron the silver . . . four hundred shekels of silver." However in the case of a Jew buying from a fellow Jew, a single penny transferred suffices to legalize the transaction, even when the property in question is worth a million.

It appears that this also applies to the relation between the sentence a man serves and the penalty he actually deserves for committing a particular sin. Just as a piece of real estate worth so many thousands can be negotiated by the transfer of a single penny, so the Almighty, when collecting a "debt," sometimes makes do with a single penny, a "particle" of the whole sentence. The Almighty does not insist that man pay the entire sum but can make do with a small nominal part of the fine, even with a tiny fraction of it, with perhaps only a penny of the total.

### *An Halakhic Element in the Reduction of Sentence*

The idea of the "trace" or "particle of something," which serves as the basis for a number of specific laws, is the first of the three elements necessary for the process of "commuting sentences" carried out on the Day of Atonement. And when one refers to "pardon" (*meḥila*), it does not imply a cancellation of the entire debt incurred by committing grave transgressions. It means that man is released from his debt, save for that "particle" which he is under obligation to render up. The measure of mercy, as it were, allows him to forego the money purchase of Ephron, about which it is written: "And Abraham weighed to Ephron the silver . . . four hundred shekels of silver," which was the entire purchase price, for a transaction along the lines of Jeremiah's acquisition of fields, which was effected by the payment of a single penny.

Man is too weak, his life too short, to pay all of his debts in full. So the Almighty makes do with the nominal payment of a single penny.

Expiation through suffering is tied up with the principle of a money transaction in yet another way. The sinner owes something to the Almighty because he stole from Him; God is the Master of the Universe, and the earth and all that fills it is the Almighty's. Not only is He the Creator of the Universe, He is also Master of everything in it, including man. Thus we say and plead in the *selihot*, the penitential prayers: "The soul is Yours and the body Your making, the soul is Yours and the body is Yours as well." Everything in this world belongs to Him. Man's powers are, so to speak, "on loan" or temporarily leased to him by God. God endows man with life for a certain period of time—for seventy years, eighty years, or for forty years; He allows man ownership over himself for the allotted period. This ownership of man by himself is utilized by him in a number of ways: through free choice, through the exercise of his intellectual powers, through his potential ability to create, and so on. By sinning, man loses the rights and privileges that were given to him.

At the conclusion of the Day of Atonement, in the *Nei'la* prayer, we say: "You extend Your hand to transgressors and Your right arm is outstretched to receive repentant sinners; You have taught us, O Lord our God, to confess our transgressions before Thee, so that we might cease from the thievery of our hands." One may well wonder: Is stealing the one and only sin for which the Jew brings himself before the Almighty and knocks on the gates of mercy and pardon, at the conclusion of the Day of Atonement? For aside from theft, all in all, another forty-four transgressions are enumerated in the *Al Het* confessional prayers! Why is theft singled out with special emphasis in the *Nei'la* service?

The fact is that "theft" actually encompasses all kinds of sin. With every sin he commits, the Jew foregoes his rights of possession over his own life. A Jew who studies for intellectual enjoyment is utilizing his power of wisdom which belongs to the Almighty, and is only temporarily placed at his disposal. The moment this intelligence is contaminated by impure intentions, man's rights to this God-given attribute expires, and any further exercise of it is seen as a form of theft. The same applies to all the other transgressions which can deprive man of ownership and the right to use his own physical and spiritual faculties. Through sin man destroys his right to life with his own hands. Through sin man foregoes his right to control the physical forces which vitalize his body. And when he goes on living a life of sin, it is an act of outright theft and extortion.

When a man repents and regrets his sinful acts, it is as if a new transaction had taken place and the contract of ownership has been renewed between him and the Creator. Henceforward he will not be living by extortion. What sort of transaction is it that takes place? It is similar to a money transaction, which is the only type of purchase applicable in sacred matters as well. In the first instance, man receives his life from the Almighty as a gift, upon birth, but after sinning he foregoes his rights of ownership. A gift is never made twice, especially when it was originally accompanied by certain contractual conditions which man failed to fulfill, abusing what he received in good faith. From now on, he must *purchase* the rights to his life. The payment man makes to the Lord of the Universe then takes the form of suffering and hardship endured as a result of his sins.

It will also be understood, in the light of this assumption, why Rabbi Ishmael ruled that man pays in the coin of suffering only for transgressions which entail the divine or the judicial death penalty. Why is there no need for "purging of suffering" for transgressions which entail the punishment of stripes? Perhaps it is because it is written: "Then I will visit their transgression with the rod, and their iniquity with stripes." But it does not state explicitly what sin is referred to in this context. How do Rabbi Ishmael and Rabbi Elazar ben Azariah know that only grave transgressions, entailing the divine or the judicial death penalty, are the subject of what is spoken of here? In light of what we have said the matter is clear: the punishments of divine or judicial execution are a concrete expression of the sinner's loss of his right to lead his own life. The sinner through his deeds loses his right to use the powers he was endowed with by the Almighty. Man is denied the right to use his bodily and spiritual powers in such cases, for after committing a sin, his exercise of them is considered as theft. Justice demands that this theft be returned, or if he wishes to regain his right to exercise these life powers, he may repurchase them, and only then is he allowed to use them again.

A sinner's repentance—especially of one who has succumbed to grave transgressions entailing death and judicial execution—means repossession of what has been lost, regaining rights over oneself, and according to the law of the Torah any such purchase is carried out along the lines of a money transaction. And what type of coin is the sinner obliged to use for repayment? Suffering! And the important question is: What is the exact fee that the Almighty will demand of us? Is the full price to be paid in suffering as in the case of the purchase from Ephron, or does part of it also suffice, as described in Jeremiah?

The answer is that the Lord of the Universe makes do with a token payment as reported in Jeremiah. The Almighty sells man his human attributes and man repurchases them by paying in the coin of suffering of the "penny purchase" variety, a transaction on the "particle" or "trace of something" order.

This is one element revealed by the quality of mercy inherent in the expiation of sins on the Day of Atonement, which is founded upon the halakhic principle of money purchase by payment of a single penny, based on the immeasurable worth of the "trace" or "particle of something." However, sometimes even this "token of suffering" is too much for a man to endure and he is utterly helpless in the face of such punishment. At this point the divine quality of mercy reappears in a second guise: in the element of redemption (*pidyon*) which, in halakhic terms, is the element of purchase by exchange.

### *A Second Halakhic Element: Exchange*

In the light of this approach, which views the suffering immanent in repentance as a form of debt to be paid by man in order to repossess his own persona, it is worth examining one further type of purchase which is similar to a money transaction. It is perhaps the most common form of transaction appearing in halakhic sources. This type of purchase is scripturally anchored in the Book of Ruth (4:7): "Now this was the custom in former times in Israel concerning redeeming and concerning exchanging, for to confirm all things a man drew off his shoe and gave it to his neighbor." This became known as a "scarf purchase" (*kinyan sudar*).

The difference between a money purchase and a "scarf purchase" lies in the fact that in the first case, though not paying the entire sum, one must at least pay a single penny, while in a "scarf purchase" acquisition is achieved without even a penny's worth changing hands. In a money transaction the penny has some monetary value, and it represents, as it were, the actual price which must be paid to finalize the deal. Though the smallest unit of capital, the penny is real money, a "token"of a whole sum as a grain of wheat is a particle of a heap of grain. It is otherwise when dealing with the scarf which is used as the instrument of exchange in a purchase that represents no value and possesses no specific worth of its own. The scarf is not even in the nature of a "particle" of money. It is not in the same category as money; it is totally worthless.

The difference between these two types of purchase is enormous. So long as we demand even a penny we are still working within the framework of the monetary system. The moment we accept something which has no real money value, we have departed from the normative economic system and have entered into the realm of the symbolic. In the purchase which takes place through symbolic exchange of a scarf, the seller receives nothing of value as payment for what he has sold. Nonetheless, the sale is valid and let us not forget that the scarf purchase is perhaps the most effective type of transaction existing in the context of Jewish civil law. It is also the only type of purchase which applies to moveable goods as well as to real estate. This type of purchase creates irrevocable obligations without anything concrete actually being exchanged.

Rabenu Tam distinguished between a purchase by exchange of two valuable goods, such as a cow for a donkey, and a purchase by exchange of something valuable for something devoid of value. In the latter purchase, what is the compensation? Not a single thing. All that the seller receives is a symbolic substitute for the money or object of value. Instead of receiving money, even in its smallest denomination, a single penny, the seller receives something in lieu of money as it was said of the *Akeda* of Isaac: "And Abraham went and took the ram, and offered him up for a burnt offering in the stead of his son" (Genesis 22:13). Is the sacrifice of the ram, indeed, comparable in any way to the sacrifice of Isaac? It certainly is not equivalent, even in a partial sense. Then why was the sacrifice of the ram accepted instead of Isaac? This is due to the divine quality of mercy which is willing to make do with a substitute for the thing itself. This is the basis of the idea of redeeming one thing for something else (*pidyon*).

As the scarf serves as a substitute for money and has only symbolic worth, even though it does not have even a "trace" of money value and is in a different category altogether, so it is regarding the suffering inflicted on the sinner. Were we to rely only on the first element which is founded on money purchase and which demands at least token payment in the currency of suffering, then we might not be able to withstand it. For who knows what a "trace" of suffering in the eyes of the Almighty amounts to, or how severe it could be? The Day of Atonement comes and its measure of mercy and grace reduces the severity of the element of a "particle of something" of money purchase by adding the possibility of exchange—the "scarf transaction." Thus, not only is the amount of suffering diminished on the basis of the "particle of something"; in addition, it is weakened and reduced on the basis of the exchange of the "scarf purchase" (which is worthless in terms of money value). In the first instance, a mere penny will suffice; in the case of the scarf exchange not even a pennyworth is required.

The suffering the sinner has to endure henceforward is merely symbolic as in the biblical examples of "A man removed his shoe and gave it to his friend," or "and he offered him up for a burnt offering in the stead of his son"—the ram offered in place of Isaac.

Let us bring an example that demonstrates this from our own lives. A Jew caused a friend distress by hounding him and persecuting him, and some may even claim that this was done "in the name of heaven," for there are those Jews who self-righteously regard the persecution of other Jews as their holy obligation. Such a Jew spread false rumors and malicious stories about another until the victim fell seriously ill. There is a limit to the persecution a man is able to endure. The victim suffered a heart attack; and our Sages said: (*Vayikra Raba* 26:5) "The Lord will care for the persecuted victim even if he be a wicked man and his tormentors righteous," as in those cases of persecution out of a supposed sense of righteousness. When the Day of Atonement came, the persecutor repented—this does happen sometimes; then one would expect according to heavenly judgment that the persecutor should suffer exactly as much as his victim—that he, too, must be hospitalized with a heart attack and spend eight weeks in bed in an intensive care unit. But the quality of mercy operative on the Day of Atonement comes into play, declaring: he can pay his debt by enduring only a "particle of suffering," not by actually undergoing a heart attack but, say, by being stricken with terrible back pains. In other words, the magnitude of the punishment has been reduced. And then the element of exchange and substitution may come into play and declare: not only must the quantity of the punishment be reduced but its quality, too, must alter. How can the quality of suffering be altered? The element of substitution causes the physical punishment to be replaced by the deep and heartfelt spiritual anguish and pangs of conscience suffered by the penitent, by the travail of discomfort and lack of tranquility. On behalf of the sinner who tormented an innocent man and made him fall ill the divine measure of mercy intercedes and commutes his sentence in the quantitative sense and posits that in place of severe bodily pains the sinner suffer terrible spiritual agony which will really trouble him.

The discomfort which befalls man as punishment can assume a number of forms: he could be hounded by someone, or he could imagine that he is not sufficiently respected and be gnawed by the feeling that society does not give him the recognition he deserves, or he could feel he is not earning as much money as he thinks he should. All these are real ways of suffering, but they do not match the punishment he deserves because of the torment he caused his hounded victim. Here is a case of "and [he] offered him up for a burnt offering in the stead of his son." The ram cannot take Isaac's place. Nonetheless, in a symbolic sense a substitution has been made.

These things are not in the teachings of the Kabbala or of Hassidism. I am a *Mitnaged* (an opponent of Hassidism), and for a *Mitnaged* there is only one source—the Talmud. Everything we have said thus far about the reduction of suffering stemming from the Day of Atonement's measure of mercy is anchored in the Talmud. In Tractate Arkhin (16b) the following question is posed: "What is the limit of suffering?"—meaning: Where is the borderline, the limit of intercession by the measure of loving-kindness in canceling the punishment inflicted on the sinner? Certainly it can protect the sinner by reducing the size of the punishment and by altering its quality—but to what degree? Where is the limit set? "Rabbi Elazar said: for example, one for whom a piece of clothing has been woven and it does not fit him." A man enters a tailor-shop and orders a suit to be made to order. But when he returns to pick it up, it becomes evident that the suit is too tight for him. Here is a case of distress which stems from a useless piece of clothing and a financial loss. According to Rabbi Elazar, therefore, the measure of how large a substitute for actual suffering must be is in the sorrow that can be caused by an ill-fitting suit. "More than this," continues the Talmud, "it can be the way a man feels if the intention was to dish out hot food and he was given it cold." A man enters a restaurant and orders a cup of hot coffee. But the waitress serves it to him cold. This angers him. He swallows the cup down in one gulp and stomps out of the restaurant fuming, without leaving even a small tip. This, according to another opinion, is "the measure of suffering." But according to a further opinion advanced in the Talmud even this is too severe. In this view, the limit of suffering is felt "when a man's gown is turned inside out." A man attempted to put on his gown and mistakenly wore it inside out. He is upset, as he must take it off and put it on again in the proper manner. This distress is a manner of suffering. The Talmud goes on to add a further example: "If a man put his hand in his pocket to extract three coins and it emerged with only two." This, too, is distressing. But the gap between real suffering and this poor substitute for it is immeasurable. It is difficult to describe the boundless benevolence evident in this passage, how much mercy our Sages had in their hearts when they set out to reduce the bitterness of the suffering which man must endure in consequence of sin. For according to the Talmud, there is no sin—especially a grave sin punishable by the divine or the judicial death penalty—which does not entail suffering, so as to purge or to consummate the expiation.

Suffering is necessary, but the Day of Atonement's measure of mercy reduces it. Without this reduction, where would we find the courage and effrontery to ask in the prayer attributed to Rav Himnona ("Lord, seal my tongue") that our sins be purged, "but not by harsh suffering"? Though we refer to the purging of sin through suffering—for without it there is no expiation—yet we ask that we be punished after it has undergone the process of reduction to a "particle of something" and the process of substitution in which the divine quality of loving-kindness has reduced our sentence. The question asked was: What is the minimum? What is necessary, what is the limit to this reduction of suffering? The Scriptures state: "Then will I visit their transgression with the rod, and their iniquity with stripes." What, then, is the least quantity of the rod's application and of the afflictions which are entailed by sin? The answer is that physical suffering is reduced to a minimum, to a "token of it." And even this "particle" can be changed through redeeming it and suffering is only symbolically felt.

This twofold process finds expression in two passages from the Scriptures: "His understanding has no limit," meaning that He can make due with a particle of something instead of the whole thing. A single penny finalizes a purchase.

"And [he] took the ram, and offered him up for a burnt offering in the stead of his son," meaning substitution, redemption, one thing in place of another.

Two passages in the Scriptures, two principles of Halakha: two rules concerning the expiation of sins through the Day of Atonement's divine quality of mercy.

## Suffering and Prayer

These two elements—the reduction of punishment or its substitution by something else—cannot function properly without the third element which must accompany either of them.

We have already mentioned that suffering is the currency in which the sinner pays the Almighty to regain ownership over himself after he repents.

How does one direct payment to the Master of the Universe? I think that we can learn the answer to this from the pre-condition made before the payment of money in a deal between a man and his fellow man. That pre-condition is that the money has to be clearly designated *for making the purchase;* otherwise it does not fulfill any purpose, even if a large sum was handed over and even if it equaled the full value of the goods or land up for sale. In the same manner, when we pay the Almighty through suffering, it must likewise first be designated for making the "purchase" and offered as a form of a sacrifice. For how else do we "give" something up to the Lord except through sacrifices. Thus Abraham offered his son to the Almighty; thus he also took the ram and offered him up as a burnt offering in the stead of his son. Every kind of giving contains the element of sacrifice. And, in truth, when the Temple existed, those punishable by a heavenly or judicial death sentence received expiation only after bringing the required sacrifice. The obligation to offer up sacrifices holds true in our times as well. But since the destruction of the Temple we cannot fulfill our sacrificial obligations as before; suffering takes the place of burnt offerings. The whole institution of *ta'anit* (fasting) is founded on the idea of suffering seen as a form of sacrifice. Thus, the following is related in Tractate Berakhot (17a): "When Rabbi Shashet kept a fast, on concluding his prayer he added the following: 'Lord of the Universe, it is known to You that when the Temple existed if a man sinned he used to offer up a sacrifice, and though all that was offered of it was its fat and blood, his sins were expiated. Now I have kept a fast and my fat and blood have been depleted. May it be Your will to accept the diminution of my fat and blood as if I had sacrificed them to You upon the altar, and that You will favor me.' " If man does not "offer up" his fast as a form of sacrifice, then it cannot be considered valid as a fast. The Day of Atonement, which is the fast day *par excellence*, is therefore seen as a great sacrifice offered up to the Master of the Universe by the entire people of Israel.

This idea is expressed also in the Concluding Prayer of the Day of Atonement when we say: "Endless are the offerings required of us, countless our guilt-sacrifices; but Thou knowest that at the end of our days wait the maggot and the worm; therefore Thou hast abundantly provided us with means of pardon." These are truly wonderful words; we do not always take note of them! The sacrifices we are obliged to offer up are numerous, but the Almighty, through His quality of mercy, "abundantly provided us with means of pardon."

A similar idea is found in the powerfully-phrased penitential-hymn for the Thursday before Rosh Hashana: "In former times the people of Israel would offer up a sacrifice; and even if my sins were scarlet, they were turned wholly white. So for all my years I have lamented the destruction of the Temple, and I have nothing except words for my offering, so I commence my song and make my supplication, asking for my soul as a return for my prayers and for my people, in answer to my plea." Here the identification of fasting with sacrifice is clearly expressed. And this has been similarly stated in Psalm 141:2: "Let my prayer come before Thee as incense; and may the lifting up of my hands be seen as an evening offering." Prayer takes the place of sacrifices because true prayer always involves deep spiritual torment. This idea is beautifully described in *Tania* by the first Rebbe of Lubavitch and in the volume *Sha'arei Hateshuva* ("The Gates of Repentance") written by the "Middle Rebbe" of Lubavitch: how low a man must feel during prayer, and how many tears he sheds over his remoteness from the Creator of the Universe, and how difficult he finds it to draw near to God. According to the teachings of the Kabbala and of Hassidism, and as it also emerges from the Halakha, true prayer is accompanied by spiritual torment, for the act of self-denigration during prayer makes man aware of his insignificance and futility, his lowliness and remoteness from the Lord on high. Through prayer, especially when offered on the Day of Atonement, a man can undergo the spiritual torment which he is obliged to endure to effect repayment and he can feel the self-inflicted limitations which confine him as a result of his sins. He must be aware of the purpose of his sufferings and see it as payment for the sake of the purchase so that he has the appropriate intent regarding his suffering such as that which accompanied the offering up of sacrifices.

### *The Third Element: Casting Lots*

The third means joining those of making a money purchase by the rule of the "particle of something" as the whole and "scarf purchase" as substitution is that which uses the *element of chance.* This element occupies a central place in the worship of the Day of Atonement, as it is written (Leviticus 16:7–8): "And he shall take the two goats, and present them before the Lord at the door of the tabernacle. And Aaron shall cast lots upon the two goats; one lot for the Lord, and the other lot for Azazel." What is "Azazel"? According to Nahmanides, "Azazel" is Samael, meaning Satan. This is a shocking idea, God help us! How could Nahmanides even suggest such a thing? Surely to sacrifice a goat to Satan is idolatry! This is indeed a horrifying explanation of the word "Azazel." As a matter of fact, Nahmanides tarries and stalls until at last he "reveals the secret" to the reader. How is it at all thinkable that the Torah should command us to offer up a sacrifice to Satan? "And we give Samael a bribe on the Day of Atonement" is how Nahmanides phrases it.

In his interpretation, Nahmanides struggles at length over this problem and attempts to provide a solution. He writes: "You must scrutinize carefully what is written in the Scriptures and in the traditional texts. You will discover that the Torah definitely prohibited the acceptance of their divinity and barred all worship of them (i.e., Satanic forces). But the Almighty ordered that on the Day of Atonement we dispatch a goat into the wilderness to the ruler who reigns over places of desolation, which is due to him because he is ruler over these places, and from the emanation of his powers come wilderness and desolation, for he rises to the constellation of the sword and the blood and the wars and the quarrels and the injuries and the blows and the disunity and the destruction . . . and his portion among the nations is Esau who is heir to the sword and of wars . . . and the Torah uses the term *"Se'irim"* (goats) since Esau and his nation are called "Se'ir".

In other words, the goat of "Azazel" is indeed a sacrifice to Satan-Samael, prince of Esau, but "it was not intended that the scapegoat offering be a sacrifice by us to Satan, God forbid, but that when making it, our intention be nothing else but to carry out our Creator's will as He commanded us" (meaning, the sacrifice is brought by command of the Almighty, though it is an offering to Satan).

"And this should be compared," said Nahmanides, "to one who gave a banquet in honor of his master who ordered him to give a portion to his servant called so-and-so," as the man giving the banquet offered nothing to the servant, considering it beneath his dignity. Rather, the man offered all the food to his master who rewarded his servant as he always did everything he was commanded to do and always obeyed him. So the master out of compassion to the man giving the banquet wanted all of his servants to speak well of the man, and none should malign him. And this is the reason for the lottery, for were the priest actually to say that he was offering them up to God and to *"Azazel,"* it would be as if he worshiped Satan. But the priest would place the goats before the Lord at the door of the tabernacle, for both were offerings to God, and He gave of them to His servant of that which was given Him. And God (not the priest) cast lots over them and separated them (that is, both are offerings to God Who hands over one of His sacrifices to Azazel). As it is written: "The lot is cast into the lap, but the disposing thereof is entirely by the Lord" (Proverbs 16:33).

Naḥmanides' explanation is quite astonishing but we shall be able to understand him better if we refer to a source in the Talmud which he used but did not cite directly. I am referring to the following passage from Tractate Kiddushin (6b–7a):

> Raba said: [If a woman says] "Give a portion to so-and-so, and I will become betrothed to thee," then she is betrothed by the law of a surety: a surety, though he personally derives no benefit [from the loan], nevertheless obligates himself [to repayment]; so this woman too, though she personally derives no benefit [from the money], obligates herself and cedes herself [in betrothal].

It stems from this that one does not necessarily have to hand over the money for the purchase to the seller—the aforementioned woman is in the position of the seller. If the seller instructs that the money be handed over to a third person, that too is sufficient for completing the sale. This rule applies not only to marriages but also to the sale of land. And this, in fact, is generally true of other transactions. There is no necessity for the money to be handed over directly to the sellers who possess the right to transfer the goods to another. The money can be given to a third party with the concurrence of the seller, and the moment the third party receives the appointed share, it is as if the seller had been given the money directly and the transaction is accomplished and concluded. Nahmanides' analogy about the lord who commands that a part of his portion be given to his servant is founded upon this ruling. Indeed the man making the banquet wanted all of it to be given to the master—but he is instructed by the master to give half of his portion to his servant, and so it is as if the master himself received the whole portion. Similarly, the two sacrifices are, in fact, offerings to God. The Torah never asked, God forbid, that a sacrifice be offered up to Satan. The priest's verbal sanctification of the goats appoints them as offerings to be made to God. They are sanctified to God alone and not to Azazel. The commandment concerning the two goats is that they both be offered up to God, but we agree that one of the offerings be set aside for Azazel because this is what God ordered us to do. It is as if the Almighty is telling the people of Israel: "You seek expiation, you wish to renew intercourse with Me, you want to sanctify yourselves to Me—then, give a portion to so-and-so." And according to the Halakha that is a binding transaction.

This is the basis of Nahmanides' interpretation. But the question still remains problematic: Why did the Torah command that one of the goats be offered up to Azazel?

Many sacrifices are offered up on the Day of Atonement—the High Priest's bullock, the High Priest's ram and the ram of the people and the goat that fell by lot to God. The blood of the High Priest's bullock and of the goat that fell by lot to God is actually brought into the Inner Sanctum and sprinkled before the cover of the ark and there they are sacrificed upon the golden altar and in white garb. And yet all these sacrifices afford no more than expiation for the defilement of the Temple and its holy objects, the same as the other goat-offerings of the festivals and of the New Moons.

What is it, then, that brings about the great universal expiation of the Day of Atonement? It is not this entire welter of sacrifices but rather the scapegoat offering *(se'ir la'Azazel)* that affords expiation for all of the transgressions mentioned in the Torah which include those deserving divine or judicial death sentences, transgressions against the negative commandments, those committed knowingly or unknowingly, and those done either with premeditation or through accident. The offering, which more than any other symbolizes the comprehensive expiation brought about by the sanctity of the Day of Atonement, the one which we have been commanded by the Torah to present in accordance with the laws of a surety, is made to none other than Satan.

In this passage, "And Aaron shall cast lots upon the two goats; one lot for the Lord, and the other lot for Azazel," the Almighty revealed the great mystery of the quality of mercy which is operative on the Day of Atonement.

Go and see the feelings of sorrow, of disappointment, of frustration and of distress that man endures, not through devotion to the Almighty but for the sake of petty human cupidity, financial covetousness and the craving for honors. Then go and see this man as he gets to a state of terrible isolation, when society turns its back upon him, when his children are contemptuous of him, and his grandchildren are alienated from him, when he feels impoverished, neglected and abandoned—and not as the result of excess devotion to God. A man who all his life studies the Torah and faithfully serves God will not feel ignored and isolated even when he grows old. This terrible feeling of alienation and loneliness usually overcomes man due to an excessive pursuit of futile vanities. The spiritual anguish, despair and frustration endured by man are not the consequence of the "lot for the Lord" but of "the lot for Azazel." The special measure of grace, of the divine quality of loving-kindness of the Day of Atonement, then intercedes and rules that all those sacrifices offered up by man to Satan which he regrets on the Day of Atonement and repents—these must all be regarded retroactively as if they had been cast as a "lot for the Lord" and the Almighty receives them as if from the beginning they were meant for Him.

A penitent who has suffered much because of his sins and now comes broken and downcast before the Almighty—after he has been abandoned and isolated because of the empty vanities to which he devoted his life—the Almighty accepts him as though the anguish he now felt was due to his devotion to God. It is seen as an offering to the Almighty and not, as it was in truth, an offering to Satan.

Suffering vouchsafes expiation—and God makes do with the reduction of the "particle of something": suffering vouchsafes expiation and God makes do with a substitute, the ram "in the stead of his son." But the suffering must be for the sake of God, as a sacrifice unto God: "for unto God is the sin-offering."

If the suffering is a consequence of our intoxication with Satan and sin, what role can it play in bringing us expiation? For then they are not in the nature of a "sacrifice," which is the major theme of the worship of the Day of Atonement. All such suffering endured by man is not seen as a sin-offering to God; so how can man expect to receive expiation of his sins through it? The passage from Arakhin which we have cited regards as "the limit of suffering"—that is, suffering that purges transgression—even the suffering endured by man not because he wished to suffer for heaven's sake (such as when he makes sacrifices, say, in order to give his children a Jewish education or sacrifices himself in order to save the lives of other Jews). The suffering which purges the transgression is usually suffering which came upon man as a result of the transgression itself, such as: he chased riches and became a pauper; he sought honors and gained obloquy; he craved social standing and met with frustration. Although sacrifices were made here, they were directed to Satan rather than to God. On the Day of Atonement the scapegoat *(sa'ir le'Azazel)* "intercedes," which demonstrates the fact that on this day the Almighty also accepts sacrifices of the type made to Satan, sacrifices that are made outside the Temple as well as those offered inside it. We have here a sacrifice which ends up in the breakage of limbs through attempting, unsuccessfully, to scale high cliffs. Had the goat not climbed to such heights, it is possible that not all of its limbs would have been broken. The scapegoat represents the sacrifice made unintentionally, the suffering endured not for God's sake. All year round, when an individual makes sacrifices that are not for God's sake, they are rejected; but on the Day of Atonement the whole of Israel offers up just such a sacrifice to Azazel and it is accepted.

When a Jew comes to the synagogue on the Day of Atonement and says, in the language used for the High Priest's confession, "I have sinned, I have transgressed, I have acted perversely," and he is wracked by suffering as he says this and this anguish is due to a sense of spiritual emptiness and disaster which are related to acts of sin and are not consequent upon his devotion to God—on this day the Almighty accepts such suffering as a qualified sin-offering. His sins are considered atoned for and he can now "repurchase" himself and make a new start in life.

The scapegoat symbolizes man who suffers because of his own failures. If he feels remorse and has second thoughts of repentance because of them, these failures are then regarded as a sacrifice offered up to God.

"And Aaron shall cast lots upon the two goats; one lot for the Lord." Blessed is the man who endures suffering through sacrifices made for the sake of God, the person who undergoes social torment because he keeps God's commandments in a hostile environment, who suffers financial loss because he observes the Sabbath and gives his children a Jewish education or he gives his money away to charity. But there is another kind of fate which befalls a greater number of people and involves far more sacrifices. A man suffers because he feels that he has gone spiritually bankrupt, even though he has made millions or gained a great deal of personal power. Sometimes a man feels alone and utterly isolated, he suffers sleepless nights; he makes sacrifices, but these are of the order of "one lot for Azazel." Nonetheless, the Almighty accepts the suffering of these people as well when they come to do penance on the Day of Atonement—as if He had retroactively sanctified their offering of pain and anguish—and by virtue of it their transgressions are completely expiated.

Upon these three elements rests the "pardon" afforded by the Day of Atonement: (1) the element of the reduction of punishment, (2) the element of transformation and substitution of punishment, and (3) the element of one lot for Azazel. "And the goat shall bear upon him all their iniquities unto a land which is cut off" (Leviticus 16:22). When the sacrifice is an animal sacrifice, then a sin-offering offered insincerely is unfit. But when it is a human sacrifice, made up of greater or lesser torments, whether they be intentional or accidental, and whether they be for God's sake or otherwise, such sacrifice is accepted on the Day of Atonement. This is the secret meaning of the scapegoat. For had it not been so ordained by God, how could a Jew coming to do penance find expiation through suffering which was not endured for the sake of God?

## *Moving Away From and Toward Him*

So far we have spoken of the commuting of a sentence on the basis of the first element of the Day of Atonement: "For the virtue of this very day shall acquit you of sin"—the erasure of transgressions by suffering after the sentence has been commuted by reduction, substitution and chance. But as we have mentioned, there is a second factor that characterizes the Day of Atonement which is referred to in the second part of the verse just quoted: "to cleanse you of all your sins." Though the transgressions have been erased, the character of the sinner still remains tainted. Man is rewarded with expiation and remission of his sentence—but how does he achieve spiritual purification, so that his soul shines as brightly as before the sin?

The Day of Atonement possesses a special power of purification not present in penitence which takes place on any other day of the year. The "essence of the Day of Atonement" does not serve only to erase transgressions but also to purify the sinner's soul. What is the manner of purification peculiar to the Day of Atonement?

There are three passages in the Torah dealing with repentance. One is in *Naso* (Numbers 5:7): "When a man or woman shall commit any sin . . . then they shall confess their sin which they have done." The second passage is in *Va'ethanan* (Deuteronomy 4:29): "But if from thence thou shalt seek the Lord thy God, thou shalt find Him, if thou seek Him with all thy heart and with all thy soul. When thou art in tribulation and all these things are come upon thee . . . if thou turn to the Lord thy God, and shalt be obedient unto His voice." The third passage dealing with repentance, the longest of them, is in *Nitzavim* (Deuteronomy 30). It is read in public, according to a regulation instituted by Ezra (so Rabbi Nissim Gaon and the Tosafot infer), before Rosh Hashana and the Day of Atonement. The episode of repentance in *Nitzavim* is directly connected with the Day of Atonement. The episode of repentance in *Va'ethanan* is read close to the date of the Ninth of Av, which is also a day of penitence that is born out of calamity and destruction: "When thou art in tribulation." The episode of repentance in *Nitzavim,* on the other hand, is read before the Day of Atonement and here the repentance issues from joy, from drawing near the Almighty. In calamity man draws apart from his God. "When thou art in tribulation . . . thou shalt seek the Lord thy God"—if there is a search here, then a loss must have occurred previous to it. This is repentance which stems from *drawing apart* as in "from afar God was revealed to me." The repentance of *Nitzavim* stems from *drawing near* (Deuteronomy 30:1): "And it shall come to pass, when all these things are come upon thee, the blessing and the curse, which I have set before thee, thou shalt bethink thyself among all the nations whither the Lord thy God hath driven thee." The feeling of remoteness from the Lord of the Universe creates in man a yearning for repentance; but even more effective is the sense of nearness he feels to the Lord of the Universe. "It shall come to pass when all these things . . . which I have set before thee."

Believe me when I tell you that I myself could never have endured the past years had I not felt the close proximity of God. I am not a Kabbalist nor a mystic, so when I speak of the nearness of God, it is something I feel when opening the pages of the Talmud in order to study. When I am thus immersed in study, I feel as if the Almighty is there standing behind me, putting His hand on my shoulder, looking with me at the text lying on the table and asking me about it. This is not something I imagine. For me this is a true-to-life experience.

Feeling remote from God is a terrible experience. What do you think of what is now happening in Russia? I spoke with a number of Jewish intellectuals who came from there, and I learned that it is a mistake to think that in Russia the awakening of a national movement is unconnected with religion. A Russian physicist whom I met told me that the phenomenon which we are witnessing in the Soviet Union is actually not limited to Jews alone. Gentiles, too, are feeling a progressive asphyxiation there due to a lack of religious faith, as they are suspended in a limbo of godlessness from which there is no room for belief in the eternality of the soul. Man is seen as nothing but a mechanical cog, here one day and gone the next. It is difficult to live in a world in which the final destination is nothing but the grave. This physicist told me that were the Pravoslavic Church more sincere, it could draw to its bosom once again hundreds of thousands of adherents. But as is well known, the Church in Russia is also an agent of the regime; it is primitive and far from religious or spiritual sincerity. As to the Jews, they have gotten to the state of "when thou art in tribulation" and have moved on to "from thence thou shalt seek the Lord thy God" and from here the road leads to the God of Israel and to the Land of Israel. This is the way the process develops and not the reverse, as some Israeli diplomats have tried to persuade me, i.e., that the return begins first with the longing for the Land of Israel. It was not only longing for the Land of Israel or wonderment that there is a Jewish army and a Jewish president that caused the first awakenings of Russia's Jews, the physicist told me. It was rather yearnings for the Lord of the Universe, and this can only bring a Jew to the God of Israel Who can be reached by the individual only when he is identified as part of *Knesset Israel.* And the place of *Knesset Israel* is of course the Land of Israel. Thus the Jews reach a state of national identity with the Land of Israel only at a later stage and not at the beginning, as some would think.

This is return which comes about due to a sense of remoteness from the Almighty: "when thou art in tribulation."

But the repentance found in *Nitzavim* originates in the act of drawing near to the Almighty. That is the nature of the repentance that takes place on the Day of Atonement, when a Jew meets God at close quarters; and when God is so near, it becomes difficult to commit a transgression.

A man may become disgusted with sin due to remoteness from the Almighty, which causes a yearning to draw near to Him. He certainly feels unable to sin when he is conscious of the proximity of the Almighty. The Day of Atonement is such an occasion, and from here stems the contiguity of the Day of Atonement and the reading of the passage from *Nitzavim.*

This passage makes reference to two basic principles of the faith: repentance and redemption. "And it shall come to pass, when all these things are come upon thee, the blessing and the curse, which I have set before thee, and thou shalt bethink thyself among all the nations, whither the Lord thy God hath driven thee, and shalt return unto the Lord thy God, and shalt obey His voice according to all that I command thee this day, thou and thy children, with all thine heart and with all thy soul; that then the Lord thy God will return thy captivity, and have compassion upon thee, and will again gather thee from all the nations, whither the Lord thy God hath scattered thee. If any of thine be driven out unto the outmost parts of heaven, from thence will the Lord thy God gather thee, and from thence will He fetch thee: And the Lord thy God will bring thee unto the land which thy fathers possessed, and thou shalt possess it; and He will do thee good, and multiply thee above thy fathers."

What is the connection between repentance and the "ingathering of the exiles" when the sovereign redeemer comes? This question has been frequently asked and there are two ways of answering it. One is given by the Sages of the Halakha and another by the Sages of the Kabbala. Both are equally true and each is infused with deep significance.

The Sages of the Halakha (cf. Maimonides in the Laws of Repentance, Chapter 7, Section 2) ruled that Israel cannot be redeemed except through repentance. It has also been promised us that in the end of days the people of Israel will repent and then be redeemed. One can find both these views in the passage from *Nitzavim:* one, that Israel will be redeemed only after doing repentance, and, two, the promise that no matter how sinful and remote from the Almighty the people of Israel may be, they are destined to return to the Land of Israel through repentance.

The Kabbalists—in the *Book of the Zohar* and in *Or Ha'hayim* and explicitly and emphatically in the *Epistle of Repentance* by the author of the *Tania,* where he speaks of repentance "on high" and repentance "on low" and especially as expounded by his son, the second Rabbi of Lubavitch, in that profound work, *Sha'arei Hateshuva*—say that the Torah is speaking here not only of the exile of Israel in the geographical-political sense, but also of the exile of the individual in a metaphysical-spiritual sense. Every sinner is really in exile, banished to a remote corner of the heavens, "dispersed" among tens of places in the sense of "the Lord hath scattered thee among the nations." Exile means the absence of a home and the sinner is someone who has lost his way from home. Though he may own magnificent palaces and villas, the sinner has no real home. A house is no home for a Jew if the Almighty is not present in it, too. The sinner, say the Sages of the Kabbala, does not have an integrated personality—and for all their naiveté, the Kabbalist Sages understood this problem's dimensions more than modern psychologists. The sinner's is a schizophrenic personality, diffuse, alienated and blown to and fro by each gust of wind; one part of him may be found in one realm while another part of him is in another realm altogether. The sinner behaves in an inconsistent manner. The curse of "and the Lord scattered thee among the nations" refers not only to a nation, but can also apply to the individual sinner. His capabilities, his spiritual powers, his emotions and his thoughts are without internal cohesion; he has no single axis around which his personality revolves. For such a person repentance leads to "the ingathering of the exiles," meaning the reunification and concentration of the personality which has been shattered to smithereens as a consequence of sin.

So says the second Rabbi of Lubavitch: "It is written: 'If any of thine be driven out unto the outmost parts of heaven, from thence will the Lord thy God gather thee.' How the matter of ingathering applies to the individual self must be understood, for normally gathering and concentration pertain to the realm of the many. But Scripture spoke metaphorically in the phrase 'be driven out unto the utmost parts' and the intention was the dispersion of the sparks of the light of the spirit (which is one) in many strange and very remote places, for 'God's light is man's soul.' " The human soul, born in God's image, is fathomless and it contains in itself vast areas in which its sparks and particles can be dispersed so that "ingathering and concentration are necessary also with every individudal, and this is the main point of the well-known phrase 'the ingathering of the exiles,' and that is what is called repentance 'on low.' "

There is great significance to this analogy which compares individual exile and the ingathering of the exiles of all of Israel in the political-geographical sense (to some extent, we see it happening now in our day, not exactly as prophesied, but there has occurred a beginning of the ingathering of Jews from all the remotest corners) to the idea of self-exile and the ingathering of the exiles in the metaphysical-spiritual sense as it applies to the sinner. Through repentance, the sinner also gathers together the dispersed sparks of his spiritual self in order to reintegrate his personality.

## *Joshua's Conquest and the Sanctification of Ezra*

How many times have the people of Israel come to the Land of Israel in the past and how many times will it return to the Land in the future? I am not referring to the historical aspect of the question but rather to an halakhic issue. According to Maimonides, only two arrivals in the Land are possible, including the past and the future, and the answer to this question determines the number of times the Land of Israel has been sanctified. For the arrival of the whole of Israel in the Land of Israel entails the sanctification of the Land, which can only happen twice.

In the Talmud (see Yevamot 16a; Shavuot 16a) there is a controversy over this matter. Among the earlier post-Talmudic Sages there are some who believe that the land of Israel has already been sanctified twice in the past: once in the days of Joshua and a second time in the days of Ezra, and that both sanctifications have since been nullified. (Thus ruled the author of *Hateruma* whose ruling serves as basis for the permission to sell the whole Land of Israel to a gentile in the Sabbatical year so that Jews might work the land. This is because the sanctity of the land expired with the destruction of the Temple and in our day the laws pertaining to the sanctity of the land are in effect only by enactment of the Sages and the gentile has the power to abrogate them.) According to this approach, there are altogether three returns to the Land of Israel; two of them have already occurred in the past, first when Joshua sanctified the Land and second when Ezra sanctified it. And the third return, God willing, will be established in the future with the arrival of the Messiah.

However, according to Maimonides (Laws of the Temple, Chapter 6), only two entries into the land are possible: Joshua's entry, sanctification of which was annulled by the Babylonian exile, and the entry in the days of Ezra, the sanctification of which is valid and operative for all time in line with the rule that "he sanctified it for the moment—he sanctified it for all time." And thus, though the arrival of the sovereign redeemer will be grander and more magnificent than all the previous arrivals, it will not innovate anything from a halakhic point of view. This will not be considered as a new entry into the Land but rather as a continuation of the return to the Land and of its sanctification that was initiated in the time of Ezra. And to tell the truth—I once heard this, but cannot recall from whom—the destruction of the Temple and of the Land of Israel has no significance from a halakhic point of view. The Halakha does not recognize such a fact as "Destruction." In the Halakha, only the first Destruction is a fact, for it was established by our Prophets. This does not hold true for the destruction of the Second Temple when there were no prophets to testify to its divine significance. This destruction therefore, halakhically speaking, has no status. Thus, the advent of the king-messiah is considered an extension of the arrival of Ezra, and what has happened and will happen in between has no effective role or specific status in the Halakha.

According to Maimonides, therefore, there have been two entries into the Land: the arrival of Joshua, which sanctified the land for that time alone, and the arrival of Ezra, which sanctified the Land of Israel for that time and for the future as well. The arrival of the king-messiah will be the continuation of the second sanctification of the Land (by Ezra). Why was Ezra's sanctification, which is operative for all time, more potent than Joshua's, which only served for that period? The question is posed by Maimonides himself; he answered it with a theory which, at first glance, appears incomprehensible.

Thus wrote Maimonides in the Laws of the Temple, Chapter 6, Section 14: "Wherever all these things are not done in this fashion and in this order, then complete sanctification does not take place. And though Ezra made two thanksgiving offerings, it was by nature of a commemoration, and it was not by his deeds that the place was sanctified, for there wasn't a king, or Urim and Thummim. How then was it considered sanctified? (Maimonides is referring here to the sanctification of the Second Temple and not to the sanctification of the land.) [It was sanctified] by the first sanctification with which Solomon sanctified it, for he sanctified the Temple Court and Jerusalem both for his own time and for all time."

Maimonides distinguished between the sanctification of the Temple, which is operative for all time, and that of the Land regarding which the first sanctification has been nullified, while its second sanctification remains operative for all times (*ibid.*, Section 16): "And why do I say of the Temple and Jerusalem, that the first sanctification sanctified for that time as well as for all time, while the sanctification of the rest of the Land of Israel for purposes of the Sabbatical year and the tithes and other matters, the initial sanctification did not qualify regarding the future? Because the sanctification of the Temple and of Jerusalem is because of the *Shekhinah* (divine presence), and the *Shekhinah* can never be withdrawn. Even though Scripture says (Leviticus 26:31): 'And I shall bring your sanctuaries unto desolation,' the Sages have said, 'Though they be desolate, their sanctity remains in force.' But the 'obligation of the land'—[the rules of] the Sabbatical year and of the tithes—is effective only because the land was conquered by the multitude when the country was taken from them. The effort of the conquest was nullified and the Land was released by the Torah, from the obligation of tithes and the rules of the Sabbatical year, for it was no longer 'the Land of Israel.' " Moreover: "And because Ezra came and sanctified it, not by an act of conquest but through right of possession, therefore every place which was taken into possession by the returnees from Babylon and sanctified by Ezra is still sanctified today, despite the fact that the Land was taken away from the Jews; and the rules of the Sabbatical year and tithes are applicable as we have explained the matter in the Laws of the heave-offering."

While the sanctity of the Temple is by virtue of the presence of the *Shekhinah* and therefore cannot be annulled, Joshua's sanctification of the Land stems from the force of conquest—thus another conquering force can come and annul it. And why isn't Ezra's sanctification annulled? Because Ezra "did not sanctify it through conquest but through the right of possession assumed by the returnees from Babylon." The scope of "right of possession" in the Halakha encompasses settlement, residence, turning wilderness into settled land—in a word, "colonization"; and how much stronger is settling on the land than military occupation! If Joshua's conquest was annulled by the Babylonian conquest, then Ezra's settlement should have been annulled by the Roman conquest of the land and destruction of the Second Temple; they laid the land waste, uprooted settlements and burned the fields! What then is the difference between Joshua's "conquest" and Ezra's "possession"—for both were terminated by acts of destruction?

It is interesting to note that even earlier on Maimonides mentions the matter of the annulment of Joshua's sanctification of the Land as opposed to the continuity of that in Ezra's time, in the Laws of the Heave-Offering and in the Law of the Sabbatical Year and Jubilee. There he does not explain why the two sanctifications are considered different. Only here, in the Laws of the Temple, after drawing a line between the sanctification of the Temple which may not be annulled and that of the Land which does not necessarily hold forever, does he get around to explaining the difference between Joshua and Ezra. It appears that the explanation of the difference between the sanctification of the Temple and the sanctification of the

Land, of that enacted by Solomon and that by Joshua, is based on the same principle underlying the difference between Joshua's sanctification of the land and Ezra's. In other words, Ezra's sanctification came about by virtue of the presence of the *Shekhinah*, while Joshua's sanctification was by virtue of conquest. And just as in the case of the Temple, the dwelling-place of the *Shekhinah*, one cannot speak of sanctification for a limited time only—since the sanctification of the *Shekhinah* is operative even when the Temple is desolate (sanctity and desolation are not mutually contradictory terms—"though desolate, their sanctity remains in force")—so it is also the case regarding Ezra's sanctification; desolation in itself does not mean that the land is denuded of its sanctity.

Conquest and desolation—these are mutually exclusive terms. Therefore, while the sanctification of the Land operative as of Joshua's conquest was later annulled (by another conquest) this was not so regarding the Second Temple's sanctity. This is because Ezra's act of sanctification was not derived from the power of conquest but came from the sanctity of the *Shekhinah* which prevailed during the Second Temple period—not only in the Temple and in Jerusalem but throughout the entire Land of Israel.

Actually, the entire distinction between "sanctified for that time" and "sanctified for all time" hangs on the issue of choice. Sanctification always comes down to the world after God chooses, and there have been four kinds of divine election. One is the election of Israel ("He who chooses his people Israel"), whose sanctity is never annulled; the same applies to the appointment of the *kohanim* (the priestly clan), the selection of the dynasty of the House of David and the choosing of the Temple site and of Jerusalem. The determination whether the sanctification was only temporary and annulable or whether it continues for all time depends upon whether the kind of sanctification under discussion is due to this element of divine choice. The four categories of holiness chosen by the Almighty Himself can never be retracted.

And what is the law of the sanctification of the Land of Israel as a whole? That is, is it a chosen land or not? It is not my intention to give either a "Zionist" or "anti-Zionist" answer to this question. I am seeking an halakhic answer. What is the status of the Land of Israel in the eyes of the Halakha? If one determines that it was sanctified temporarily but not for all time in both instances (the view of *Sefer Hateruma*), then the element of chosenness no longer pertains to the Land. But Maimonides did not judge the matter this way. When he ruled that the element of choice pertained to Jersualem, he did not wish to distinguish Jerusalem as apart from the rest of the Land of Israel. So he ruled that though the sanctity of the land by virtue of Joshua's conquest was null and void, its sanctification from the days of Ezra was still operative, that is, the land was divinely chosen. Were you to ask me, I would say that I agree with Maimonides, not because I am a "Zionist" or a member of Mizrachi, but because the sources indicate this to be so. With regard to Jerusalem, it is written (1 Kings 8:16): "Since the day that I brought forth My people Israel out of Egypt, I have not chosen any city of any of the tribes of Israel," meaning that in the whole Land of Israel I chose no city other than Jerusalem. But the Land of Israel itself was also given sanctity, for thus we have read in the Mishna (*Kelim* 1:6): "There are ten sacred things, the Land of Israel being holier than all other lands"; after which, in rising order of sanctity, come walled cities, Jerusalem, the area within the city walls, the Temple Mount, the Temple courtyard and so on until we reach the pinnacle of sanctity, the "Holy of Holies," into which no one enters save the High Priest on the Day of Atonement during worship. From this mishna we learn that the Land of Israel is likened to the base of a multi-storied pyramid of sanctity; without that base, the whole pyramid would topple over. Were not the Land of Israel in itself also chosen, it would not have been cited among the ten sacred things.

The meaning of the sanctity brought about by chosenness means the sanctity of holiness bestowed by the presence of the *Shekhinah.* In the days of Joshua and throughout the First Temple period, the country did not possess the sanctity that is derived from chosenness, but rather the sanctity due to conquest. This type of sanctity can be nullified, while the sanctity that comes from chosenness can never be annulled. On the other hand, the sanctity of the land in the time of Ezra was due to chosenness, characterized by the holy presence of the *Shekhinah.* Thus said our Sages (Mekhilta, *Petihata* 25): "The *Shekhinah* never reveals itself in foreign lands," and in Jonah it is written, "For he fled from the presence of the Lord" (Jonah 1:3). Where did he flee to hide from God's presence? He fled abroad.

In Joshua's day this sanctity of chosenness was not possible since the *Bet Habehira* (the "chosen house"—the Temple) had not yet been built and the sanctity of the Land of Israel is derived from that of the Holy Temple. All of the "ten special sanctities" evolve around what is really divine choice. At the time of Joshua's conquest the Temple had not been built. (The whole of Psalm 132 in the Book of Psalms deals with pinings after the Temple; the chosenness of Jerusalem first becomes evident in the time of King David after the purchase is made of the threshing-floor from Arnon the Jebusite.) The conquest by Joshua occurred at a time when there was no established "sanctity of Jerusalem" and no Holy Temple to radiate its sanctity through the whole Land of Israel. The conquest led by Joshua began with a battle for the border lands, from Jericho down to the Negev, and from there to the Mediterranean seashore, along the coast up to Acre, and thence to Galilee and the land of Naphtali. Every area seized was considered sanctified by virtue of the act of conquest. Thus, sanctification by conquest proceeded from place to place until it got to Jerusalem years later in the time of David. And only afterward, in the days of Solomon, was the Holy Temple built in Jerusalem. Thus, the Land of Israel received sanctity by conquest *even before* the Holy Temple existed. And that same pristine sanctification by Joshua was brought about by conquest and it was later annulled by a subsequent conquest by others. It contained nothing of that element of divine chosenness which confers unnullifiable sanctity. The first Temple was built after the Land of Israel had already been sanctified. There occurred here, so to speak, a process of sanctification going from the peripheries inward, from the outlying areas sanctified by conquest to the central core: the Temple in Jerusalem.

However, the situation was different during the time of Ezra. When Maimonides speaks of the "possession with which the returnees from Babylon possessed the land," where did this occur? Not in the peripheries but first of all right in the center, in Jerusalem. Ezra did not go about reclaiming areas of the Land of Israel; he first set about to build the Temple and to restore the walls of Jerusalem. To achieve that, naturally Jews had to live in Israel, so that the Temple should not be rebuilt in a country inhabited mainly by gentiles. Thus it is written (Ezra 1:5–6), "Then rose up the chief of the fathers of Judah and Benjamin, and the priests and the Levites, with all those whose spirit God had raised, to go up to build the House of the Lord which is in Jerusalem. And all they that were about them strengthened their hands with vessels of silver, with gold, with goods and with beasts, and with precious things." And it is also written (Ezra 2:1): "Now these are the children of the province that went up out of the captivity . . . and came again unto Jerusalem." The center, for the return in the days of Ezra, was Jerusalem.

How was the land sanctified in the days of Ezra? By the right of possession? Possession in itself does not bring any sanctification! When the holy Temple, the chosen dwelling place for the *Shekhinah,* was built, it bestowed sanctity on the whole Land of Israel. This time the sanctification did not gravitate inward from the circumference, from the outer peripheries toward the center. Quite the contrary, the sanctity was established first in the center itself and from there it spread outward, like a fountain gushing forth, overflowing into the Jerusalem environs and, from thence, to the rest of the Land of Israel, until all of it was completely sanctified.

That which sanctified the Land of Israel in Ezra's day was the Temple, the dwelling-place of the *Shekhinah.* This is why Maimonides ruled that the sanctification of the Land by Ezra was in the same category as that of the Temple, whose sanctification by Solomon was not terminated because the *Shekhinah* cannot be withdrawn.

The Talmud in Tractate Shavuot (16a) notes that Ezra made two great thanksgiving offerings when he sanctified Jerusalem and asks: According to those who are of the opinion that Solomon sanctified Jerusalem for his time and for all time, why did Ezra have to make the two great thanksgiving offerings? The Talmud answers: "[He was not obliged to] but did it as a commemoration." Maimonides as well, in chapter 6 of the Laws of the Temple, writes: "And though Ezra made two thanksgiving offerings, it was by nature of a commemoration, and not by his actions that the place was sanctified."

What was the purpose of this act of commemoration?

The explanation of this is that indeed Ezra did not have to consecrate the Temple, for its sanctity invoked in the days of Solomon, still held true. Nor was it necessary to endow Jerusalem with sanctity. But in order to consecrate the whole Land of Israel he had to build the Temple and reconstruct Jerusalem. Therefore, he placed the two thanksgiving offerings upon the wall of the city to show that the rebuilt walls held it in their power to radiate sanctity upon their surroundings and to bestow the holiness of the *Shekhinah* upon the entire Land of Israel. And this is what the Talmud meant: "[He was not obliged to] but did it as a commemoration."

### *Returning from the Exile of Sin*

The analogy we previously drew between exile, destruction and the ingathering of the exiles on the one hand and sin and repentance on the other is pertinent to the present issue as well. We have shown that there are two types of repentance: the first by conquest and the second which involves the *Shekhinah,* just as there are two ways of obtaining sanctification when going to dwell in the Land of Israel—that obtained through conquest, as when Joshua conquered and consecrated one area after another, and the sanctification brought about by Ezra, when the Temple was built at the center while the rest of Israel was still under alien rule and its enemies still harassed it. The same applies to penitent people: there are those who sanctify themselves through acts of conquest and there are others who attain sanctity by inspiration received from the *Shekhinah.*

"Then the Lord thy God will turn thy captivity, and have compassion upon thee, and will return and gather thee from all the nations, whither the Lord thy God hath scattered thee" (Deuteronomy 30:3). At first glance, it seems questionable why the Torah should have had to repeat "and will return and gather thee from all the nations, whither the Lord thy God hath scattered thee"—for it has already stated: "will turn thy captivity, and have compassion upon thee." It appears that there are two separate promises here: one, "that then the Lord thy God will turn thy captivity and have compassion upon thee," and, two, "and will return and gather thee from all the nations, whither the Lord thy God hath scattered thee." The first promise means that quite suddenly God will act to redeem the entire people of Israel or an individual Jew in the act of doing penance. Sometimes the Almighty aids the penitent and causes a sudden revolution to take place in his way of thinking, transforming his whole worldview, affecting the total essence of his being. For many years his personality had been schizophrenic and fragmented; he had been pulled along by dark impulses and instincts; all his life he had been an outsider everywhere he went; he had been driven by dark spirits; his own soul was in a state of exile. And then, through a sudden ray of illumination, he discovered the focal point of his existence, and he was transformed into another person. A new light shone in the depths of his soul, new aspirations filled his being, he was released from the bonds that held him back, the fragments of his personality were collected and reunited to form an integrated person. The sparks which had gone far astray into infinite space assembled and burned as a single flame. The penitent regained control over his own self. All at once God freed him from his captivity: "Then the Lord thy God will turn thy captivity, and have compassion upon thee."

We all know some cases of this type of penitent. Take, for example, what happened to the German-Jewish philosopher, Franz Rosenzweig. He was an outsider and an exile who almost reached the point of apostasy. During the First World War, he entered a small hassidic *bet midrash* (house of learning) on the Day of Atonement and left it a different man. Suddenly, the outsider and exile vanished; the apostate, too, disappeared, as did the assimilated and self-hating Jew. The great Jew, Franz Rosenzweig, had made his appearance.

That is the repentance meant by "Then the Lord thy God will turn thy captivity, and have compassion upon thee." This is repentance which stems from the spontaneous eruption of the divine flame which possesses man's soul, "God's candle." It bursts outward in the same manner as Ezra's sanctification.

This kind of sanctification is not the same as it was with Joshua's conquest; there is no need to assault Ai or Jericho, no need to conquer bastions, to topple walls or to conduct wars against the five kings. All Ezra had to do was to construct the Temple at the center, and from there the light radiated and invaded every corner of the Land from one end to the other. Similarly, there is a type of repentance which springs forth from the core of the personality, from the secret interior of the soul, which erupts from its inner depths and spreads over all of man's spiritual faculties and talents, throughout his body and limbs, overtaking his thoughts and feelings. The route in this type of repentance runs from the "Holy of Holies" to the circumference round about; even the alienated elements are, so to speak, resuscitated. My father, of blessed memory, told me in the name of Rabbi Haim that the verse from Zechariah, "Not by might, nor by power, but by my spirit, saith the Lord of hosts," refers to the type of sanctification invoked by Ezra, in contrast to that by Joshua. And this is also referred to in the verse, "Then the Lord thy God will turn thy captivity, and have compassion upon thee."

But this is not always the path of repentance. Sometimes it is analogous to the events of Joshua's conquest. At other times repentance does not come and suddenly overtake the whole man. Rather, man is called upon to advance step by step, to proceed from one struggle to another, to make one conquest after another. This is an arduous and protracted route—but in the end it leads to the establishment of the Holy Temple. It is in relation to this type of repentance that the Torah repeats: "and will return and gather thee from all the nations, whither the Lord thy God hath scattered thee." This is a slow and drawn-out ingathering of the soul's scattered fragments. But it is ultimately rewarded, and with God's help the soul attains the goal of redemption. And we are assured that "if any of thine be driven out unto the outmost parts of heaven, from thence will the Lord thy God gather thee, and from thence will He fetch thee; and the Lord thy God will bring thee unto the Land which thy fathers possessed, and thou shalt possess it; and He will do thee good, and multiply thee above thy fathers."

There are those who attain repentance of the order of Ezra's sanctification and there are those who attain repentance through Joshua's way of sanctification. But concerning both, Tradition has bequeathed us a fine rule: For him who comes to be purified, the way is cleared and he is extended a helping hand.